2-25

5/04.

UNIVERSITY

ELEMENTS OF THE NATURAL MOVEMENT OF POPULATION

ELEMENTS OF THE NATURAL MOVEMENT OF POPULATION

by

EGON VIELROSE

Translated from the Polish by
I. DOBOSZ

Translation edited by
H. INFELD, P. F. KNIGHTSFIELD

PERGAMON PRESS
OXFORD · LONDON · EDINBURGH · NEW YORK ·
PARIS · FRANKFURT

PAŃSTWOWE WYDAWNICTWO EKONOMICZNE
WARSAW

PERGAMON PRESS LTD.
Headington Hill Hall, Oxford
4 & 5 Fitzroy Square, London W.1

PERGAMON PRESS (SCOTLAND) LTD.
2 & 3 Teviot Place, Edinburgh 1

PERGAMON PRESS INC.
122 East 55th Street, New York 22, N.Y.

GAUTHIER-VILLARS ED.
55 Quai des Grands-Augustins, Paris 6

PERGAMON PRESS G.m.b.H.
Kaiserstrasse 75, Frankfurt am Main

First edition 1965

Library of Congress Catalog Card Number 64-8193

Printed in Poland

CONTENTS

PREFACE

THIS book is the fruit of more than twenty years' work on problems of demography. These problems affect everybody to a varying degree, in one way or another, be it the need to support a family or the care of a home. For this reason they are, and will always be, actual and of vital importance.

It is important, therefore, to investigate the pattern of demographic phenomena. To arrive at a thorough knowledge of these phenomena a very superficial study is not enough. A student of these phenomena must examine them in detail and analyse the various elements which cause some phenomenon to take a certain form and not another. Only when a phenomenon is known precisely is it possible to proceed to finding out its cause. Such investigations may prove, however, to be outside the scope of demography, while in my present work I wish to confine myself to statistical and demographic problems only.

It is evident that with this aim in view a work of this kind had to be based on ample statistical data. The United Nations Demographic Yearbooks are the main source of statistical information contained in this book. I have also consulted statistical yearbooks of various countries, as well as special publications on particular subjects. I quoted this material in the text whenever needed to prove a point, either fully or (especially if such quotations were too extensive) in a summary form, as necessary. I have not tried to bring the material quoted up to date, as it would not change the argument and would require much time and wasted effort.

I have frequently resorted to diagrams since, in my opinion, they not only provide a graphic presentation of the problem but are also an instrument of guidance for further research, leading to certain conjectures in a much more tangible way than mere figures could convey.

The contents of this book can be divided as follows.

The first two chapters are an introduction explaining the

1

nature and quality of statistical sources, the degree of their reliability and the results that may be expected.

Chapter 3 deals with the structure of population by sex, age and marital status, as it is essential to examine the statics of a problem before proceeding to its dynamics. The next three chapters are concerned with the three main elements of the natural movement of population: marriages (and divorces), births, and deaths. I have endeavoured to write all these chapters according to a uniform scheme. I begin with a general description of the present pattern of a phenomenon in various countries and of its variations within one country. I then analyse its different elements, and finally, I examine how these elements change with time. This procedure reveals obvious dependencies in the changes of various elements. Everything changes, but with an internal consistency. In some cases these relationships are so close that they can be used to assess approximate values of unknown elements from known values of related elements. Such interrelations can be "traced" only when the statistical material available is sufficiently ample. Studies of this type can be classified as comparative demography.

These studies are useful, not only because they make it possible to penetrate more deeply into the essence of demographic phenomena, which in itself is of great significance, but also because they provide an instrument which helps us—by approximate evaluations—to supplement our knowledge about elements on which no direct statistical data are available, but are revealed only by means of analogy and comparison. Indeed, information which is not quite accurate is always better than no information at all. This is how some data concerning Poland have been obtained which are not covered by official statistics.

It is hard to say which, if any, ideas contained in this book are entirely new. Demography has been an excellent field for exercising human ingenuity ever since the times of Graunt, if not earlier. Obviously some concepts have occurred to many researchers simultaneously or, if not simultaneously, at least independently. To give an example, the notion of reproduction rates, popularized by Kuczynski, had been introduced half a century earlier in Böckh's works.

At any rate, coming back to what I said at the beginning, I should like to emphasize one point: if we want to make a really good analysis of a demographic phenomenon we must not confine ourselves to a superficial study; we must examine the phenomenon from all possible aspects and divide it into components, each of which must be the subject of a separate study. Otherwise, we can never hope to attain full knowledge.

EGON VIELROSE

CHAPTER 1

SOURCE AND QUALITY OF INFORMATION ON THE STATE AND MOVEMENT OF POPULATION

THE PHENOMENA of the movement of population are usually studied in relation to the existing state of the population. Thus, the number of births is compared to that of females of child bearing age, the number of married couples to that of the marriageable population, etc. Hence, when studying the population movement it is not sufficient to analyse statistics of birth, death, marriage and divorce; additional information on the number and structure of the population distributed by sex, age, marital status and perhaps some other demographic characteristics, is no less necessary.

Let us examine, therefore, the methods of collecting such information and their degree of reliability.

Information on the number and structure of the population of a particular country is usually obtained by means of population censuses. In many countries population censuses are taken periodically, approximately every ten years. In some countries, however, not a single census has been taken so far; in others, censuses have been discontinued. Occasionally, only part of the territory is covered by the census or a section of the population is counted (e.g., only the white population in colonial countries). Since it is imperative to have more or less accurate information on the total number of population of a given country, attempts have been made to fill gaps in statistics by means of indirect estimates based on registers of taxpayers, numbers of families or households, on statements by heads of households or chiefs of tribes. One of the methods used is to make an accurate count of a section of the population and on this basis to estimate approximately the total population. The accuracy and comparability of information obtained in this manner is, of course, not very high.

As a result, the available data on the population of some countries are partly based on conjectures and, hence, not fully reliable. In fact, even the figures yielded by population censuses may occasionally be not very accurate. Consequently, a comparison of data obtained in succeeding censuses does not always present the true picture of actual changes; it may to a certain extent be only a reflection of gradual improvements in the quality of information collected.

Even in cases of correct census procedures the results may not be completely comparable, as the definition of the population covered by the censuses may vary. In some cases all inhabitants are counted, whether residing in their native land or staying abroad. In others, temporary absentees are taken into account, but those who have left the country for a longer period are excluded. Occasionally, all persons present in one area of a given country at a given moment are enumerated. Different methods of counting the population are related to the notions of *resident* population and *present-in-area* population. There is a tendency to use for the purposes of international comparisons the number of present-in-area population, excluding foreign armed forces stationed in the country, but counting the troops of the given country stationed abroad. The accuracy of census results depends on a great many factors. In countries where censuses have been taken regularly for a long time, and the population has become used to them, census results are much more accurate as a rule than in countries where a population census is taken for the first time. The efficiency of census organization and the proper choice of census methods are, of course, of great importance.[1]

Although census results contain errors of varying importance they are usually published without even an approximate evaluation of the magnitude of these errors, and they all appear to be equally accurate and reliable. The impression of complete reliability is all the stronger as census results are not stated in round numbers but seem to be given very exactly, "to one man".

---

[1] For information on census methods see *Handbook of Population Census Methods*, United Nations, New York 1954.

In so far as the structure of population is concerned, we are interested in its distribution by sex, age, and marital status.

The sex structure presents no problem; the number of males and females obtained in a census can be regarded as true to fact provided, of course, that the census was really general and covered all territorial, national and other groups of the population.

The age structure is a less simple matter. The problem of age can be interpreted in different ways. Census questionnaires may ask the informant to furnish the exact date of his birth or to name the number of years completed. The question dealing with age is simple enough, but the reply is not always quite accurate.

Replies on age are often given in round numbers; hence ages ending in 5 or 0 are more numerous than the adjacent ones. Statisticians also note a tendency of people to state ages in even rather than in odd numbers, which causes a pile up of replies giving the age in numbers ending with 2 and 8. Also, some people do not know their exact age.[1]

Differences in the distribution of a population by age groups are another obstacle when comparing the age structures of different countries. In some countries where the death rate is high, the number of old people is relatively small and, consequently, there is no detailed classification of age groups above 65 or 60; in other countries the age distribution of the population is given in single years of age or in 5-year groups until the age of 100 or more.

It may happen that the number of a population distributed by sex and age is not the same as the population total enumerated in the census; the former may have been obtained for the resident population while the total enumeration covers the present-in-area population. Information on the sex and age structure may also include only a section of the population selected for a certain purpose.

Besides the tendency to state age in round numbers, considerable disproportions may occur between the number of males and females of the same year of birth or belonging

---

[1] The difficulties of fixing the age in population censuses are described by E. ROSSET in his *Aging Process of Population* (Pergamon Press, Oxford).

to the same age group, as well as between the numbers of adjacent age groups. Characteristically, such disproportions can be noted even in countries where censuses have a long tradition and where illiteracy is virtually nonexistent.[1]

Distribution of a population by marital status also gives rise to many problems and doubts. The terms used are usually a reflection of the customs prevailing in different societies and are influenced by legal, religious and political factors. The only uniform, internationally acceptable approach may be towards marriages formally contracted in accordance with the laws of a given country. The interpretation of the term union varies in different countries, which leads to great difficulties in comparing statistics.

The Statistical Office of the United Nations recommends that both legal and consensual unions be counted as marriages since in some countries non-formalized unions outnumber legal marriages. Hence, to list the number of legal unions in a separate group in such countries would be artificial and unrealistic.

It is worth noting that in Poland non-formalized conjugal unions and separations were classified in separate groups as early as in the 1931 census. Such classification makes it possible to fix the total number of couples cohabiting in legalized or non-legalized unions, excluding those whose marriage is de facto dissolved.

Natural movement statistics are based on registers of demographic facts recorded under the existing legal regulations. A birth certificate is, generally speaking, an identification card which has to be presented on certain occasions. A death certificate must be issued to obtain permission to bury the

---

[1] The Statistical Office of the United Nations has prepared a method of classifying census figures on the age structure from the point of view of these disproportions, facilitating an objective evaluation of the reliability of the data obtained. The method is derived from the observation that, in the absence of unusual circumstances, large differences in the numbers of adjacent age groups as well as in the sex structure of adjacent age groups are caused by census inaccuracies. For a detailed description of this method see "Accuracy Tests for Census Age Distributions Tabulated in Five-year and Ten-year Groups", United Nations, Department of Social Affairs, Population Division, *Population Bulletin* No. 2, Document STSOA, Ser. n. 2, New York, October 1952, pp. 59—79.

deceased, to receive inheritance or to collect insurance. A marriage certificate is the legal basis for establishing a family.

Apart from this information, important from the judicial point of view, registers of demographic facts record many purely demographic data. The general tendency is to extend the scope of such records.

Registration of demographic facts is complete if it covers the whole area of a particular country and all inhabitants of that area. If registration is to cover the entire area, the country must be divided into relatively small units of territorial administration which, taken together, embrace the total area of the country without exception. This calls for sufficiently wide-spread organization which is attainable only at a certain level of socio-economic development. This is the reason why vital records of demographic facts do not exist as yet in some countries, while in some others they are incomplete and cover some parts of the country or sections of the population only.

Such limitations may also be of an administrative origin. In certain countries, for instance, demographic facts are recorded as fully as possible in special "registration areas" only. Those are mostly areas in and near large towns, i.e. areas which are easily accessible for administrative bodies and where contact with administrative offices is easy for the population. In registration areas the number and structure of the population are fixed as accurately as possible, this being the basis for calculating various rate values. Such registration areas exist to day in Burma, Ghana, India and Venezuela. In certain other countries, registration covers one or several large towns only. By gradually expanding the area of registration it is possible to bring vital records of demographic facts throughout the country to a satisfactory level, as was done, for example, in the United States.

In some countries, certain areas are excluded from compulsory registration because of their inaccessibility and sparseness of population. Thus, demographic facts are not recorded in northern Canada and in the inaccessible regions of Argentina and Peru.

In colonial countries, vital records often cover the white population or persons of European descent only, since the introduction of compulsory registration for the whole population would entail organizational difficulties and large scale expenses.

Disdain for the native on the part of colonial authorities also plays a significant part in this respect.

All this makes it very hard to compare natural movement statistics for different countries and different years. Moreover, even when compulsory registrations cover the whole area of a given country, not all facts pertaining to the natural movement of the population are entered in vital records. This is particularly true for countries where such records are of recent date; consequently, registration is often regarded as unnecessary if not onerous. The result is that in many cases the rates computed from registers of demographic facts are of little value. However, the shortcomings are often relatively small and not easily detected.

One method of checking whether birth registers are complete is to collate registration results with the data on the number of the youngest age groups enumerated in a population census. By means of such procedure it was established, for example, that in 1950, in Alaska, registration covered 92·1% of all births; in 1941, in Canada—98%; in 1940, in Puerto Rico—86·3%; in 1950, in the United States—97·9%. This shows that even in those countries where vital statistics have been kept fairly accurately for a long time, birth registration is far from complete. To quote the example of some other countries, the percentage of births entered in registers was 97% in Argentina, 80% in Sarawak, 75% in Nicaragua, 80% in Peru, 98·5% in Honduras.

It is much more difficult to check the completeness of death statistics.

Generally speaking, registration is never complete when the state is not interested in having statistics of the natural movement and of the state of the population, or when the registration is hindered by illiteracy or by the inaccessibility of large and sparsely populated areas of the country. If the entry of a demographic fact in the register entails cash payment, the tendency to avoid registration becomes very pronounced.

The question is, to what extent can the registration results in different countries be compared? This can be divided into two questions: (1) what is the scope of facts covered by registration in different countries? and (2) what kind of information is collected at registration?

In so far as births and deaths are concerned, the terms are usually so interpreted that stillbirths are counted neither as births nor as deaths. Since the term stillbirths has different meanings, there may also be different interpretations of what to include in live births and deaths. Here the completeness of registration coverage depends on the time-limit for registration. If the time-limit is short, such as twenty-four hours, records of live births can be regarded as more accurate than those allowing a time-limit as long as one year; for in the latter case there is a tendency not to record the births of children who died soon after birth. The births and deaths of such infants are thus not entered in the registers, which detracts from the value of infant birth and death rates. Similar in effect is the practice in some countries of including among stillbirths all infants that die before their births are recorded.

When studying population movement it is always essential to know the number of facts which actually occurred within a certain period (e.g., within a given calendar year) and not the number of facts which were recorded in the said period. If the time-limit for registration is not very short, the two figures may differ substantially. Here, too, there is no uniform approach to the problem. In the countries where registers of natural movement have been kept for a long time the period which elapses between the occurrence and the registration of demographic facts is usually short, in most cases not longer than one month. In some other countries, however, the facts registered within a given year may have actually occurred during any of several preceding years.[1] In some countries provisional data based on the number of facts registered within a given period are prepared; they are replaced

---

[1] In forty-four out of the seventy countries listed in United Nations demographic statistics, natural movement figures are based on facts which occurred within a given period; in the remaining twenty-six countries statistical figures are based on facts registered within a given period. The latter group should probably be expanded to include those countries which for lack of adequate information cannot be listed in United Nations demographic publications.

by final data computed at a later date, on the basis of facts which actually occurred within the given period.[1]

The problem seems to be relevant in the case of births only, since deaths must be registered without delay, and marriage registration is part of the wedding ceremony.

Lack of uniformity in birth statistics may also be caused by the fact that in most countries actual births are recorded, but in a few others registration covers confinements. Here, too, the meaning of confinement varies: in some countries only confinements resulting in live births are taken into account, while in some others all confinements are counted, whether the infant was born alive or dead.

The classification of births by age of the mother in some countries covers all births, and in some others legitimate births only. The order of birth is determined by considering only live births in some countries and all births in some others. The order of births may occasionally be considered only for legitimate children, or for legitimate children from the last marriage.

It is pertinent to note here that in some countries of South America and Asia consensual marriages are very numerous. Any classification confined to legitimate births in those countries would, of course, be of little value.

Birth classification in relation to the time of marriage reveals certain systematic deviations since, if the birth occurred soon after the wedding, the time of marriage may not be reported at all. Here again, there is no uniform approach, as in some countries only the year of marriage and in some others the exact date of marriage must be entered in the register.

Death statistics, apart from the question of whether or not to take into account stillbirths, involve the problem of deaths caused by hostilities. No uniform interpretation exists in this respect, either. In some countries war casualties are excluded from natural movement statistics, in some others they are counted along with other deaths.

Marriage statistics may deal with three different facts: (1) religious or civil marriage ceremony, (2) marriage registration, and (3) the issue of a marriage licence. If the latter is taken

---

[1] *Demographic Yearbook 1954*, pp. 20—21.

into account, then marriage statistics contain exaggerated figures since not every case for which a licence is obtained results in an actual marriage. Also, as I have mentioned above, in some countries common-law unions are so numerous that the value of data on legal marriages contracted in those countries is rather dubious. Lack of uniformity may also result from the fact that the legal minimum age at marriage differs from country to country or even within the same country.

Divorce statistics are hard to compare on an international scale as the relevant legal regulations vary in different countries. Some countries still refuse to recognise the institution of divorce, in others a decree of divorce is easy to obtain. In no cases do divorce statistics reflect the number of broken marriages. Where a divorce is hard to obtain, many couples remain married only *de jure*; such marriages, though *de facto* dissolved, will never be covered by divorce statistics.

Divorces have another aspect in countries where polygamy is permissible by law. Divorce is then relatively easy; in some countries, such as Egypt, there are several types of divorce.

Divorce statistics are always complete, in the sense that they include every case for which a decree on the dissolution of marriage has been granted by the authorities concerned. But the decree follows only some time after the actual dissolution of the marriage.

CHAPTER 2

DEGREE OF ACCURACY OF
DEMOGRAPHIC RATES

APART from absolute figures denoting the number of the population, births, marriages, deaths, etc., demographic statistics deal with various relative figures indicating rates of birth, marriage, death, etc. Rates for different areas and periods of time are compared and various computations are made on this basis.

It is important to know, therefore, the degree of accuracy of these rates. Those containing an error of considerable magnitude obviously cannot be a good basis for comparisons, and any conclusions drawn from them must be considered with utmost caution.

Generally speaking, rates computed for large populations are more reliable than those computed for smaller populations. Smaller populations can be taken into account when a certain error is permissible; however, below a certain minimum size the error becomes so large that no accurate numerical values can be ascribed to a given rate. For example, if the general conditions of population reproduction in a particular country remained unchanged, the birth rate computed for the whole country would remain virtually constant (unless some noticeable shifts occurred in the age structure of the population). Analogous rates for one province would probably also remain stable. But if we made a further territorial division of the country, we might find that chance fluctuations in one locality or one block of flats reach considerable dimensions. In the same block of flats the number of births in one year may be several times as large as in another year, even though the general birth rate changes very slowly or not at all. The same can naturally be said about mortality rates, marriage rates, etc.

Accordingly, the population group for which rates are computed must not be too small. How small a population may be used depends on the purpose of the study and the use to be made of the rates computed. Should we only want to establish whether the rates for a given area are lower or higher than for another, the minimum group can be smaller than when we want to fix the exact value of the rate. In the former case, correct conclusions can be drawn even if the two rates contain considerable errors; in the latter case, no error is permissible.

However, errors depend not only on the size of the population for which the rates are computed but also on the value of the rates. The larger the rate the smaller can be the population; and, conversely, the lower the rate the larger must be the population.

Demography deals with low rate values. Birth rates very seldom exceed 40 per thousand, or 0·04; death rates are usually even lower; marriage rates are the lowest, mostly about 0·01. If demographic phenomena are studied in greater detail, e.g. in relation to age, the rates may be considerably lower.

Hence, the population studied should be quite large, numbering at least scores of thousands. In the case of Poland, this represents approximately the population of a county.

This can be formulated mathematically as follows: if the size of the population is n, p—the probability of the occurrence of a certain event (birth, death, marriage etc.) within one year (annual periods are most frequently used in demographic studies), it is to be expected that if the probability is constant over a long period of time, on the average there will be $A = np$ such events within one year. The standard deviation of the number of such events is $\sigma = np(1-p)$. Since the probability p is small, $1-p$ will approximately equal 1 and

$$\sigma = \sqrt{np}.$$

If we want the chance error with fair certainty (i.e., with 0·95 probability) not to exceed k times the arithmetic mean A, i.e. the error not to exceed kA, a necessary condition is that

$$2\sqrt{np} < knp.$$

Hence, after simple transformations:

$$n > \frac{4}{pk^2}$$

If $p = 0.01$ and $k = 0.1$ (10%), then $n > 40,000$;

if $p = 0.03$ and $k = 0.05$ (5%), then $n > 53,333$, etc.

Accordingly, in any studies of a quantitative character the minimum population must not be less than that of a county area, or a similar territorial unit. Otherwise it might happen that differences resulting from chance fluctuations would be interpreted—though without the slightest reason—as significant differences. This does not mean, of course, that small changes (or small differences) are always due to chance; it only means that they may have arisen by chance. If, therefore, we notice a small change (or a small difference), we are not entitled to say solely on the basis of rate values that the change in question is essential and not due to chance.

Table 1 shows the minimum population size where the error is almost certainly not larger than k times the given rate (considering different rate values and different values of k).

TABLE 1

Relative rate error (k)	Rate values (p)						
	0·01	0·02	0·03	0·04	0·05	0·06	0·07
	Minimum population size						
0·1 (10%)	40,000	20,000	13,333	10,000	8000	6667	5714
0·05 (5%)	160,000	80,000	53,333	40,000	32,000	26,667	22,856
0·02 (2%)	1,000,000	500,000	333,333	250,000	200,000	166,667	142,857
0·01 (1%)	4,000,000	2,000,000	1,333,333	1,000,000	800,000	666,667	571,429

If, for example, we want the error with fair certainty not to exceed 0·1, or 10% of the rate value, which amounts to some 0·02, the population must not be smaller than 20,000. If the rate value reaches some 0·05 and the permissible error must not be larger than 0·02 (2%), the population cannot be smaller than 200,000.

This can be presented graphically. In Figure 1, the horizontal axis represents rates and the vertical axis (in the logarithmic scale)—the minimum population size. Each curve thus corresponds to the value of (k) marked on it.

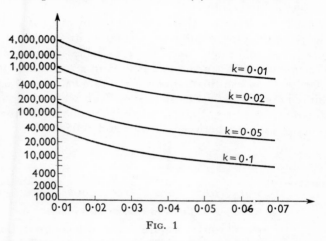

FIG. 1

The problem may be tackled from another angle. We may try to find the relative error in the rate if its order of magnitude is known and also the population group for which it has been computed (Table 2).

TABLE 2

Population size (n)	Rate values (p)						
	0·01	0·02	0·03	0·04	0·05	0·06	0·07
	maximum relative error						
1000	0·6324	0·4471	0·3637	0·3162	0·2799	0·2584	0·2391
10,000	0·2000	0·1414	0·1150	0·1000	0·0895	0·0817	0·0756
100,000	0·0632	0·0447	0·0364	0·0316	0·0280	0·0258	0·0239
1,000,000	0·0200	0·0141	0·0115	0·0100	0·0089	0·0082	0·0076
10,000,000	0·0063	0·0045	0·0036	0·0032	0·0028	0·0026	0·0024
100,000,000	0·0020	0·0014	0·0012	0·0010	0·0009	0·0008	0·0008

Table 2 reveals that if the rate is 0·02 and the population group amounts to 10,000 units, the error almost certainly will not exceed 0·1414 (14·14%) of the rate value. Similarly, if the rate is 0·05 and the population group consists of 1,000,000 units, the error will not exceed 0·0089 (0·89%) of the rate value.

On the basis of Table 2 may be computed the limits within which the rate values will almost certainly range, allowing for random fluctuations.

From Table 3 we see that, when the rate value is 0·02 and the population group numbers 10,000 units, under the influence of random fluctuations, the rate values may vary from 0·0172 to 0·0228. When the rate is 0·05 in a population group of 1,000,000, random fluctuations of the rate values will almost certainly range from 0·0496 to 0·0504. Even when the population group numbers 10,000,000 units, random fluctuations may occur ranging between 0·0499 and 0·0501.

TABLE 3

Population size (n)	Rate values (p)						
	0·01	0·02	0·03	0·04	0·05	0·06	0·07
	limits of random fluctuations						
1000	0.0037	0.0111	0.0191	0.0274	0.0360	0.0445	0.0533
	0·0163	0·0289	0·0409	0·0526	0·0640	0·0755	0·0867
10,000	0.0080	0.0172	0·0266	0·0360	0·0455	0·0551	0·0647
	0·0120	0·0228	0·0334	0·0440	0·0545	0·0649	0·0753
100,000	0.0094	0·0191	0·0289	0·0387	0·0486	0·0585	0·0683
	0·0106	0·0209	0·0311	0·0413	0·0514	0·0615	0·0717
1,000,000	0·0098	0·0197	0·0297	0·0396	0·0496	0·0595	0·0695
	0·0102	0·0203	0·0303	0·0404	0·0504	0·0605	0·0705
10,000,000	0·0099	0·0199	0·0299	0·0399	0·0499	0·0598	0·0698
	0·0101	0·0201	0·0301	0·0401	0·0501	0·0602	0·0702
100,000,000	0·0100	0·0200	0·0300	0·0400	0·0500	0·0600	0·0699
	0·0100	0·0200	0·0300	0·0400	0·0500	0·0600	0·0701

The contents of Table 3 can also be presented graphically (Fig. 2) in curves bounding the range of rate fluctuations for different sizes of the population group for which the rate has been computed (Fig. 2).

The graph shows that the range of random fluctuations, quite large in the case of a small population, is gradually reduced and, in the case of very large population groups, does not affect even a ten-thousandth part of the rate value.

Thus, when the population group numbers 1000, the area of fluctuation of the 0·05 rate overlaps the area of fluctuation of the 0·03 rate. In other words, if the population under study numbers 1000 and the rate equals 0·05 in a particular year, there is no certainty whatever that the rate will not drop to 0·03 the next year. In this case, random fluctuations may result in nearly doubling the rate value.

We shall now proceed to some examples.

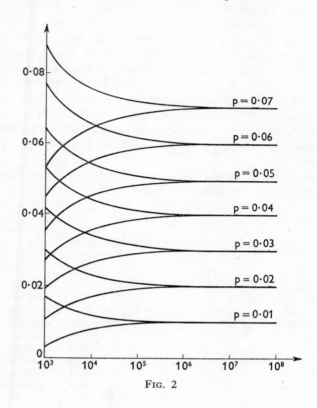

$$p = 0·07$$

$$p = 0·06$$

$$p = 0·05$$

$$p = 0·04$$

$$p = 0·03$$

$$p = 0·02$$

$$p = 0·01$$

Fig. 2

Let us begin with live births in England and Wales in 1958.[1]

The general live birth rate throughout the country was 16·4 per thousand inhabitants. Let us see whether birth rates in different parts of the country equalled the overall national figure. It may be anticipated that birth rates varied from region to region; we want to ascertain, however, whether the differences between regional and national rates were due to random fluctuations or whether they were real.

We begin with the northern region. Its population was 3,203,000 and the number of live births 59,344; the birth rate thus equalled 18·5‰. Given this particular population, random fluctuations in either direction should not exceed 0·2‰. Had the birth rate in the northern region been the same as in the whole country, due to the influence of random fluctuations, it might have deviated from the national figure by 0·2‰ in either direction. Fluctuations would thus have ranged between a minimum of 16·4—0·2 and a maximum of 16·4 + 0·2, i.e. between 16·2‰ and 16·6‰. But the actual birth rate in the northern region is 18·5‰, i.e. it exceeds the upper limit of the range of random fluctuations. This means that the birth rate in the northern region differs significantly (and not due to chance) from the birth rate for the whole country.

Similar computations have been made for other regions, and the results are given in Table 4.[1]

TABLE 4

Region	Birth rate	Range of fluctuations	Difference between local and national birth rates
Northern.	18·5	16·2—16·6	significant
East and West Ridings	16·6	16·3—16·5	significant
North Western	16·8	16·3—16·5	significant
North Midlands	16·8	16·3—16·5	significant
Midlands	17·0	16·2—16·6	significant
Eastern	17·1	16·3—16·5	significant
London and South Eastern . .	15·1	16·3—16·5	significant
Southern	16·7	16·3—16·5	significant
South Western	15·6	16·3—16·5	significant
Wales	16·2	16·2—16·6	may not be significant

It should be noted that in relation to Wales we use the formulation "the difference may not be significant." This denotes that the available statistics are not sufficient to establish whether the difference is significant or not. For it is conceivable

[1] Source of data: *The Registrar General's Statistical Review of England and Wales for the Year 1958,* Part II. Marriage and death statistics mentioned later in this book are taken from the same source.

taht it was purely by chance that the birth rates in Wales rose to 16·2, thus remaining within the permissible range of fluctuations. Had more abundant data been available, covering at least several years, and had the birth rates in Wales proved to remain constantly slightly lower than the national figure, we might have arrived at another conclusion.

Statistics for the year 1958 enable us to state that in nine out of ten regions the difference between regional and national birth rates was significant, and in Wales it may not have been significant. The birth rates ranged from 15·1 to 18·5‰.

An objection might be raised here against comparing rate values for populations with different age structures; one must first eliminate the effect of differences in the age distribution of the population of various regions. In fact, in the publication quoted the rates are standardized and on this basis the ratio is computed indicating the relation of the (adjusted) birth rates in each region to the national rate (Table 5).

TABLE 5

Region	Ratio of birth rate to national rate
Northern.	1·11
East and West Ridings	1·01
North Western	1·02
North Midlands	1·02
Midlands	1·01
Eastern	1·04
London and South Eastern . .	0·89
Southern	1·05
South Western	1·01
Wales	1·01

The results are the same as in the case of crude (uncorrected) birth rates; hence, in all regions except Wales the deviations from the national birth rate are certainly significant. The range is not very large: from 0·89 (89%) to 1·05 (105%) of the national birth rate.

If instead of large regions we take into account smaller administrative units, such as counties (their number in England and Wales is 62), the range of fluctuations will be larger: from 12·5 to 19·3‰, or from 0·89 to 1·23 times the national

rate (after adjusting the rates to eliminate the effect of differences in age structures). The range between minimum and
maximum birth rates for counties is thus more than twice
as large as that for regions. The respective quantities are
listed in Table 6.

TABLE 6

Ratio of birth rate to national rate	Number of administrative units
0·85—0·89	5
0·90—0·94	6
0·95—0·99	13
1·00—1·04	18
1·05—1·09	9
1·10—1·14	6
1·15—1·19	2
1·20—1·24	3
Total	62

In 13 out of 62 counties the birth rates can be considered
to be consistent with the national rate within the range of
random deviations. Actual birth rates in the 13 counties ranged
between 15·3 and 16·7, i.e. they remained rather close to
the national rate (16·4‰).

If the administrative units taken into account are still
smaller the situation will change again: the range between
the extreme values of birth rates will increase. Birth rate
data for 1470 administrative districts, numbering from 700
to more than one million inhabitants, are classified in Table 7.

The lowest birth rate (in crude figures, not adjusted to
take into account the difference in age structures) is 4·2‰,
and the highest, 31·4‰; the difference is thus still larger
than for regions and counties. After correcting the data to
eliminate the influence of difference in age structures, the
resulting rates range between 0·33 and 1·78 times the national
figure.

The lowest rate to be considered as perhaps not differing
significantly from the national figure is 6·3‰, and the highest,
which shows no significant difference from the national
birth rate, is 24·5‰. As ratios of the national rate (after making
corrections for age) these equal from 0·58 to 1·48. Naturally,

TABLE 7

Ratio of birth rate to national rate	Number of administrative units
0·30—0·34	1
0·35—0·39	1
0·40—0·44	1
0·45—0·49	—
0·50—0·54	5
0·55—0·59	5
0·60—0·64	2
0·65—0·69	18
0·70—0·74	47
0·75—0·79	47
0·80—0·84	88
0·85—0·89	144
0·90—0·94	191
0·95—0·99	208
1·00—1·04	185
1·05—1·09	173
1·10—1·14	118
1·15—1·19	92
1·20—1·24	65
1·25—1·29	27
1·30—1·34	20
1·35—1·39	12
1·40—1·44	6
1·45—1·49	5
1·50—1·54	2
1·55—1·59	3
1·60—1·64	2
1·65—1·69	1
1·70—1·74	—
1·75—1·79	1
Total	1470

this does not mean that all administrative districts with birth rates ranging from 6·3 to 24·5 reveal no significant difference in relation to the national rate. Within these limits there may be some administrative districts with a population so numerous that random fluctuations cannot be very large; hence, even though their birth rates are closer to the national figure, the deviation from the national rate cannot be explained by the influence of mere chance. Anyhow, in this case the number of administrative districts with birth rates not differing significantly from the national rate will be certainly still greater than in the previous case (when the country was divided into 62 units, 13 of which did not reveal significant differences from the national rate). We have not verified which of the 1470 smaller administrative districts have birth rates not differing significantly from the national rate, as this would entail too great an effort in comparison with the results that could be obtained.

The course of our reasoning can be summarized in a table (Table 8).

TABLE 8

Number of administrative units	Number of administrative units where birth rates may not differ significantly from national rates	Minimum and maximum birth rates	
		in all units	in units where birth rates may not differ significantly from national rates
10	1	15·1—18·5	16·2
62	13	12·5—19·3	15·9—16·4
1470	—	4·2—31·4	6·3—24·5

The distribution of territorial units by birth rates followed a certain pattern; the difference between the lowest and the highest rates was relatively small in the case of a small number of large units, and it gradually increased as the units under study grew smaller and smaller. The distribution of birth rates can be presented in a graph (Fig. 3); the total number of administrative units in each case is taken as 100%.

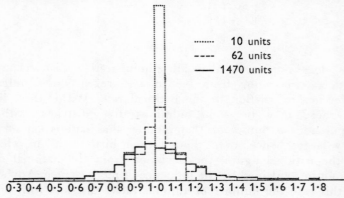

FIG. 3

A similar picture is obtained when examining death rates. Again, in one out of ten regions, death rates may not differ significantly from the national figure.

For counties, the minimum death rate was 9·2‰ and the maximum 13·9‰. In 17 out of 62 counties death rates may not differ significantly from the national figure. Death rates in these 17 counties range from 11·3 to 12·6; in corrected rates (taking into account the influence of age) this represents as from 0·86 to 1·15 times the national ratio respectively.

We have not analysed the smaller administrative districts since it can be safely assumed that the result would be the same as in the case of birth rates. But it should be noted that in the event of an administrative division of 1470 units the range of death rates is very large: varying from 3·0 to 28·4‰, or, after making the corrections for age structures, at a ratio of 0·36 to 1·78 of the national mortality rate.

The summarized results are presented in Table 9.

TABLE 9

Number of administrative units	Number of administrative units where death rates may not differ significantly from national rate	Minimum and maximum death rates	
		in all units	in units where death rates may not differ significantly from national rate
10	1	10·6—12·8	11·8
62	17	9·2—13·9	11·3—12·6
1470	—	2·8—32·0	—

We have also examined analogous marriage statistics, but only for administrative divisions of 10 regions and 62 counties, as there are no data available on the number of marriages for each of the 1470 smaller administrative districts. Neither have corrections for age structures been introduced; presumably they would be similar to those in the case of birth rates.

The marriage rate for the whole country was 7·6 per thousand inhabitants (this is the proportion of the number of marriages to the total population, computed per thousand inhabitants, and not the ratio of the number of persons contracting marriage to the total population).

The results of computations for marriage rates are presented in Table 10.

TABLE 10

Number of administrative units	Number of administrative units where marriage rates may not differ significantly from national rate	Minimum and maximum marriage rates	
		in all units	in units where marriage rates may not differ significantly from national rate
10	6	6·2—8·1	7·4—7·8
62	20	5·6—10·0	7·0—7·8

It seems safe to assume that analogous computations made for other countries would yield results of a very similar nature.

An analysis of all the data relating to birth, death and marriage rates leads to the following general conclusions:

(1) the intensity of demographic phenomena within one country varies considerably; differences between various parts of the same country are often larger than between various countries;

(2) the smaller the administrative units under study, the more variable the intensity of a given phenomenon; however, when the units under study are too small, the rates may contain random errors of such magnitude that their usefulness for purposes of comparison and drawing conclusions is reduced;

(3) hence, a student of the problem should not carry territorial divisions too far, but should stop at sufficiently large units for which reliable rates can be computed.

However, these are not the only difficulties involved. Rates may contain errors not only in the case of small territorial units but also when computed for small population groups. This is true both for a detailed division into territorial units and for a division by any non-territorial characteristic, whenever it involves too small a population group.

Such small population samples are sometimes arrived at when examining mortality by age. If the distribution by age is given in great detail, e.g. by individual years of age, then the number of deaths in the years of childhood and adolescence may be very small and the death rates for these years will be subject to large random fluctuations. The error will be even larger if, for instance, divisions by sex or by urban and rural population were additionally accounted for. That is why mortality tables are usually based on larger divisions, e.g. five-year age groups.

The values of possible errors and of the range of fluctuations computed for Polish mortality tables for 1955/56 are presented in Table 11. Probabilities of death are based on data for five-year age groups. The computations have been made separately for both sexes (as the largest group) and for urban females (as the smallest group). Errors, given in percentages of the respective rates, are listed in Table 11.

TABLE 11

Age groups	General population	Urban females
Under 1 year	0·9	1·9
1—4	2·4	5·5
5—9	4·0	9·5
10—14	5·5	15·4
15—19	4·1	10·9
20—24	3·3	8·2
25—29	3·0	7·3
30—34	3·0	6·6
35—39	3·2	7·1
40—44	2·6	5·8
45—49	2·0	4·7
50—54	1·8	4·2
55—59	1·6	3·6
60—64	1·5	3·4
65—69	1·3	2·9
70—74	1·3	2·7
75—79	1·3	2·7
80—84	1·5	3·0
85 and more	1·8	3·5

The relative error initially rises to its maximum in the 10—14 age group, then gradually drops to a minimum in the 75—79 group, and subsequently increases again.

The largest range of fluctuations exists in infancy and in older (but not the oldest) age groups. Most difficult to compute accurately is the probability of death in childhood and adolescence, i.e. in the age groups having the lowest mortality.

Using the values of relative errors obtained it is possible

to compute the range of fluctuations in probabilities of death
due to the influence of random factors (assuming that the
probabilities of death shown in the 1955/56 tables are
"reliable"). As in the previous case, the results of computations are listed for both sexes and for urban females. The
computations refer to the median year of birth in every class
(Table 12).

TABLE 12

Age group	Range of fluctuations in probabilities of death	
	general population	urban females
0	0·07547—0·07727	0·06023—0·06235
3	0·00175—0·00183	0·00143—0·00159
7	0·00089—0·00097	0·00069—0·00083
12	0·00065—0·00073	0·00038—0·00052
17	0·00100—0·00108	0·00064—0·00080
22	0·00162—0·00172	0·00094—0·00110
27	0·00186—0·00198	0·00121—0·00141
32	0·00210—0·00222	0·00152—0·00174
37	0·00275—0·00293	0·00209—0·00241
42	0·00341—0·00359	0·00268—0·00302
47	0·00516—0·00538	0·00384—0·00422
52	0·00833—0·00863	0·00618—0·00672
57	0·01315—0·01357	0·00962—0·01034
62	0·02140—0·02206	0·01669—0·01787
67	0·03316—0·03404	0·02606—0·02762
72	0·05211—0·05349	0·04314—0·04554
77	0·07804—0·08030	0·06708—0·07080
82	0·11058—0·11396	0·09767—0·10371
87	0·14900—0·15446	0·13478—0·14424

Immediately after infancy, during which the deviation in
absolute figures may be quite large, it drops very low and
remains at approximately the same level until the age of 20,
following which it gradually rises, first slowly and then at
an increasingly faster rate. The process is presented graphically
(in logarithmic scale) in Fig. 4.

Since such comparatively large fluctuations may already be
noted in the middle age groups, it is conceivable that the
configuration of death rates by age for populations which are
not too large will not follow the smooth course of mortality
usually encountered in life tables. Deviations from the normal
course may be revealed not only in too low or too high death

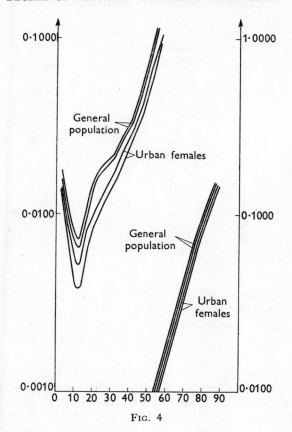

FIG. 4

rates for certain age groups but also in a reversal of the course of mortality in relation to age: instead of increasing with age, mortality declines in some age groups. This is illustrated in Table 13 listing death rates in certain voivodships of Poland in 1955.

A graphic representation of these rates is given in Fig. 5. The most regular of the three is the pattern of death rates for females in Warsaw. However, the minimum in the 10 to 14 age group seems to be too low as compared with the adjacent groups, and certain irregularities are revealed above the age of 40: while the distance between death rates in subsequent age groups should increase, in actual fact the distance

TABLE 13

Age groups	Warsaw (females)	Olsztyn voivodship (males)	Szczecin voivodship (males)
0—4	0·0089	0·0261	0·0283
5—9	0·0006	0·0012	0·0013
10—14	0·0003	0·0011	0·0018
15—19	0·0011	0·0019	0·0029
20—24	0·0010	0·0027	0·0026
25—29	0·0012	0·0026	0·0033
30—34	0·0017	0·0030	0·0033
35—39	0·0021	0·0027	0·0034
40—44	0·0032	0·0052	0·0057
45—49	0·0040	0·0071	0·0069
50—54	0·0069	0·0112	0·0109
55—59	0·0092	0·0193	0·0180
60—64	0·0157	0·0257	0·0286
65—69	0·0221	0·0392	0·0350

between the 40 to 44 and 45 to 49 age groups is smaller than that between the 35 to 39 and 40 to 44 age groups; similarly, the distance between the 50 to 54 and 55 to 59 age groups is smaller than that between the 45 to 49 and 50 to 54 age groups.

In the Olsztyn voivodship, the death rate for males aged between 25 and 29 is smaller than for those aged from 20 to 24; similarly, it is smaller for the 35 to 39 than for the 30 to 34 age group. We are thus faced with a reversal of the normal process. In the Szczecin voivodship, death rates for males are the lowest in the 5 to 9 age group and not, as might have been expected, in the 10 to 14 group; also, the 25 to 29 and 30 to 34 age groups have equal mortality rates, and the rate in the next age group, from 35 to 39, is nearly the same as that in the preceding two groups.

The situation is much better as far as birth rates by age of mother and marriage rates by age of spouses are concerned, since the range of random fluctuations is smaller in this case. This is due to the fact that births and marriages are concentrated in some age groups, unlike deaths which are scattered over all age groups but reveal the highest concentration in the two extreme groups—infancy and old age.

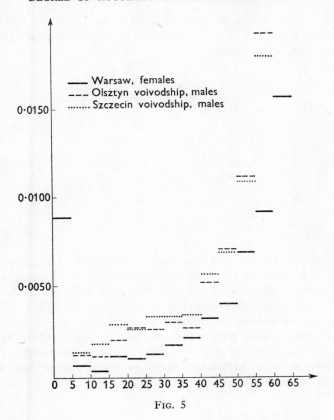

FIG. 5

The results of computations for the total female population and for urban females are listed in Table 14.

TABLE 14

Age of mother	Birth rates per 100 females			
	total	range of fluctuations	urban	range of fluctuations
15—19	4·6	4·6	4·8	4·7—4·9
20—24	21·6	21·5—21·7	19·8	19·7—19·9
25—29	19·5	19·4—19·6	17·5	17·4—17·6
30—34	13·0	12·9—13·1	10·4	10·3—10·5
35—39	7·5	7·4—7·6	6·4	6·3—6·5
40 and more	1·4	1·4	0·8	0·8

Thus, the range of random deviations in birth rates by age of the mother is so small that the rates can as a rule be considered as accurate.

TABLE 15

Age groups	Marriage rates per 100 females			
	total	range of fluctuations	urban	range of fluctuations
15—19	5·5	5·5	6·4	6·4
20—24	10·0	9·9—10·1	9·9	9·8—10·0
25—29	3·5	3·5	3·5	3·4—3·6
30—34	1·4	1·4	1·5	1·5
35—39	0·9	0·9	1·0	1·0
40—49	0·4	0·4	0·5	0·5
50 and more	0·2	0·2	0·4	0·4

Table 15 shows that the range of random fluctuations is also very small in the case of marriage rates distributed by age; hence, these rates are accurate as a rule.

Consequently, the following remark can be added to the general conclusions formulated on page 26:

(4) demographic phenomena are very strongly influenced by age; in analysing the available data on these phenomena it is advisable to study sufficiently large age groups rather than carry age differentiation too far.

CHAPTER 3

STRUCTURE OF THE POPULATION BY AGE AND MARITAL STATUS

WE SHALL endeavour to trace the existence of some patterns in the structure of the population by age and marital status, i.e. to see whether the ratio of various age groups to the total number of the population as well as to the number of married population reveals certain interrelations or is due to a smaller or greater degree to chance.

The existence of certain regularities can be safely assumed, if only because of the fact that amongst the great variety of age structures there exist some types of structures which have their equivalence in characteristic shapes of the age pyramid (Fig. 6). According to Sundbärg,[1] the typical structures are:

— a progressive age structure, giving a cone-shaped age pyramid starting on a broad base and rapidly tapering towards the top;

— a stationary structure, giving a bell-shaped age pyramid; and

— a regressive structure, giving a narrow-bottomed pyramid which slightly broadens upwards and then gradually tapers off.

Infancy and childhood cohorts are the most numerous in the case of a progressive age structure, less numerous in a stationary structure, and relatively very small in a regressive age structure. Old age cohorts reveal a reverse interrelation: relatively small in a progressive age structure, they are more numerous in a stationary and relatively very numerous in a regressive age structure.

Not always does the age structure follow such a regular

---

[1] Cf. G. Sundbärg, Sur la répartition de la population par âge et sur les taux de la mortalité, *Bulletin de l'Institut International de Statistique*, vol. XII, 1900.

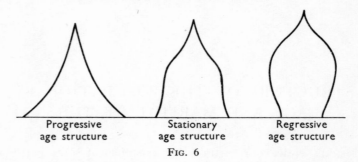

| Progressive age structure | Stationary age structure | Regressive age structure |

FIG. 6

pattern; for the age pyramid may be marked by indentations (caused by epidemics, war, emigration, economic depression etc.) or protuberances (e.g. as a result of immigration). It should be noted that any such indentation or protuberance leads in turn to another indentation or protuberance in the age pyramid some time later. Indeed, when cohorts much more or much less numerous than the adjacent ones enter the reproductive age, this results in a corresponding increase or decrease in the number of births as compared with the preceding period. These secondary disturbances cover a longer period of time than the original ones and, though less intense, can often be easily observed. Their influence on natality in the next generation (their grandchildren) is, of course, much less distinct if not quite unnoticeable.

Hence, if we want to establish the existence of some regular patterns in the age structure we must take into account data as free from the influence of such disturbances as possible. Consequently, the data examined should not cover the first post-war years, unless the country under study was non-belligerent and did not suffer from any direct consequences of the war. Moreover, the statistics under examination should represent countries demographically old, with a regressive age structure, as well as countries demographically young, with a rapidly growing population and a progressive age structure (countries with a stationary age structure are virtually nonexistent, since they are the border-line cases which by definition are extremely rare). Such statistics are listed in Table 16.[1]

---

[1] *Demographic Yearbook 1948.*

It should be borne in mind that data on the age structure
may contain errors of varying magnitude resulting from
inaccurate age enumeration in population censuses. The error is particularly frequent in the less developed countries.
But even though such inaccuracies indubitably exist, the
statistics listed here reveal a certain general trend; namely,
the larger the proportion of infants and children the larger
also the proportion of early age groups and the smaller the
proportion of adult and old-age groups. The 20 to 29 age
group marks the division between the age groups which
follow the same trend in proportional changes as do childhood groups and those whose proportional changes are in
a reverse direction. The 20 to 29 age group reveals neither
a distinctly rising nor a declining trend.

The farther we move in either direction from the 20 to
29 age group the more distinct are the differences between
the progressive and the regressive age structures. Characteristically, differences in absolute numbers of old age groups are
quite small; this is caused by the fact that old age groups
are never numerous, not even in the case of a highly regressive
age structure.

All these interrelations are clearly revealed in diagrams
where the horizontal coordinate axis denotes the proportion
of the 0—9 age group (marked A_{0-9}) and the vertical axis
denotes the proportion of any other age group (Fig. 7a, b,
c, d, e). The points thus obtained form certain more or less
regular shapes and are scattered over larger or smaller areas.

Diagrams for the later age groups have not been shown
here; their configuration follows the pattern of the 50—59
age group, only at a lower level. Thus, in the 60—69
age group the maximum and minimum proportions are 2·5 and
8·8 respectively, and in the 70 group and over the equivalent
figures are 1·0 and 6·0.

The diagrams reveal that the points, though scattered,
are grouped in strips along more or less straight lines.

In Fig. 7a, two points clearly deviate from the general pattern, as they show a very high proportion of the 0—9 age
group and a relatively small proportion of the 10—19 age
group. They stand for Mozambique and Turkey, two countries
where statistics are quite new and the coverage is so in-

3

TABLE 16

Country	Year	Age groups							
		percent of total population							
		0—9	10—19	20—29	30—39	40—49	50—59	60—69	70 and over
Angola	1940	29·4	18·8	17·5	15·2	9·9	4·1	3·9	3·7
Egypt	1937	27·2	20·5	15·1	14·7	10·0	6·0	3·6	2·7
Mozambique	1940	36·1	14·1	18·8	16·1	7·6	3·8	2·5	1·0
South Africa —white population .	1946	21·5	17·9	16·2	15·5	11·0	8·4	5·8	3·7
Canada	1941	18·3	19·3	17·4	13·9	11·4	9·5	6·2	4·0
Cuba	1941	25·2	20·7	18·7	14·5	8·4	6·9	3·5	2·1
Dominican Republic . .	1935	33·2	23·6	16·8	11·2	7·0	3·7	2·5	2·0
Guatemala	1940	30·5	23·5	15·9	12·1	8·5	4·7	3·2	1·6
Honduras	1945	29·8	23·0	17·5	12·0	8·2	4·8	2·9	1·8
Mexico	1940	28·9	22·4	16·0	13·7	8·7	5·3	3·3	1·7
Puerto Rico	1940	28·5	23·1	18·9	10·9	8·3	4·9	3·3	2·1
United States	1940	15·9	18·3	17·2	15·0	13·0	9·9	6·5	4·0
Brazil	1940	29·6	23·7	17·4	11·9	8·3	4·9	2·6	1·6
Chile	1940	25·0	22·3	17·6	13·4	9·6	6·2	3·7	2·2
Colombia	1938	29·6	22·6	17·4	12·2	8·1	5·0	3·0	2·1
Peru	1940	30·3	21·2	16·4	12·2	8·4	5·1	3·3	3·0
Venezuela	1941	28·6	22·8	17·1	12·1	8·8	5·1	2·8	1·7

Japan	1940	24·5	21·7	16·0	12·7	9·6	7·5	5·3	2·7
Korea	1944	31·3	21·4	14·1	11·6	8·8	6·6	4·1	2·1
Philippines	1939	31·8	21·6	17·9	11·2	7·4	4·6	3·4	2·1
Thailand	1937	30·9	21·3	16·9	12·6	8·1	5·4	3·3	1·5
Turkey	1935	31·4	16·4	16·9	13·8	8·3	6·0	4·2	3·0
Austria	1939	13·2	16·4	14·0	17·2	13·8	11·6	8·7	5·2
Belgium	1939	16·7	14·2	17·6	15·6	13·0	11·1	7·4	4·4
Bulgaria	1934	23·7	19·2	18·2	14·0	9·7	7·4	4·6	3·2
England and Wales	1931	15·8	16·6	17·1	14·6	13·1	11·2	7·3	4·3
Finland	1940	16·7	18·6	17·0	16·1	11·8	8·9	6·2	3·7
France	1936	16·2	14·0	15·2	15·9	12·5	11·4	8·8	6·0
Greece	1930	21·5	20·8	15·7	14·2	10·1	7·9	5·8	4·0
Italy	1936	20·5	17·7	17·1	13·7	11·0	8·8	6·5	4·7
Netherlands	1930	21·1	18·9	17·1	13·8	11·0	8·7	5·8	3·6
Norway	1930	18·4	19·7	16·8	14·3	10·6	8·6	6·2	5·4
Poland	1931	24·8	18·1	19·1	13·2	9·3	7·0	5·1	3·4
Portugal	1940	21·5	20·1	16·1	13·6	10·4	8·2	5·9	4·2
Rumania	1930	25·9	19·1	18·0	12·8	10·3	6·6	4·6	2·7
Spain	1940	19·4	20·4	16·4	14·1	11·1	8·5	6·3	3·8
Sweden	1945	15·7	12·9	15·7	16·3	14·1	11·1	8·2	6·0
Switzerland	1940	14·6	15·6	15·4	16·5	14·0	10·8	8·3	4·8
Yugoslavia	1931	27·5	17·5	18·7	12·2	9·1	6·8	5·0	3·2
Australia	1933	18·1	18·7	16·9	14·4	13·1	8·9	6·2	3·7
New Zealand	1945	18·3	15·4	14·1	15·0	12·6	10·5	8·8	5·1

3*

complete that the data may be expected to contain an error
by under-enumeration of the 10—19 age group (possibly
to the benefit of the 0—9 group). Except for the two deviating
points, the general contour is quite regular.

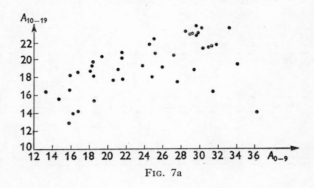

FIG. 7a

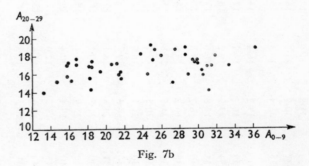

Fig. 7b

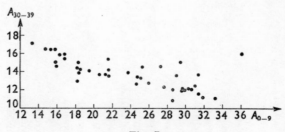

Fig. 7c

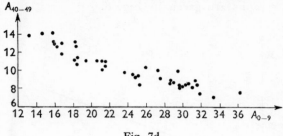

Fig. 7d

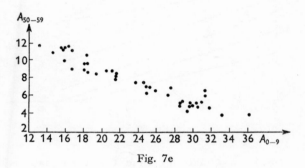

Fig. 7e

In Fig. 7c, the point denoting Mozambique is again far from the others; this confirms our belief that the population census in Mozambique was not quite efficacious and that the data collected are questionable.

By hazarding a theory that the interrelation should follow a straight line and that any deviations are due to census errors we would obtain some simple regression lines. The equations for these lines (arrived at by Hellwig's point method) are:

$$A_{10-19} = 0{\cdot}38\,A_{0-9} + 10{\cdot}3$$
$$A_{20-29} = 0{\cdot}04\,A_{0-9} + 15{\cdot}7$$
$$A_{30-39} = -0{\cdot}16\,A_{0-9} + 17{\cdot}6$$
$$A_{40-49} = -0{\cdot}30\,A_{0-9} + 17{\cdot}4$$
$$A_{50-59} = -0{\cdot}37\,A_{0-9} + 16{\cdot}3$$
$$A_{60-69} = -0{\cdot}34\,A_{0-9} + 13{\cdot}3$$
$$A_{70-\text{and over}} = -0{\cdot}25\,A_{0-9} + 9{\cdot}4$$

Their graphs are given in Fig. 8.

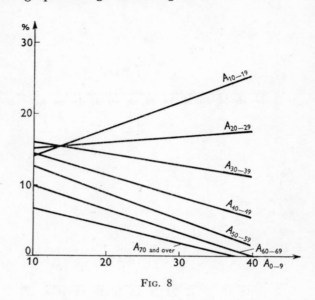

FIG. 8

It is not to be assumed, of course, that the equations denote accurate, error-less relations between the proportions of different age groups. We must emphasize that our intention was only to depict the prevailing trends so as to be able to reach more concrete conclusions than would be possible solely from age structure statistics.

The equations show, first and foremost, that if the proportion of the earliest age group (0—9) changes, a noticeable change in the same direction takes place in the proportion of the adjacent group (10—19). The 20—29 group remains practically unchanged, but subsequent age groups undergo changes in the reverse direction to those in the youngest age group. From the 55—59 age group on, the changes grow gradually smaller in absolute value.

We can now pass to computing theoretical age structures derived from different values of the initial proportion of the youngest age group (0—9). The results are listed in Table 17.

The list begins with an intensely progressive age structure (it might even be called a primitive structure) which gradually

TABLE 17

Population	Age groups							
	0—9	10—19	20—29	30—39	40—49	50—59	60—69	70 and over
	percentage of population							
100·0	35·0	23·6	17·1	12·0	6·9	3·4	1·4	0·6
100·0	30·0	21·7	16·9	12·8	8·4	5·2	3·1	1·9
100·0	25·0	19·8	16·7	13·6	9·9	7·1	4·8	3·1
100·0	20·0	17·9	16·5	14·4	11·4	8·9	6·5	4·4
100·0	15·0	16·0	16·3	15·2	12·9	10·8	8·2	5·6
100·0	10·0	14·1	16·1	16·0	14·4	12·6	9·9	6·9
100·0	5·0	12·2	15·9	16·8	15·9	14·5	11·6	8·1

becomes distinctly regressive. The youngest age group (0—9) initially dominates; as its proportion declines, the next youngest group (10—19) takes top place, to be gradually replaced by subsequent groups. The last line in the table mirrors a strongly regressive age structure, with the largest percentage in the 30—39 age group. It can be seen that the regression of population begins when the earliest age group no longer dominates; this occurs when the proportion of this group equals 16—17% of the population. Accordingly, a proportion of more than 16 or 17% in the 0—9 age group denotes a progressive age structure, a smaller proportion—a regressive structure, and a proportion equal to 16—17% — a stationary structure of the population.

We can also compute relative changes on passing from a progressive or primitive to a regressive age structure. The result corroborates the conclusions drawn above that the greatest changes occur in the extreme age groups and the smallest, in the 20 to 29 age group. This is graphically presented in Fig. 9, where the point of departure (100%) for every age group is equivalent to 35% in the 0—9 age group.

The question arises which age group or which cohort of a single year retains its proportion while gradually passing from a progressive to a regressive type of age structure. This is true for the ten-year group between the ages of 21 and 30, and for the 25- and 26-year cohorts.

The equations listed on page 39 lead to further conclusions. The proportion of the 10—19 age group to the total

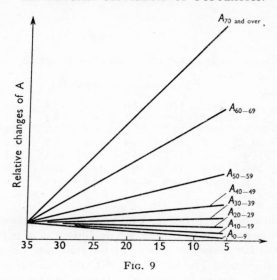

FIG. 9

population cannot be less than 10·3% (otherwise the A_{0-9} index, which denotes the proportion of the 0—9 age group, would be negative). Similarly, the proportion of the 20—29 age group cannot fall below 15·7%. Thus, the proportions of these two age groups have fixed lower limits. The remaining age groups have fixed upper limits: the 30—39 age group cannot exceed 17·6%, the 40—49 group—17·4%, the 50—59 group—16·3%, the 60—69 group—13·3%, and the 70 and over group cannot exceed 9·4% of the total population.

Calculations show that if the proportion of the 0—9 age group exceeds 37% of the population, there will be no old people over the age of 70; if the 0—9 age group exceeds 39% of the population, there will be none above the age of 60.

To pass from abstraction to reality, we can say that in a normally developing population, whether its age structure is progressive or regressive, certain proportions must be maintained, automatically imposed by the very nature of events; never can a population be composed predominantly of children or predominantly of old people. For children must have parents, and old people must leave progeny.

As to the changes in the age structure with time, a decline in the proportion of the earlier age groups in favour of older groups is noted nearly everywhere; this is evidence of the ageing process of the population.[1]

We shall now proceed to analyse the data on the age structure in some countries where vital statistics have been faithfully recorded for a long time.

The age structure of the French population since 1851, i.e. since the question on age was first included in the population census, is shown in Table 18.[2]

TABLE 18

Year	Age groups						
	0—9	10—19	20—29	30—39	40—49	50—59	60 and over
	percentage of population						
1851	18·5	17·4	16·3	14·7	12·4	10·2	10·5
1856	18·7	17·3	16·0	14·8	12·6	10·1	10·5
1861	18·5	17·3	16·0	14·5	12·7	9·9	11·1
1866	18·6	16·8	16·0	14·3	12·7	10·1	11·5
1872	18·3	17·1	16·0	13·9	12·5	10·4	11·8
1876	18·5	17·3	15·8	13·8	12·4	10·3	11·9
1881	18·3	17·1	15·8	13·8	12·4	10·3	12·3
1886	17·9	17·3	16·6	14·5	12·1	10·2	12·4
1891	17·5	17·5	16·3	13·8	12·3	10·1	12·5
1896	17·2	17·6	16·2	14·3	12·1	10·1	12·5
1901	17·7	16·9	16·1	14·2	12·2	10·4	12·5
1906	17·8	16·5	16·0	14·4	12·5	10·2	12·6
1911	17·4	16·5	15·8	14·7	12·7	10·2	12·7
1921	13·9	17·7	15·1	14·2	13·8	11·5	13·8
1926	14·8	16·2	16·6	13·9	13·4	11·4	13·8
1931	17·3	13·1	16·7	14·7	13·8	11·5	13·9
1936	16·2	14·0	15·2	15·9	12·6	11·4	14·7
1946	14·1	15·7	13·2	14·8	14·9	11·4	15·9
1954	17·0	15·0	14·5	11·8	13·9	12·8	14·8

The statistics listed reveal distinct irregularities caused by the two world wars (the wars waged by France in the second half of the 19th century do not seem to have had any striking influence on population dynamics). The percentage of children immediately after the end of the First World War was relatively small; as the generations born during the war grew up, the

---

[1] The problem is examined in detail by E. ROSSET in his book *Aging Process of Population* (Pergamon Press, Oxford).

[2] *Annuaire Statistique de la France 1957*, p. 11 (pink).

drop in their proportion affected increasingly older age groups causing a disequilibrium in the more and more ageing groups. Thus the 1921 census showed a relatively small proportion of generations in the 0—9 age group; the same, though to a less marked degree, was observed in 1926. By 1931 and 1936 the drop due to war reached the 10—19 age group, by 1946 the 20—29 age group, and by 1954 the 30—39 age group. The drop caused by the Second World War was reflected in the 0—9 age group in 1946, and by 1956 shifted to the 10—19 age group.

Notwithstanding these irregularities the table reveals a general trend towards a decline in the proportion of earlier in favour of later age groups. The smallest and least consistent changes are noted in the middle age groups, from 30 to 39 and from 40 to 49; after a small initial decline, their proportion has grown somewhat larger in later years.

The age structure of the United States population is shown in Table 19.[1]

TABLE 19

| Year | Age groups | | | | | | |
| | 0—9 | 10—19 | 20—29 | 30—39 | 40—49 | 50—59 | 60 and over |
	percentage of population						
1830[a]	33·0	23·6	17·4	10·9	6·8	4·3	4·0
1840[a]	31·6	23·0	18·1	11·6	7·3	4·4	4·0
1850	29·2	23·3	18·4	12·1	8·0	4·8	4·2
1860	28·8	22·5	18·3	12·8	8·3	5·0	4·2
1870	26·8	22·9	17·7	12·6	9·1	5·8	5·1
1880	26·7	21·4	18·2	12·7	9·1	8·2	5·6
1890	24·4	21·7	18·2	13·6	9·5	6·4	6·0
1900	23·9	20·5	18·4	13·9	10·1	6·8	6·4
1910	22·2	19·8	18·8	14·7	10·6	7·2	6·6
1920	21·7	19·0	17·5	15·0	11·5	7·9	7·4
1930	19·6	19·2	17·0	14·9	12·2	8·7	8·5
1940	15·9	18·3	17·2	15·0	13·0	9·9	10·5
1960	19·5	14·4	15·7	15·1	12·7	10·6	12·0

[a] White population only. The age structure of the total population differs very little from that of the white population, as evidenced by the following statistics for the year 1850 on page 45.

[1] *Historical Statistics of the United States*, Washington 1949; *Demographic Yearbook 1954*.

TABLE 19 (*cont.*)

Population	Age groups						
	0—9	10—19	20—29	30—39	40—49	50—59	60 and over
Total population	29·2	23·3	18·4	12·1	8·0	4·8	4·2
White population	28·7	23·2	18·5	12·4	8·1	4·9	4·2

The general trend is very similar to that of France: a steady drop in the proportion of children under 10; a declining tendency (quite obvious in recent years) in the percentage of the 10—19 age group; an initial rise followed by a decline in the proportion of the 20—29 age group; and a growing proportion of the older age groups.

The rise in the proportion is most noticeable in the oldest group (60 years and over).

Statistics on the age structure of the Swedish population,[1] dating back to as early as the mid-18th century, are listed in Table 20.

In Sweden, changes in the age structure of the population are much slower than in the United States but more rapid than in France where the proportion of some age groups remained virtually unchanged for several decades prior to the First World War.

It remains to be seen whether the changes in the age structure of various countries follow a similar pattern or differ from country to country and have their own peculiarities in each case. To find the answer to this question we shall draw a graph similar to that in Fig. 7, but depicting simultaneously the changes in several age groups (Fig. 10). As in the previous graph, the horizontal axis denotes A_{0-9} indices in descending order in accordance with the prevailing trend of changes (in an ageing population the proportion of the 0—9 age group declines). The vertical axis denotes the values of A_{10-19}, A_{30-39} and $A_{60 \text{ and over}}$. It is impossible to show the remaining indices of A; the many crisscrossing lines

---

[1] G. SUNDBÄRG, *Bevölkerungsstatistik Schwedens 1750—1900*, Stockholm 1907; *Statistik Arsbok för Sverige*, different yearbooks.

TABLE 20

Year	Age groups						
	0—9	10—19	20—29	30—39	40—49	50—59	60 and over
	percentage of population						
1750	23·7	18·5	16·7	13·1	10·3	7·9	9·8
1760	24·2	19·0	15·7	13·9	10·6	7·8	8·8
1770	22·9	19·9	16·2	13·3	11·4	8·2	8·1
1780	22·2	18·8	17·3	13·6	10·9	8·9	8·3
1790	23·0	18·2	16·3	14·6	11·3	8·6	8·0
1800	22·8	18·4	15·7	13·7	11·9	8·7	8·8
1810	21·6	19·8	16·2	13·5	11·3	9·2	8·4
1820	23·4	18·0	13·1	13·5	11·9	8·5	7·6
1830	25·2	19·2	15·0	13·9	10·6	7·9	8·2
1840	23·1	21·2	16·4	12·5	11·1	7·8	7·9
1850	23·3	19·2	17·9	13·6	9·9	8·3	7·8
1860	23·9	18·8	16·1	14·7	10·9	7·4	8·2
1870	23·4	19·7	15·2	13·1	11·9	8·5	8·2
1880	23·0	19·5	15·7	12·3	10·7	9·4	9·6
1890	23·1	19·2	14·5	12·4	10·3	8·9	11·6
1900	22·1	19·8	15·2	11·9	10·5	8·6	11·9
1910	21·7	19·3	15·6	12·5	10·2	8·8	11·9
1920	19·3	19·4	16·3	13·3	10·2	8·6	12·1
1930	15·9	18·0	17·4	14·3	12·0	9·6	12·8
1940	13·4	15·1	17·0	16·3	13·5	10·8	13·9
1950	16·9	12·4	14·0	15·5	14·6	11·5	15·1

would make the graph indecipherable. The lines between points denoting successive indices of A_{0-9} represent changes in the respective indices which accompany changes in the A_{0-9} index. The lines for the United States and Sweden start at the points for which the proportions of the 0—9 age group in those countries have fallen below 25% of the total population. An analogous graph for France would not be illustrative enough in view of the small changes in some indices.

The A_{10-19} indices show the closest resemblance in the United States and Sweden; in accordance with our previous reasoning, they both show a declining trend following the drop in the proportion of the 0—9 age group. These lines are so close as to be nearly identical. Other indices show marked differences, not only in value but sometimes also in direction. In the United States the proportion of the 30—39 age group, after a slow initial rise, remains on the same level.

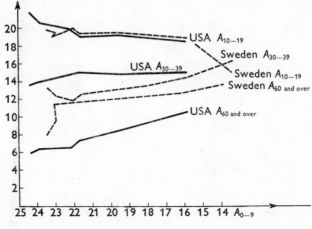

FIG. 10

In Sweden, the analogous index starts with a decline and then gradually increases. The proportion of the 60 and over age group in Sweden far exceeds that throughout the United States. After a very rapid initial rise, its rate of growth is now nearly the same in the two countries.

All this proves that changes in the age structure, including the ageing of the population, do not follow the same pattern everywhere but have their own specific characteristics in each country.

To complete the picture, age structures in some other countries around the year 1950 are presented in Table 21.

Some typical shapes of the age pyramid are shown in Fig. 11.

The first three pyramids represent progressive age structures. The Maoris in New Zealand have a very high fertility rate; hence, their age pyramid has a very broad base and rapidly narrows towards the top.

Yugoslavia and Poland also have progressive age structures, as witnessed by the broad base of their age pyramids; the gaps caused by the two world wars are quite obvious, somewhat smaller for females than for males. In later age groups, and in Poland also in middle age groups, males are outnumbered by females.

TABLE 21

Country	Year	Age groups							
		0—9	10—19	20—29	30—39	40—49	50—59	60—69	70 and over
		percentage of population							
Bechuanaland	1953	23·1	24·6	17·0	13·6	9·3	5·0	3·8	3·6
Bermuda	1950	23·7	17·5	16·6	14·1	12·4	7·7	4·7	3·3
Canada	1950	22·8	15·6	15·4	14·5	11·7	8·7	6·5	4·8
Haiti	1950	25·8	22·8	17·5	13·5	9·4	5·1	3·9	2·8
Mexico	1950	29·6	22·3	16·7	11·8	8·9	5·3	3·5	2·1
Paraguay	1950	29·5	22·8	16·0	12·1	7·6	5·4	3·7	2·4
Puerto Rico	1950	19·5	14·4	15·7	15·1	12·9	10·3	7·3	4·9
United States	1950	31·0	20·0	15·4	11·9	9·7	6·4	3·6	2·0
Venezuela	1950	30·5	21·2	17·4	12·5	8·4	5·3	2·8	1·9
Burma	1954	26·2	21·0	18·6	13·5	9·4	6·2	3·5	1·6
India	1953	26·1	21·4	17·1	13·5	9·8	6·4	3·5	2·2
Israel	1953	24·5	15·4	16·1	14·2	14·2	8·6	4·5	2·5
Japan	1952	24·0	20·7	17·3	12·1	10·2	7·6	4·9	3·2
Turkey	1950	27·0	22·6	16·4	11·4	10·0	6·4	4·9	1·4
Austria	1952	14·6	14·5	14·2	12·0	15·3	13·4	9·3	6·7
Belgium	1952	15·0	12·9	15·2	12·8	14·9	12·9	9·2	7·1

Denmark	1950	18·9	14·2	14·3	14·6	13·7	10·9	9·8	5·6
England and Wales	1953	15·9	12·7	13·4	14·5	15·0	12·3	9·1	7·1
Finland	1952	21·9	16·0	15·5	13·5	13·4	9·5	6·3	3·9
France	1953	16·4	12·8	15·2	12·0	14·0	12·3	8·8	7·5
German Fed. Rep.	1952	14·0	16·7	14·5	13·6	15·7	14·4	8·4	5·7
Greece	1956	17·9	17·4	18·4	13·5	12·2	9·6	6·2	4·8
Ireland	1950	22·8	16·4	16·2	13·2	11·1	9·3	5·8	5·2
Netherlands	1953	21·4	15·8	14·9	13·5	12·1	9·9	7·0	5·4
Norway	1952	18·3	12·6	14·2	15·6	13·8	11·4	7·7	6·4
Poland	1955	24·1	15·2	17·3	12·6	12·5	9·8	5·4	3·2
Portugal	1952	19·9	18·6	17·3	13·1	11·8	8·7	6·3	4·3
Sweden	1950	17·0	12·3	14·1	15·4	14·6	10·6	8·5	6·5
Switzerland	1950	16·9	13·4	15·0	14·1	14·7	11·6	8·2	6·1
Yugoslavia	1953	20·7	20·4	18·6	10·7	12·3	8·7	5·4	3·2
Australia	1953	20·6	13·9	15·0	15·1	13·0	9·9	7·6	4·9
Fiji Islands	1956	31·4	21·5	16·4	12·0	7·8	5·0	3·2	2·7
Hawaii	1950	23·3	16·8	20·0	16·1	10·8	6·6	4·1	2·3
New Zealand —white population	1953	21·2	14·6	14·2	14·2	12·8	9·6	7·6	5·8
New Zealand —Maori population	1953	33·4	24·1	16·0	10·5	7·7	4·4	2·6	1·3

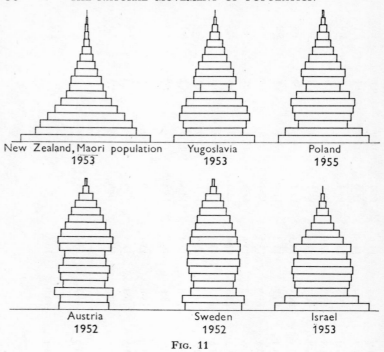

| New Zealand, Maori population 1953 | Yugoslavia 1953 | Poland 1955 |

| Austria 1952 | Sweden 1952 | Israel 1953 |

FIG. 11

Austria and Sweden have distinctly regressive age structures; their age pyramids are narrow at the bottom and slightly expand instead of narrowing towards the top. The age pyramid of the Austrian population reveals some traces of war losses.

As far as fertility rates are concerned, the Israeli population occupies one of the leading places among civilized nations;[1] this is why its age pyramid is broad at the base. But the age structure of the Israeli population is greatly influenced by immigration; consequently, the middle age groups are comparatively numerous. Instead of gradually narrowing towards the top, the age pyramid in its upper parts resembles the regressive type of structure, with approximately equal proportions of several consecutive age groups.

We shall now pass on to examine the distribution of popu-

---

[1] Gross and net reproduction rates in Israel are among the highest (cf. Table 69).

lation by marital status. The first problem is the number of the married population.

As has already been pointed out, the actual number of married couples is never accurately recorded in statistics, although some population censuses clearly attempt to do so. Nuptiality statistics can be based either on a *de jure* or on a *de facto* criterion. While the advantage of a *de jure* criterion is that it leaves no margin for arbitrary interpretation, statistics thus obtained may be rather remote from reality. However, if the *de facto* situation is accepted as the basis, it may happen that the information supplied will be untrue (as far as consensual unions are concerned) or that the information will not be supplied at all.

Nor is there any uniformity in the processing of marriage statistics. There are national variations in statistical definitions of consensual unions; in some countries they are listed in a separate group, in others, persons in consensual unions are included with the single or with the married population. Separated persons are sometimes included in and sometimes excluded from the married population. Persons who have not answered the question on marital status are usually enumerated in a special group, but in some statistics (e.g., the percentage of married population over the age of 15) may be included in the single population. It is because of these limitations that statistics on marital status in different countries are not entirely comparable.

The proportion of married persons above the age of 15 to the total population according to official statistics in various countries is shown in Table 22.[1]

TABLE 22

Country	Year	Males	Females
		percentage of married population	
Algeria			
—Moslem population . . .	1954	62·7	67·7
—European population . .	1954	65·3	57·2
Egypt[a]	1947	63·4	62·9

[1] Demographic yearbooks for various years.

4

TABLE 22 (*cont.*)

Country	Year	Males	Females
		percentage of married population	
Libya	1954	60·4	66·7
Morocco	1952	72·5	70·3
Mauritius	1952	56·0	59·1
Mozambique	1950	59·4	69·1
Portuguese Guinea	1950	59·6	80·7
Tunisia:			
—Moslem population . . .	1946	59·4	63·8
South Africa:			
—Bantu population	1946	55·6	56·7
—white population	1946	62·0	62·2
Alaska	1950	47·6	73·6
Canada	1951	63·6	64·3
Costa Rica	1950	44·2	43·2
Cubab	1953	54·2	60·0
El Salvadorb	1950	60·6	49·9
Guatemalab	1950	50·8	59·0
Haitib	1950	60·8	52·0
Mexico	1950	50·5	45·2
Nicaraguab	1950	54·4	50·7
Puerto Ricob	1950	50·0	57·1
United States	1950	67·2	64·8
Argentinac	1947	45·2	47·7
Bolivia	1960	59·7	56·2
Brazil	1950	54·1	54·1
Chileb	1952	52·1	50·1
Colombiab	1951	48·8	48·2
Ecuadorb	1950	56·5	55·9
Paraguayb	1950	50·1	46·2
Venezuela	1950	47·1	48·4
Burma:			
—urban	1953	62·5	60·8
—rural	1954	65·2	61·0
Ceylonb	1953	56·6	64·8
Federation of Malaya	1947	59·6	67·0
India	1951	71·5	73·0
Iraq	1947	57·9	53·4
Israel	1948	63·2	67·7
Japan	1955	59·8	55·8
Korea, South	1955	64·0	63·3
Nepal	1952—1954	75·9	74·3
Philippines	1956	59·8	55·9
Thailand	1947	60·4	60·5
Turkey	1950	67·6	67·4

POPULATION BY AGE AND MARITAL STATUS 53

TABLE 22 (cont.)

Country	Year	Males	Females
		percentage of married population	
Austria	1951	63·0	52·5
Belgium	1947	64·1	61·3
Bulgaria	1948	69·5	69·2
Czechoslovakia	1947	64·1	59·6
Denmark.	1950	64·6	62·4
England and Wales	1951	68·7	64·8
Finland	1950	60·6	62·8
France	1954	64·5	57·4
Germ. Dem. Rep.	1950	70·1	56·1
Germ. Fed. Rep.	1950	64·5	55·7
Greece.	1951	54·5	51·6
Hungary	1949	64·5	59·0
Iceland	1950	49·8	49·3
Ireland	1951	41·9	44·8
Italy.	1951	58·3	54·9
Netherlands	1947	59·7	58·0
Norway	1950	59·3	57·2
Poland	1954	64·9	57·8
Portugal	1950	56·4	51·6
Spain	1940	53·2	47·6
Sweden	1950	61·0	59·6
Switzerland	1950	59·5	53·4
Yugoslavia	1953	63·6	58·4
Australia	1954	63·6	64·0
Fiji Islands	1956	60·3	66·5
Hawaii.	1950	53·3	63·2
New Zealand:			
—white population	1951	64·9	64·1
—Maori population	1951	54·8	62·0

a Out of 3,635,000 married males 117,746 had 2 wives, 6573 had 3 wives, and 888 had 4 wives.

b ‖Includes persons consensually married.

c Percentages computed on the population of 14 years and over.

The percentage of the married population varies a great deal from country to country. The lowest percentages are in Iceland (males 49·8, females 49·3) and Ireland (41·9 and 44·8); the highest, in some subtropical countries: Nepal (75·9 and 74·3), India (71·5 and 73·0), and Morocco (72·5 and 70·3). The proportion of married females is nearly the same as that of males; exceptions to this rule are observed in countries with large family immigration where women are far outnumbered by men and, hence, the proportion of married females is very high. Two such countries are listed in Table 22: Alaska (47·6 and 73·6) and Portuguese Guinea (59·6 and 80·7).

Some countries have reported extremely low proportions of married population. In the Dominican Republic, for example, the percentage of married population in 1950 was 27·8 for males and 30·6 for females. The actual percentage could hardly be so small; the explanation is that in developing countries marriage registers are incomplete and the statistics unreliable. This is why those data are not listed in our table.

In most cases the percentage of married population varies from 50 to 60. A list of percentages in an ascending order is given in Table 23.

TABLE 23

Percentage of married population	Males	Females
40—44	2	2
45—49	5	8
50—54	12	10
55—59	16	19
60—64	25	19
65—69	7	8
70—74	3	4
75—79	1	—
80—85	—	1
Total	71	71

The 60—64% proportion is the most frequent, closely followed by proportions equalling 55—59% and 50—54%. The three groups cover some 70% of the countries enumerated in Table 22.

Data on consensual unions, in those countries where they are separately recorded, are presented in Table 24.

Table 24 reveals that in some countries consensual unions are very numerous, sometimes outnumbering legal marriages (El Salvador, Guatemala, Haiti).

The proportion of married population varies in different

TABLE 24

Country	Year	Type of marriage	Males	Females
Cuba	1953	formal	35·9	38·7
		consensual	18·3	21·3
El Salvador	1950	f.	25·6	24·8
		c.	24·3	26·0
Guatemala	1950	f.	18·8	19·4
		c.	40·2	41·4
Haiti	1950	f.	14·3	14·4
		c.	37·7	40·0
Nicaragua	1950	f.	29·5	28·3
		c.	21·2	21·7
Puerto Rico	1950	f.	43·9	44·8
		c.	13·2	14·6
Chile	1952	f.	48·7	46·7
		c.	3·4	3·4
Colombia	1951	f.	39·8	38·7
		c.	9·0	9·5
Ecuador	1950	f.	44·1	42·7
		c.	12·4	13·2
Paraguay	1950	f.	34·9	31·9
		c.	15·2	14·3
Venezuela	1950	f.	28·9	28·1
		c.	18·2	20·3
Ceylon	1953	f.	40·6	46·9
		c.	16·0	17·9

age groups. Relatively small at very early ages, it increases
rapidly since most marriages are contracted within an age
span of a few years. After a certain maximum the proportion
declines; new marriages are rarely contracted in later ages,
and with increasing age the existing marriages are more and
more often dissolved by death, so that the marriages dissolved
increasingly outnumber the new unions.

Percentages of married population by age groups in selected
countries are listed in Table 25.[1]

Differences in the percentage distribution are enormous.
Only the general trend of proportions by age of the married
population remains the same: initial rapid rise, followed by

---

[1] *Demographic Yearbook 1954.*

TABLE 25

Age groups — percentage of married population

Country	Year	Sex	15—19	20—24	25—29	30—34	35—39	40—44	45—49	50—54	55—59	60—64	65—69	70—74	75 and over
Algeria —Moslem population	1948	m	4.5	29.8	59.8	76.3	84.4	87.1	88.3	88.8	88.0	86.0	84.3	80.2	74.3
		f	31.4	71.7	83.3	86.4	83.1	75.9	65.7	50.6	40.0	26.2	19.0	12.0	7.9
Egypt	1947	m	2.8	26.2	61.1	81.6	89.9	92.1	93.6	92.2	92.2	88.7	87.4	82.3	73.8
		f	24.2	73.9	87.2	87.6	86.7	74.3	72.7	46.8	54.1	25.5	30.6	13.3	9.5
Mozambique	1940	m	26.2	61.6	81.8	88.9	92.0	92.3	91.8	90.2	87.6	85.3	83.6	81.2	79.5
		f	60.9	82.0	84.5	84.3	81.2	74.1	62.2	52.9	38.3	30.0	24.7	22.8	18.1
South Africa	1946	m	1.4	20.2	53.4	74.3	82.6	86.0	87.5	87.2	86.8	83.8	81.6	76.1	68.2
		f													
Alaska	1950	m	1.1	12.5	45.8	57.7	63.4	64.2	57.5		49.2		39.4		26.3
		f	20.8	73.5	85.5	86.8	84.3	82.2	76.8		63.9		40.7		20.7
Canada	1951	m	1.0	25.5	64.6	79.9	84.2	85.2	84.6	83.7	82.8	80.1	74.6	67.3	51.7
		f	7.9	51.2	78.5	84.4	84.8	83.2	81.2	77.6	72.7	65.5	56.3	43.0	23.0
Costa Rica	1950	m	1.5	25.4	58.4	73.8	80.7	83.2	83.7	81.6	80.2	75.5	71.3	63.7	54.1
		f	14.7	50.0	68.1	74.7	75.5	72.6	68.6	59.8	54.2	42.3	36.7	24.7	15.6
El Salvador	1950	m	3.2	28.8	53.8	67.1	73.7	75.6	76.6	75.1	74.1	69.5	64.5	59.3	51.5
		f	19.2	51.7	66.2	70.1	70.0	63.9	60.2	52.4	47.7	36.3	32.6	24.5	18.6
Haiti	1950	m	0.5	10.6	41.9	67.4	80.1	84.9	86.5	85.4	84.6	81.9	79.4	75.0	48.3
		f	5.1	37.2	65.6	77.1	81.0	77.9	74.6	66.3	64.3	52.9	47.5	38.6	30.0
Nicaragua	1950	m	4.1	28.9	54.7	67.3	75.1	77.2	79.9	77.9	77.5	71.8	69.9	65.0	54.0
		f	18.8	49.9	64.3	68.3	70.0	65.1	60.9	51.4	48.6	35.6	30.7	23.3	19.4
United States	1950	m	3.1	40.0	74.2	84.3	86.8	87.1	86.2	85.0	83.1	79.3	74.0	67.5	53.4
		f	16.7	65.6	83.3	86.2	85.5	83.1	79.8	75.0	73.1	60.1	48.9	36.6	18.7

Country	Year	Sex													
Brazil	1940	m	1·1	23·2	57·5	72·9	78·1	80·0	80·6	79·0	78·3	74·0	71·5	65·7	54·6
		f	14·1	50·7	67·9	72·7	72·8	68·6	65·3	55·9	51·3	37·6	32·7	22·5	13·3
Ecuador	1950	m	2·7	30·4	62·4	76·5	81·9	83·8	84·4	83·4	82·1	78·7	76·5	71·3	62·6
		f	17·4	55·9	72·4	76·0	75·7	71·4	68·8	60·9	57·2	45·2	42·4	32·1	23·5
Peru	1940	m	2·1	27·8	58·6	63·6	79·8	81·1	82·1	80·2	79·2	75·7	74·1	68·4	60·5
		f	14·4	48·8	64·0	70·1	70·7	68·1	64·7	57·6	52·5	41·2	37·3	29·0	23·5
Ceylon	1946	m	1·1	18·9	55·1	84·1	84·1	85·9	85·9	83·2	82·1	77·6	70·7		
		f	23·9	68·4	84·4	87·1	85·4	78·4	71·4	61·2	54·2	43·1	30·8		
Federation of Malaya	1947	m	3·7	30·5	62·7	75·8	79·5	80·3	79·4	76·9	74·0	72·3	69·0		66·2
		f	37·5	78·6	87·6	86·9	83·6	75·4	67·6	54·5	48·1	32·4	27·4		15·1
India	1931	m	44·5	62·6	82·1	85·9	86·3	85·1	81·1	78·6	72·6	69·8	64·0		57·7
		f	83·0	90·0	87·3	82·6	70·0	62·2	46·6	40·0	26·8	21·9	17·2		13·4
Israel	1948	m	1·2	19·8	54·6	75·1	85·1	88·8	90·4	90·6	89·3	87·9	84·6	77·9	63·6
		f	10·9	60·4	82·0	86·6	87·6	85·6	82·0	75·7	68·5	57·1	46·6	28·8	18·7
Japan	1950	m	0·4	16·7	64·0	90·0	94·6	95·0	93·2	90·4	86·8	78·6	71·1		
		f	3·2	42·7	79·0	93·2	82·5	82·0	78·5	72·0	61·9	50·0	34·4		
Philippines	1948	m	2·8	34·1	70·5	84·0	87·8	88·1	87·9	84·6	83·5	71·8	69·3	64·0	49·7
		f	14·3	56·1	75·7	78·8	79·8	75·8	72·8	64·8	62·7	30·1	36·3	17·8	7·4
Taiwan	1930	m	6·9	46·8	78·1	86·7	88·3	87·3	84·8	81·3	77·1	75·5	64·0	62·1	52·6
		f	31·3	83·5	92·6	92·4	88·8	82·1	71·6	59·0	44·2	41·4	17·8	22·0	14·0
Thailand	1947	m	3·1	37·9	73·2	86·3	88·9	88·9	87·4	84·8	81·4		84·8	78·5	68·9
		f	17·9	64·2	81·5	85·1	83·8	79·4	72·9	63·4	53·0		24·0	17·3	12·7
Turkey	1945	m	14·1	42·0	73·1	87·4	91·5	92·4	92·8	91·3	90·8	87·3	70·5		
		f	25·8	78·4	90·8	91·3	89·4	82·7	75·7	59·0	48·7	30·8	32·7		
Austria	1951	m	0·3	15·8	50·5	71·4	80·4	83·6	84·8	85·4	84·5	82·0	77·0	68·5	51·2
		f	3·5	32·8	59·7	68·5	70·6	71·7	70·1	66·2	59·1	49·8	39·2	28·3	14·7
Belgium	1947	m	0·7	21·8	60·5	78·1	82·6	84·8	86·7	87·0	85·0	80·2	73·4	63·6	44·8
		f	4·6	43·3	73·5	81·8	83·5	83·0	80·5	76·3	69·6	61·9	51·8	39·5	20·5

TABLE 25 (cont.)

Country	Year	Sex	Age groups — percentage of married population												
			15—19	20—24	25—29	30—34	35—39	40—44	45—49	50—54	55—59	60—64	65—69	70—74	75 and over
Czechoslovakia.	1947	m	0·4	14·9	53·4	81·0	87·6	90·0	91·1	90·9	89·2	85·5	79·3	69·6	51·3
		f	5·7	44·7	74·0	83·1	83·9	81·6	77·5	71·0	61·7	52·3	42·2	31·0	16·8
Denmark . . .	1950	m	0·2	17·7	59·3	78·7	83·7	85·5	86·1	85·9	85·0	81·4	75·2	66·6	46·6
		f	4·6	47·8	77·3	83·9	83·5	81·0	77·1	72·5	67·1	59·9	50·9	39·2	21·3
England and Wales	1951	m	0·6	24·1	64·9	80·3	85·5	87·2	88·0	88·0	86·2	82·7	76·3	68·1	50·9
		f	4·4	48·1	77·2	83·0	83·3	81·2	77·9	74·6	66·9	57·0	47·1	36·8	20·3
Finland . . .	1950	m	1·0	21·1	60·1	77·6	83·0	84·2	84·2	83·3	81·6	77·9	72·9	64·4	46·9
		f	4·3	40·4	68·7	75·2	74·5	71·7	67·5	61·4	53·6	44·0	34·2	24·5	12·5
France . . .	1946	m	0·8	22·2	53·9	71·7	79·7	83·1	84·9	85·2	83·6	80·0	74·6	67·1	51·4
		f	5·3	41·1	69·0	78·8	80·0	78·4	74·1	67·5	58·9	50·6	40·7	29·5	15·0
Germ. Fed. Rep.	1950	m	0·2	16·4	52·2	74·6	84·4	88·0	89·7	90·4	89·7	86·5	80·2	69·5	49·2
		f	2·4	31·7	61·1	70·8	74·1	75·5	74·6	70·7	64·5	55·2	45·7	34·4	17·8
Iceland . . .	1950	m	0·6	20·2	52·4	67·3	74·5	75·8	77·1	77·4	77·4	73·3	67·9	60·9	45·2
		f	5·8	42·1	68·6	76·5	77·1	73·4	69·2	66·5	60·4	53·9	42·2	35·8	16·8
Ireland . . .	1951	m	0·1	5·1	23·2	41·6	54·4	62·6	65·5	65·8	64·8	61·1	56·3	30·3	18·3
		f	1·1	17·6	45·2	62·5	69·2	69·1	66·2	62·1	56·0	47·9	40·0	30·3	18·3
Netherlands . .	1947	m	0·6	13·6	52·1	76·8	84·5	80·9	88·0	87·9	85·1	80·4	73·1	62·9	43·6
		f	3·2	30·2	65·4	78·1	80·2	80·0	79·0	76·4	71·5	64·7	55·0	42·6	22·5
Norway . . .	1950	m	0·3	11·9	44·7	68·8	78·2	81·2	81·6	81·1	80·2	76·5	72·0	64·8	47·4
		f	3·1	34·1	65·6	77·7	79·3	76·6	72·2	67·8	62·8	56·0	48·2	38·2	20·9
Poland . . .	1954	m	1·1	24·0	67·1	89·2		92·8		91·1			76·8		
		f	6·3	50·0	76·3	80·1		74·2		63·3			36·0		

Country	Year	Sex													
Portugal	1950	m	0·6	16·0	55·7	75·7	81·0	83·3	83·8	83·9	83·0	79·1	74·9	67·4	54·0
		f	4·1	34·3	63·3	72·8	75·2	74·3	71·5	66·4	61·0	52·0	42·5	32·5	18·2
Spain	1940	m	0·2	6·3	36·6	69·1	81·1	85·0	86·3	84·6	82·4	76·5	71·3	61·8	47·4
		f	1·2	20·6	52·3	69·2	74·2	73·5	71·9	66·3	61·3	50·4	40·9	29·5	16·1
Sweden	1950	m	0·2	12·6	47·5	68·5	76·3	78·8	79·9	79·8	77·7	74·2	68·4	60·3	41·6
		f	3·0	36·0	68·2	77·3	77·6	74·5	71·1	67·3	61·2	55·0	46·8	37·0	19·6
Switzerland	1950	m	0·1	9·6	45·4	70·4	79·1	82·0	82·9	82·7	81·5	78·3	72·3	63·9	46·3
		f	1·2	25·8	60·8	74·3	76·4	74·9	71·9	67·6	61·6	52·7	42·9	31·9	15·9
Yugoslavia	1948	m	7·8	35·4	66·8	83·9	88·5	90·0	89·7	88·1	85·7	82·1	76·7	69·0	52·8
		f	13·3	53·6	73·6	78·4	79·5	78·5	74·5	69·1	59·0	50·9	40·3	32·1	21·0
Australia	1947	m	0·7	23·3	61·0	76·4	81·1	82·4	82·0	81·8	80·4	77·3	71·7	64·9	49·4
		f	5·5	47·8	76·8	83·1	83·3	81·3	78·6	74·3	67·6	58·6	47·6	36·0	19·1
Hawaii	1950	m	1·2	20·6	57·6	75·9	72·2	68·9	71·6	71·6	71·4	71·4	62·1		43·4
		f	7·9	50·2	78·4	85·9	86·1	83·9	78·2	78·2	63·1	63·1	41·9		20·4
New Zealand —European population.	1951	m	0·4	20·2	62·3	79·8	84·4	86·5	86·0	84·5	82·9	79·6	75·0	68·2	52·8
		f	4·3	49·6	79·7	85·1	85·4	83·5	80·5	76·3	70·0	61·2	52·3	41·5	23·3
New Zealand: —Maori population.	1951	m	2·0	33·5	66·4	80·7	83·9	85·0	84·3	78·6	76·3	72·7	60·9	52·4	42·4
		f	11·3	60·7	80·7	86·7	87·8	85·8	82·4	76·4	65·4	54·7	50·9	37·1	20·9

a gradual decrease and an increasingly rapid decline after a certain maximum. However, the maximum level, the age at which the maximum is attained, and the rate of decline after the maximum, differ greatly. The maximum for males varies from 65·8% to 95·0% (Ireland and Japan), and for females from 69·2% to 92·6% (Ireland and Taiwan). In Hawaii, the largest percentage of married males is to be found in the 30—35 age group; in Iceland, an equally large percentage is noted in two groups: from 50 to 55 and from 55 to 60. Other countries show a maximum proportion midway between these two groups. For females, the earliest age group having a maximum is 20—25 (India) and the latest, 40—45 (Austria and the G.F.R. (German Federal Republic)). The rate of post-maximum decline also varies, as witnessed by the different percentages of the married population in the latest age groups: from 50·8 to 82·3 for males and from 13·3 to 43·0 for females in the 70—75 age group. Finally, in some countries marriages are usually contracted earlier than in others, as revealed by the large proportion of married population in the 20—24 age group. Percentages in this group vary from 5·1 to 62·6 for males and from 17·6 to 82·0 for females.

Nevertheless, the countries listed can be arranged in groups with similar distributions of marital status by age.

The first group comprises Eastern European countries: Poland, Czechoslovakia and Hungary; the G.F.R. has a similar age--specific marital structure. Marriages in those countries are performed rather early, and the proportion of persons remaining single all their life is quite small. This is revealed in the high percentage of married persons in the early age groups and the high maximum index (over 90% for males and about 80% for females). In some respects, Czechoslovakia's structure approaches that of the next group of countries.

The second group includes Scandinavian countries: Sweden, Norway, Denmark and Iceland, with similar structures in the Netherlands and Switzerland. Marriages in this group of countries are contracted rather late and the percentage of single persons is quite large. The proportion of married males in all age groups in these countries is lower than in Eastern European countries, but the proportion of married females is nearly the same.

The third group consists of Western European countries: Belgium, France and England; some British Commonwealth countries: Canada, Australia and New Zealand (white population) — have a similar age structure, and so has Finland.

Early marriages are the rule in those countries, but since many persons remain single the maximum index is comparatively low.

The fourth group covers Moslem countries: Algeria, Egypt and Turkey, where marriages start very early and the percentage of married males is very high even in the oldest age group, in contrast with married females whose post-maximum proportion rapidly declines with age. The maximum comes early for females and late for males. A similar marital structure by age exists in Israel and South Africa, with the single difference that in these two countries marriages are contracted somewhat later and the proportion of married females in the later age groups is distinctly larger than in Moslem countries.

Finally, *the fifth group* embraces Central and South American countries: El Salvador, Costa Rica, Nicaragua, Brazil, Ecuador and Peru. They reveal a certain similarity to Western European countries, but females in the fifth group of countries marry earlier and the general percentage of married persons is smaller.

Figure 12 represents typical distributions by marital status in the five groups of countries.

The elements of marital structure which make it possible to arrange countries in five groups are listed in Table 26.

Elements within each group of countries have a similar structure, but differences between groups are very large. The configuration of indices for males differs characteristically from that of the respective indices for females.

To show the range of differences between marital structures by age, two extreme structures are represented graphically (Fig. 13): in India, where early marriages are very frequent, and in Ireland, where marriages are contracted very late and many persons remain single all their lives.

The data quoted above reveal the following regularities:

(1) in the 20—24 age group the proportion of married females is everywhere larger than that of males; this means that women marry earlier than men. The larger the percentage

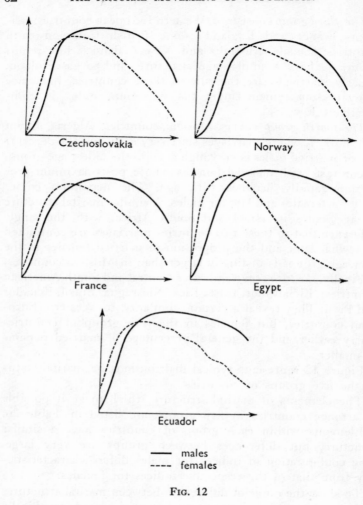

FIG. 12

of married males the larger also the percentage of married females;

(2) in the 75 and over age group, the proportion of married females is everywhere smaller than that of males; this is to be explained by the fact that widowed or divorced men are more apt to remarry than women.

TABLE 26

Country	Males			Females		
	maximum % of married persons	% of married persons in 20—24 age group	age group at maximum	maximum % of married persons	% of married persons in 20—24 age group	age group at maximum
Poland	92·8	24·0	40—49	74·2	50·0	35—40
Czechoslovakia	91·1	14·9	45—50	83·9	44·7	30—35
Hungary . . .	90·8	14·9	45—50	79·8	47·5	35—40
Denmark . . .	86·1	17·7	45—50	83·9	47·6	35—40
Norway . . .	81·6	11·9	45—50	79·3	34·1	35—40
Sweden . . .	79·9	12·6	45—50	77·6	36·0	35—40
Iceland	77·4	20·2	50—55	77·1	42·1	35—40
England . . .	88·0	24·1	45—55	83·3	48·1	35—40
Belgium . . .	87·0	21·8	50—55	83·5	43·3	35—40
France	85·2	22·2	50—55	80·0	41·1	35—40
Egypt	93·0	26·2	45—50	87·6	73·9	30—35
Turkey	92·8	42·0	40—46	91·3	78·4	30—35
Algeria	88·8	29·8	50—55	86·4	71·7	30—35
Ecuador . . .	84·4	30·4	45—50	76·0	55·9	30—35
Costa Rica . .	83·7	25·4	45—50	75·5	50·0	35—40
Peru	82·1	27·8	45—50	70·7	48·8	35—40
Brazil.	80·6	23·2	45—50	72·8	50·7	35—40
Nicaragua . .	79·9	28·9	45—50	70·0	48·9	35—40
El Salvador . .	76·6	28·8	45—50	70·1	51·7	30—35

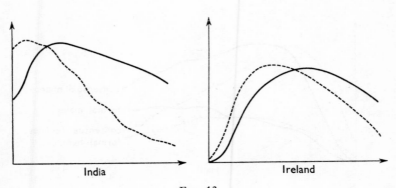

India   Ireland

FIG. 13

No regularities can be traced in respect to the maximum percentage of married persons. The proportion may be larger among males in some cases, and among females in others. However, there is a certain prevailing trend, namely:

(3) the larger the maximum proportion of married males, the larger also the maximum proportion of married females, and *vice versa*.

Finally, with regard to the age for which the maximum proportion is noted, the following seems to be the rule:

(4) among males, the maximum percentage of married persons is reached at a later age than among females.

Marital structures classified by formal marriage incidence and by consensual unions in certain countries are presented in Table 27.

The proportions of formally and consensually married males and females according to their age in Haiti are graphically presented in Fig. 14. Haiti has been chosen because it has a high preponderance of consensual unions. The graph demonstrates that consensual unions among males and females reach their maximum proportion at a much earlier age than do legal marriages. From about the age of 30 on, the percentage of formal marriages reveals a trend towards stabilization. The conclusion seems to be that consensual unions usually prevail in earlier ages, while if a marriage is contracted at an older age it is usually a legal union.

It is not difficult to establish the prevailing trend in the percentage changes of married population with time.

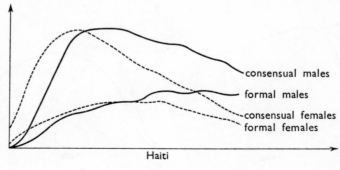

Haiti

FIG. 14

TABLE 27

Country	Year	Sex	Marriage	Age groups												
				percentage of married persons												
				15-20	20-25	25-30	30-35	35-40	40-45	45-50	50-55	55-60	60-65	65-70	70-75	75 and over
Costa Rica	1950	m	formal	1·2	20·3	48·4	62·5	68·8	71·8	72·8	71·9	71·7	67·1	64·6	58·9	49·3
			consensual	0·3	5·1	10·0	11·3	11·9	11·4	10·9	9·7	8·5	8·4	6·7	4·8	4·8
		f	f.	11·7	41·7	57·2	63·5	64·3	63·7	61·1	54·3	50·4	39·2	34·6	23·5	14·6
			c.	0·3	8·3	10·9	11·2	11·2	8·9	7·5	5·5	3·8	3·1	2·1	1·3	1·0
El Salvador	1950	m	f.	0·9	10·9	24·1	32·3	35·8	39·6	42·3	44·7	45·9	44·0	44·4	40·4	35·7
			c.	2·3	17·9	29·7	34·8	37·9	36·0	34·3	30·4	28·2	25·5	21·8	18·9	15·8
		f	f.	6·9	20·9	29·4	33·4	33·9	34·2	34·4	32·5	32·6	24·4	22·8	16·3	11·9
			c.	12·3	30·8	36·8	36·7	36·1	29·7	25·8	19·6	15·1	11·9	9·8	8·2	6·7
Haiti	1950	m	f.	0·1	2·2	9·3	16·5	18·5	21·8	23·9	27·2	30·2	27·9	30·4	28·4	27·9
			c.	0·4	8·4	32·6	50·9	61·6	63·1	62·6	58·2	54·4	54·0	49·0	46·6	40·4
		f	f.	0·7	7·6	13·5	17·4	19·5	21·8	23·7	23·6	25·4	20·8	20·0	16·2	13·1
			c.	4·4	29·6	52·1	59·7	61·5	56·1	50·9	42·7	38·9	32·1	27·5	22·4	16·9
Ceylon	1946	m	f.	0·7	12·0	37·5	52·7	57·3	59·4	58·8	58·3	57·9	56·9		54·2	
			c.	0·4	6·9	17·6	22·5	26·8	26·5	27·1	24·9	24·2	20·7		16·5	
		f	f.	14·2	46·5	56·8	59·0	57·3	54·1	50·2	45·2	41·0	33·2		24·1	
			c.	9·7	21·9	27·6	28·1	28·1	24·3	21·2	16·0	13·2	9·9		6·7	

The influence of the constant decline in mortality rates is obvious enough. Thus, assuming that the disposition to contract marriage remains more or less unchanged, owing to the decline in mortality rates marriages last longer and longer and are less and less often dissolved by the death of one of the spouses. As a result, the percentage of married population is bound to rise. This is confirmed by data on countries where population censuses were started long ago and, consequently, vital statistics have a long record (Table 28).

TABLE 28

Country	Year	Males	Females
		percentage of married persons	
Austria	1869	53·0	51·1
	1910	54·4	52·0
	1934	53·9	48·6
	1951	63·0	52·5
Bulgaria	1881	70·9	73·1
	1905	67·0	69·8
	1926	67·0	66·3
	1946	69·5	69·2
England	1851	52·8	50·4
	1911	54·3	50·6
	1931	59·3	53·4
	1951	68·7	64·8
France	1851	54·4	52·7
	1911	58·8	56·0
	1931	63·0	57·5
	1954	64·5	57·4
Ireland	1861	44·3	42·1
	1911	38·5	38·6
	1951	41·9	44·8
Italy	1861	56·5	53·3
	1911	55·4	54·6
	1931	55·0	52·5
	1951	58·3	54·9
Netherlands	1849	45·3	44·5
	1909	52·9	50·8
	1930	56·0	54·5
	1947	59·7	58·0

With a few exceptions, the table reveals a steady rise in the percentage of married persons. The exceptions can be explained by objective reasons. The drop in the percentage of married population in Austria in 1934 as compared with 1910 was the result of the large territorial changes brought about by World War I. The drop noted in Ireland in 1911 as compared with 1861 was caused by the great number of emigrants who went abroad to escape poverty at home, thus reducing the frequency of marriages. Besides, it is evident that one of the inevitable consequences of war is a temporary drop in the percentage of married population; war casualties are especially large among men, and the number of widows rises considerably.

Since the percentage of married persons tends to increase in the course of time, the number of existing marriages rises at a somewhat more rapid rate than does the total number of the population. The balance of marriages newly contracted against those dissolved is thus not very large; the elements from which it has been compounded are often much larger. The figures computed for selected countries are presented in Table 29.

TABLE 29

Country	Year	Marriage dissolved by			Newly con-tracted mar-riages	Mar-riage in-crement
		death of husband	death of wife	divorce or annul-ment		
		percentage of existent married couples				
Algeria — European popul-ation	1954	1·22	0·49	0·18	3·76	1·87
South Africa — white population	1951	1·32	0·63	0·66	4·60	1·99
Dominican Republic	1950	0·95	0·70	0·53	4·53	2·35
Guadeloupe	1954	1·56	0·98	0·23	5·92	3·15
Martinique	1954	1·37	0·91	0·24	5·02	2·50
United States . . .	1950	1·24	0·61	1·10	4·62	1·67
Argentina	1947	1·93		—	5·32	3·39
Chile	1952	1·26	0·82	—	5·55	3·47
Colombia	1951	1·43	1·01	—	4·92	2·48
Venezuela	1950	1·57	0·68	0·17	5·91	3·49
Japan	1955	1·04	0·50	0·44	4·18	2·20
Philippines.	1956	1·28		—	3·61	2·33

TABLE 29 (cont.)

Country	Year	Marriage dissolved by			Newly con-tracted mar-riages	Mar-riage in-crement
		death of husband	death of wife	divorce or annul-ment		
		percentage of existent married couples				
Austria	1951	1·67	0·84	0·68	4·19	1·00
England and Wales .	1951	1·42	0·78	0·26	3·28	0·82
Finland	1950	1·41	0·65	0·47	4·33	1·76
France	1954	1·46	0·67	0·29	3·14	0·72
Germ. Fed. Rep. . . .	1950	1·57	0·77	0·72	4·83	1·77
Hungary	1949	1·31	0·70	0·60	5·14	2·53
Iceland	1950	1·06	0·54	0·42	4·97	2·95
Ireland	1951	0·70	0·37	—	1·25	0·18
Italy	1951	1·25	0·67	—	3·40	1·48
Norway	1950	0·98	0·60	0·33	3·81	1·90
Portugal	1950	1·26	0·72	0·06	4·13	2·09
Spain	1950	1·30	0·69	—	3·86	1·87
Sweden	1950	1·05	0·68	0·49	3·34	1·12
Switzerland	1950	1·23	0·49	0·42	3·62	1·68
Australia	1954	1·20	0·60	0·32	3·47	1·35

The number of marriages dissolved by the death of the husband exceeds the number of marriages dissolved by the death of the wife; the ratio between the two figures varies from 40% to 70% (in the countries listed in Table 29) and in most cases is about 50%. Thus, the increment for widows is larger than for widowers. Divorce and annulment indices vary from country to country. In some countries (Ireland, Italy, Spain, Latin American countries) divorces are still non-existent; in others it is comparatively easy to obtain a divorce. This has a marked bearing on the number of marriages dissolved and, indirectly, on the number of remarriages. In the United States, for example, the number of marriages dissolved by divorce is much greater than that of marriages dissolved by the death of the wife and nearly equals the number of marriages dissolved by the death of the husband; in South Africa (white population), Japan, the German Federal Republic and Switzerland divorces are nearly as frequent as marriages dissolved by the death of the wife.

If we classify the countries enumerated in Table 29 in an ascending order by percentage of marriages dissolved by the death of either husband or wife, the list will be as follows:

Ireland	1951	1·07	South Africa			
Philippines	1956	1·28	—white population	1951	1·95	
Japan	1955	1·54	Portugal	1950	1·98	
Norway	1950	1·58	Spain	1950	1·99	
Iceland	1950	1·60	Hungary	1949	2·01	
Poland	1956	1·62	Finland	1950	2·06	
Dominican Republic	1950	1·65	Chile	1952	2·08	
Algeria:			France	1954	2·13	
—European popu-			England and Wales	1951	2·20	
lation	1954	1·71	Venezuela	1950	2·25	
Switzerland	1950	1·72	Martinique	1954	2·28	
Sweden	1950	1·73	Germ. Fed. Rep.	1950	2·34	
Australia	1954	1·80	Colombia	1951	2·44	
United States	1950	1·85	Austria	1951	2·51	
Italy	1951	1·92	Guadeloupe	1954	2·54	
Argentina	1947	1·93				

The list is chaotic: highly developed countries are to be found both at the beginning and at the end of the list, which means that the percentage of marriages dissolved by death in those countries may be high as well as low. However, a closer scrutiny reveals that the less developed countries are towards the end of the list, i.e. they have large percentages of marriages dissolved by death. As to the economically advanced countries, the proportion of marriages dissolved by death is also high in those that were belligerents in the Second World War (France, England, GFR, Austria) and, hence, have a special distribution of population by age and marital status. As a result of war casualties a great many marriages were dissolved by the death of the husband; also, the number of newly contracted marriages was comparatively small. Hence, at the end of the war there were very few young married couples and relatively many older ones in which the husband had passed the age of military service. After the war new marriages were contracted by young people, but the gap caused by war losses remained in the middle age groups. As a result, the proportion of older couples continued to be much larger than before the war, and the reduction in marriages caused by the death of one of the spouses had to be more rapid than in the countries where the age structure of the population had not undergone such violent changes. As a rule, any improvement in mortality rates should lead to a reduction in the percentage of marriages dissolved by death. For the same reason, the most advanced countries should have a low percentage, and the developing countries—a high percentage of marriages dissolved by death.

The same conclusions can be drawn when examining changes with time in the proportion of marriages dissolved by death in Sweden (Table 30).[1]

TABLE 30

Decade	Marriages dissolved by		Newly contracted marriages
	death	divorce	
	annual mean in % of number of marriages at beginning of decade		
1750—1759	4·22	—	5·64
1760—1769	4·06	—	4·76
1770—1779	4·16	—	4·67
1780—1789	4·21	—	4·36
1790—1799	3·99	—	4·95
1800—1809	4·44	—	4·60
1810—1819	4·21	—	5·12
1820—1829	4·05	—	5·03
1830—1839	3·92	0·02	4·30
1840—1849	3·60	0·02	4·63
1850—1859	3·57	0·02	4·87
1860—1869	3·28	0·02	4·16
1870—1879	3·08	0·03	4·40
1880—1889	2·91	0·03	3·88
1890—1899	3·01	0·04	3·68
1900—1909	2·93	0·06	3·80
1910—1919	2·93	0·10	3·96
1920—1929	2·58	0·18	3·97
1930—1939	2·46	0·26	4·66
1940—1949	—	0·46	4·59

The picture is quite clear. Apart from decades marked by hostilities, the proportion of marriages dissolved by death reveals a steady decline, with rare deviations. Mortality rates

---

[1] *Statistik Årsbok för Sverige*, various yearbooks.

in Sweden are known to have gradually diminished during the period in question. The decline in mortality was thus accompanied by a drop in the percentage of marriages dissolved by the death of one of the spouses. The proportion of marriages dissolved by divorce, on the contrary, constantly increased. Hence, the proportion of newly contracted marriages fluctuated rather irregularly between periods of rise and decline.

CHAPTER 4

MARRIAGE AND DIVORCE

A MARRIAGE contract or a divorce decree does not change the number of population but affects the legal status of the spouses towards each other and towards their children. Since marriages are of primary importance from the point of view of the trends in reproduction rates, they cannot be excluded from a study of the natural movement of the population.

The structure of population by marital status has already been dealt with. It is usually established on the basis of population censuses. Statistics on newly contracted marriages and divorces are supplied by civil registers. The completeness of these statistics varies from case to case; sometimes they are compiled for a part of the population only (white population); sometimes they fail to cover certain inaccessible areas of the country.

The simplest and most common measure of relative marriage frequency is the marriage rate, which gives the ratio of the number of marriages contracted within one year to the total population (the ratio of the number of newly married persons to the total population used in some statistics, is twice as high). Marriage rates per thousand in various countries about the year 1957 are listed in Table 31.[1]

The rates fluctuate over a large range: from 1·3 to 12·3, or nearly tenfold. South and Central American countries, where the percentage of consensual unions is large, have low marriage rates; the developing countries, in which statistics are not very reliable as yet, belong to the same group. In Ireland, where marriages are contracted relatively very late and where a sizeable segment of the population remain single, the 5·0 rate can be regarded as accurate. A marriage rate of 5·0 per thousand is roughly the limit below which a steady decline begins in the number of existing marriages;

---

[1] *Demographic Yearbook 1958.*

TABLE 31

Marriage rates

under 3·9		from 4·0 to 5·9		from 6·0 to 7·9		8·0 and over	
Angola	3·5	Bahamas	5·9	Argentina	7·2	Albania	8·0
South Africa		British Gui-		Australia	7·6	Austria	8·1
—Bantu pop-		ana	4·1	Algeria		Alaska	8·1
ulation	3·5	Bolivia	4·3	—Moslem		Algeria	
Dominican		Colombia	5·9	popula-		—European	
Republic	3·7	El Salvador	4·0	tion	6·8	popu-	
Honduras	3·7	Guadeloupe	5·1	Belgium	7·6	lation	8·3
Iraq	3·8	Guatemala	4·9	British		Bermuda	9·6
Mozambique	1·3	Ireland	5·0	Honduras	6·3	Bulgaria	8·9
Nicaragua	3·3	Mauritius	4·9	Ceylon	6·0	Canada	8·0
Panama	3·5	Martinique	5·4	Costa Rica	6·9	Cyprus	8·1
Spanish Gui-		Paraguay	4·7	Chile	7·5	Egypt	8·1
nea	1·7	Peru	4·2	Czechoslo-		Germ. D.R.	8·5
Thailand	1·8	Philippines	5·4	vakia	6·8	Germ. F.R.	9·0
		Venezuela	5·5	Denmark	7·3	Greece	8·1
		Zanzibar		Ecuador	6·1	Hawaii	8·0
		and Pem-		England		Hungary	10·0
		ba	5·9	and		Iceland	8·0
				Wales	7·7	Iran	8·1
				France	7·0	Japan	8·5
				Finland	7·2	Jordan	11·5
				Italy	7·5	Lebanon	8·5
				Israel	7·9	New Zea-	
				Luxembourg	7·4	land	8·0
				Mexico	6·5	Netherlands	8·5
				Norway	6·9	Poland	9·1
				Syria	7·5	Portugal	8·1
				Sweden	7·0	Puerto Rico	8·4
				Uruguay	7·7	Rumania	11·4
				Taiwan	7·9	Spain	8·5
						South Africa	
						—white pop-	
						ulation	8·8
						Switzerland	8·1
						United	
						States	8·9
						USSR	12·3
						Yugoslavia	8·6

marriage rates are then certainly too low to provide replacement for the marriage decrement caused by the death of one of the spouses (or possibly even by divorce). Hence, marriage rates under 5·0 per thousand can safely be considered to be the outcome of incomplete marriage registration rather than the indicator of actual marriage frequency. In Europe, marriage rates are relatively low in Czechoslovakia, the Scandinavian countries and France. The countries of western and south-western Europe have higher rates, and the highest rates are noted in the Eastern European countries which belong to the socialist camp. Marriage frequencies in Arab countries are also quite large.

Marriage rates computed per thousand inhabitants are not a very precise way of measuring marriage frequency; the number of marriages should be given as a ratio of the marriageable part of the population rather than of the total population. With the exception of countries where polygamy is recognized by law, the marriageable population comprises persons over a certain age limit (the minimum age at marriage laid down by law is usually different for the two sexes), who are free to contract a marriage. Such rates are usually computed separately for males and for females.

Table 32 contains such marriage rates in selected countries. For the purposes of comparison, average rates per thousand inhabitants are also included.[1]

In most countries marriage rates are nearly the same for males and females. Exceptions to this rule can be found in countries which have a large influx of immigrants; since the majority of them are men, these have lower marriage rates; also, in the countries which were belligerents in the world war men are outnumbered by women and, therefore, marriage rates among males are higher. Alaska, Argentina and Israel belong to the first group, and the second comprises all the European countries, including Poland, which took part in the last world war.

Classified by marriage rates per 1000 marriageable persons, the countries listed retain approximately the same order as when classified by marriage rates per 1000 inhabitants.

Figure 15 represents the relation between marriage rates per thousand inhabitants and marriage rates per thousand marriageable males (the results for marriageable females would be nearly the same). The countries specified are those

---

[1] *Demographic Yearbook 1958.*

TABLE 32

Country	Years	Marriage rates per 1000		
		marriageable persons		inhabit-ants
		males	females	
Alaska	1949—1951	52·6	204·9	14·1
Algeria				
—Moslem population .	1953—1955	95·7	110·5	9·8
—European population	1953—1955	70·7	50·2	7·9
Argentina	1946—1948	42·3	47·0	8·4
Austria	1950—1952	69·3	44·2	8·9
Australia	1953—1955	63·1	66·3	7·9
Bahamas	1952—1962	70·5	49·4	9·1
Bermuda	1949—1951	77·9	69·8	10·9
British Honduras	1945—1947	39·0	35·2	6·9
Bolivia	1949—1951	57·2	47·7	7·3
Canada	1955—1957	69·1	72·6	8·2
Ceylon.	1952—1954	33·1	42·9	6·3
Chile	1951—1953	54·4	49·9	4·3
Colombia	1950—1952	34·4	32·8	5·5
Costa Rica	1949—1951	50·5	49·3	7·8
Denmark.	1949—1951	68·8	62·5	8·8
Dominican Rep.	1949—1951	16·6	16·8	3·3
Ecuador	1949—1951	42·3	39·4	6·7
Egypt	1946—1948	127·9	121·0	14·2
El Salvador	1949—1951	22·1	20·6	4·6
England and Wales . . .	1950—1952	70·2	51·6	8·1
Finland	1949—1951	65·4	47·3	8·4
Fiji Islands	1955—1957	65·5	85·1	7·2
France	1953—1955	57·0	42·2	7·2
German Dem. Rep. . .	1949—1951	113·2	56·9	10·8
German Fed. Rep. . . .	1949—1951	83·5	56·0	10·5
Greece.	1950—1952	48·1	41·3	7·5
Guadeloupe	1953—1955	31·4	27·1	5·7
Guatemala	1949—1951	15·4	15·4	3·6
Hawaii.	1949—1951	61·6	101·3	11·1
Honduras	1950—1951	18·1	17·8	3·8
Hungary	1948—1950	89·8	69·6	11·3
Iceland	1949—1951	46·0	45·1	8·0
Ireland	1950—1952	25·7	27·9	5·4
Italy.	1950—1952	49·9	42·2	7·5
Israel				
—Jewish population .	1947—1949	93·2	113·7	12·4
Japan	1954—1956	61·9	52·5	8·0
Martinique	1953—1955	34·4	27·9	6·2
Mexico	1949—1951	50·7	39·2	6·7
Mozambique	1949—1951	19·4	17·1	1·5

TABLE 32 (cont.)

Country	Years	Marriage rates per 1000		inhabit-ants
		marriageable persons		
		males	females	
New Zealand	1955—1957	69·6	68·5	8·1
Nicaragua	1949—1951	23·7	21·2	4·5
Norway	1949—1951	55·2	50·5	8·3
Peru.	1939—1941	17·9	15·5	3·1
Philippines	1956—1957	52·9	48·1	5·5
Poland	1949—1951	96·2	63·9	10·9
Portugal	1949—1951	54·1	43·1	7·8
Puerto Rico	1949—1951	52·0	52·0	8·3
Spain	1949—1951	46·1	36·4	7·4
Sweden	1949—1951	52·6	49·5	7·8
Switzerland	1949—1951	54·1	42·1	7·9
Taiwan	1934—1936	26·9	28·8	8·6
United States	1949—1951	96·9	87·3	10·7
Venezuela	1949—1951	23·6	23·5	4·9
Yugoslavia	1952—1953	85·1	66·6	10·2

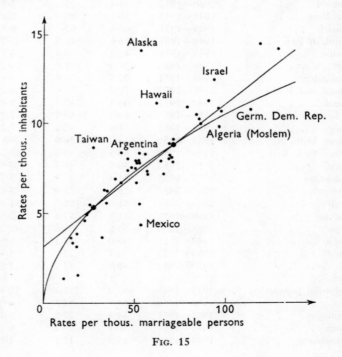

FIG. 15

in which certain factors (wars, migrations) caused marked
deviations from the pattern obtained in other countries. The
graph shows that the relation between the two rates is approximately linear; but it is not very clear, as the dispersion
of points around the straight line (e.g., regression line) ap-
proximating them, is quite large. Hence, if we estimate marriage rates among marriageable persons (such rates cannot
be directly computed when the marital structure of population
by age is unknown) on the basis of marriage rates per thousand inhabitants we must allow for a certain error, particularly
when the structure of population in a given country has
for some reason undergone serious disturbances. The graph
indicates that the error may amount to as much as 20 per
1000, although in most cases it is under 10 per 1000. The
formula for the regression, found by the point method (corresponding points on the graph are marked with circles), is:

$$r_m = 12 \cdot 5\, r_t - 39 \cdot 2$$

where:
r_m is the rate computed for the marriageable population, and
r_t is the rate computed for the total population.

We have also tried to draw a parabola for the same points,
with the additional assumption that the two rates take on
the value 0 simultaneously. But, as the graph shows, the
effect is even less satisfactory.

Using the regression formula given above, we can estimate
approximately the marriage rates among the marriageable population in some of the more important countries:

Belgium	56
Czechoslovakia	46
Netherlands	67
U.S.A.	72
U.S.S.R.	115

Since these are approximate figures only, decimals have
been omitted. In any case, it is obvious that marriage frequency among the marriageable population is very high in
the Soviet Union and quite low in the other countries accounted for in the computation, particularly in Czechoslovakia.

The question therefore arises of the comparability of rates
and, consequently, of their standardization. Marriage rates
computed for the marriageable population do not require

TABLE 33

Country	Years	Sex	Age groups											
			15—19	20—24	25—29	30—34	35—39	40—44	45—49	50—54	55—59	60—64	65—69	70—74
Australia	1953—1955	m	0·0037	0700	0858	0533	0206	0156	0104	0073	0082	0057	0038	0038
		f	0·0287	0929	0584	0296	0146	0085	0054	0035	0020	0011	0011	—
Austria	1950—1952	m	0·0080	0945	0542	0208	0114	0079	0060	0050	0044	0038	0037	0037
		f	0·0528	1103	0319	0138	0088	0007	0052	0038	0028	0022	0022	—
Canada	1955—1957	m	0·0126	1029	0596	0211	0099	0062	0050	0043	0039	0041	0043	0043
		f	0·0044	0984	0322	0123	0071	0052	0045	0038	0031	0032	0032	—
Chile	1951—1953	m	0·0097	0667	0603	0339	0194	0137	0108	0086	0062	0062	0062	0062
		f	0·0427	0586	0379	0225	0128	0102	0076	0049	0036	0023	0023	—
Egypt	1947	m	0·0098	1110	1227	0646	0413	0245	0233	0140	0150	0076	0064	0064
		f	0·0310	1066	0485	0266	0167	0091	0066	0024	0016	0006	0006	—
England and Wales	1950—1952	m	0·0062	0991	0628	0262	0134	0080	0059	0050	0044	0039	0040	0040
		f	0·0389	0899	0377	0161	0092	0061	0047	0034	0024	0018	0018	—
Poland	1949—1951	m	0·0084	1083	0977	0435	0238	0131	0086	0063	0063	0041	0041	0041
		f	0·0448	1001	0520	0225	0104	0066	0042	0020	0020	0006	0006	—
Portugal	1949—1951	m	0·0049	0679	0674	0263	0123	0076	0054	0043	0037	0031	0031	0031
		f	0·0288	0778	0394	0163	0088	0055	0037	0024	0016	0016	0016	—
Sweden	1949—1951	m	0·0042	0672	0716	0316	0155	0088	0059	0044	0034	0023	0014	0014
		f	0·0320	0998	0502	0195	0109	0066	0044	0026	0014	0006	0006	—

standardization; they can be used as they are, without further calculations, for purposes of comparison between different countries or between different periods of time in the same country. To be sure, it would be conceivable to compute such rates for a definite age structure of the marriageable population but this would not be quite satisfactory since the age structure everywhere is predominantly influenced precisely by the marriage frequencies in the various age groups (Table 33). Accordingly, to assume a uniform age structure of the marriageable population would be inconsistent with the actual trends in marriage frequencies of various countries.

However, the influence of the age structure can be taken into account when computing marriage rates based on the total population. Table 34 presents the results of such computations based on an age distribution typical for a population with a stationary age structure according to the Polish life tables for 1952—1953. This table illustrates the trends in the probability of marriage among men and women of various age groups in the course of the year.

TABLE 34

Age groups	Males	Females
	in thous.	
15—19	434	446
20—24	429	442
26—29	422	438
30—34	416	433
35—39	409	427
40—44	400	420
45—49	387	412
50—54	369	400
55—59	341	382
60—64	303	336
65—69	233	317
70—74	191	
Total	5860	6430

We have assumed that the probability of marriage for men aged 75 and over and women aged 70 and over is negligible.

The standard age structure has been computed on the basis

of Polish life tables for 1952—1953, by adding together the numbers of survivors in consecutive five-year age groups and rounding off the figures obtained. Only those age groups have been considered within which marriages can be contracted, i.e. between 15 and 74 years.

The total number of population is obtained from the life table by multiplying the initial number of infants (100,000 in our case) by the average expectation of life at birth (58·6 years for males and 64·3 years for females).

Standardization can be based on marriage rates for either sex. The purpose of our calculations is to establish the number of marriages among males (or females) if their age structure corresponded to that in the Polish life tables for 1952—1953, and the marriage frequencies by age were similar to those actually prevailing in that country at the given period. The result gives the hypothetical number of marriages per 5860 thousand males (or 6430 thousand females). The next step is to calculate how many females (or males) there ought to be if the distribution by sex is to correspond to the one actually existing in the given country and period; on this basis we can establish the hypothetical total number of population. It is on this total number of males and females that standardized marriage rates are computed.

There is a difference between rates based on the probability of marriage among males and among females, but the difference is rather slight. The divergence between crude and standardized marriage rates can be much larger. It is possible to state in advance that if the actual age structure in a given country is more progressive than the standard structure, the standardized marriage rate will then exceed the crude rate. If, on the other hand, the age structure of a given population is more regressive than the standard structure, then the standardized rate will be below the crude rate.

The results of our computations are listed in Table 35.

Chile shows the largest difference between crude and standardized rates. The explanation is that the youngest age groups in Chile are very numerous and thus the age structure of the Chilean population is distinctly progressive. The same phenomenon, though to a less marked extent, is noted among males in Egypt. In Portugal, the situation is reversed: crude

TABLE 35

| Country | Years | Marriage rates | | |
| | | crude | standardized on the basis of age structure | |
			males	females
Australia	1953—1955	7·9	7·9	8·6
Austria	1950—1952	8·9	9·6	8·9
Canada	1955—1957	8·2	8·5	7·9
Chile	1951—1953	4·3	8·4	7·1
England and Wales . . .	1950—1952	8·1	8·2	7·3
Egypt	1947	14·2	15·1	12·1
Poland	1949—1951	10·9	10·6	8·9
Portugal	1949—1951	7·8	7·0	6·6
Sweden	1949—1950	7·8	7·7	7·8

rates are higher than standardized rates, which is evidence of an age structure less progressive than the standard structure. In the case of Poland and of England and Wales, the rates are influenced by war gaps in natality; this lowers the standardized rates *among females*. Gaps in middle age groups among males affect the rates in a reverse direction, which explains the large disparity between the standardized rates for the two sexes in Canada. Characteristically, in Sweden and Australia the rates are almost identical.

Knowing the marriage rates by age groups, based on the total number of a certain age cohort (and not on marriageable persons) we can find the gross marriage rates (analogous to gross reproduction rates). Gross marriage rates give the average number of marriages per person for given marriage frequencies by age on the assumption that there is no mortality. Gross marriage rates can also be defined as the average number of marriages per person who has reached the age when marriage can no longer be expected to occur (according to our assumption, the age in question is 75 years for males and 70 years for females).

Gross marriage rates are obtained by summing the marriage rates of men and women by age during the whole period when marriage can be expected to occur (Table 36).

Among the countries listed in Table 36 Egypt has the highest gross marriage rates. Assuming that marriage frequencies in Egypt remained unchanged for a long time, a man

TABLE 36

Country	Years	Gross marriage rates	
		males	females
Australia	1953—1955	1·117	1·202
Austria	1950—1952	1·463	1·229
Canada	1955—1957	1·191	1·187
Chile	1951—1955	1·247	1·032
Egypt	1947	2·233	1·761
England and Wales	1951—1953	1·213	1·060
Poland	1949—1951	1·641	1·229
Portugal	1949—1951	1·043	0·932
Sweden	1949—1951	1·088	1·143

aged 75 would score an average of 2·233 marriages, and a
woman aged 70, 1·751 marriages. The rates in Poland and
Austria are also comparatively high. In the remaining countries,
the rates are slightly above 1.

In the majority of cases, gross marriage rates among males
are higher than among females, but in Sweden and Australia
the reverse is the case.

Gross marriage rates may be divided by age groups. Let us
consider here (Table 37) such a division into two groups
from the point of view of marriage frequencies: the younger
(under 29) and the older (30 years and over).

TABLE 37

Country	Years	Gross marriage rates			
		males		females	
		under 29	30 and over	under 29	30 and over
Australia . . .	1953—1955	0·784	0·333	0·975	0·227
Austria	1950—1952	0·797	0·666	0·900	0·329
Canada	1955—1957	0·876	0·315	0·975	0·212
Chile	1951—1955	0·684	0·563	0·696	0·336
Egypt	1947	1·218	1·015	1·431	0·320
England and Wales . . .	1951—1953	0·839	0·374	0·833	0·227
Poland	1949—1951	1·070	0·571	0·985	0·244
Portugal	1949—1951	0·701	0·342	0·730	0·202
Sweden	1949—1951	0·715	0·373	0·910	0·233

The table indicates that marriage frequencies are distributed very unevenly between the two groups. One thing is certain; the proportion of the older group among females is smaller than among males. Apart from this, there is no other distinct regularity. The same proportion of the younger age group has a high equivalent in the older group in some cases and a low one in others. Austria and Australia for instance, have nearly equal marriage rates among males (0·797 and 0·784) in the younger group, but the rates for the older group in Austria are exactly twice as high as in Australia (0·666 against 0·333). Among females, marriage rates in the older group in Egypt, Chile and Austria are almost the same (0·320, 0·336 and 0·329), but the younger group in Egypt has a rate more than twice that in Chile and one and a half times the rate in Austria (1·431 against 0·696 and 0·900).

There is no apparent connection between gross marriage rates among males and females, though a certain general interrelation is bound to exist; for the more men marry the more women get married; higher marriage rates among males should mean higher marriage rates among females. A certain interrelation is also to be expected between the rates of the two sexes in younger age groups, even though we are unable to establish it from the material available.

Similarly, an interrelation should exist between gross marriage rates and marriage rates computed per thousand marriageable persons.

Marriage frequencies by age per thousand marriageable persons in selected countries are listed in Table 38.

Changes in marriage frequencies by age reveal a characteristic trend. The increase in marriage frequencies, very slow in the beginning, becomes more and more rapid until a maximum is reached, which is followed by a gradual decline. Among females, in most cases maximum frequencies are noted in the 20—24 age group, and among males, in the next group, from 25 to 29. The probability of marriage in the earlier age groups is higher among females than among males; the reverse is true for later age groups. The maximum for women generally exceeds the maximum for men, since among women marriages are concentrated around a certain age while the range of age at marriage among men is far more extended.

6

TABLE 38

Country	Year	Sex	Marriages per 1000 marriageable persons — age groups										
			15—19	20—24	25—29	30—34	35—39	40—44	45—49	50—54	55—59	60—64	65 and over
Alaska	1950	m	6·4	28·3	71·3	70·2	64·3	57·1	25·6	12·0			3·0
		f	79·0	263·6	250·4	259·4	171·0	121·1	53·2	7·2			—
Australia	1954	m	7·8	126·9	148·0	99·9	68·3	50·4	39·8	31·4	23·5	18·8	7·9
		f	57·8	266·9	194·5	111·5	71·3	45·3	28·9	16·2	9·0	4·9	1·5
Austria	1951	m	3·8	86·2	178·3	189·1	136·4	95·5	67·8	51·7	42·2	32·3	7·7
		f	30·8	142·4	146·4	96·1	49·8	29·8	18·4	10·3	5·1	2·2	0·6
Canada	1956	m	12·9	144·2	176·3	109·8	68·9	46·2	37·1	27·2	23·6	20·3	8·6
		f	71·5	222·7	171·8	94·1	55·5	35·3	26·2	17·3	11·2	7·9	2·4
Chile	1952	m	9·5	82·7	115·9	94·8	65·9	50·9	41·8	31·9	27·9	13·9	
		f	46·3	93·4	90·8	66·6	44·0	30·7	20·4	9·4	5·5	1·8	
Colombia	1951	m	6·0	47·7	65·9	53·7	37·1	31·0	24·6	19·0		11·2	
		f	43·6	61·3	37·0	26·8	16·5	12·1	7·6	3·8		1·1	
Costa Rica	1950	m	9·9	84·2	111·1	76·3	52·1	43·4	40·4	24·8		14·0	
		f	60·1	95·2	66·0	42·0	26·9	21·8	15·3	5·8		2·0	
Denmark	1950	m	3·4	106·7	204·0	156·3	103·5	76·6	55·0	41·0	36·4	17·3	5·2
		f	45·2	226·1	216·2	115·5	68·6	38·9	24·0	12·0	4·6	2·2	0·7
Egypt	1947	m	13·2	141·1	298·2	336·5	410·1	313·8	371·4	180·4	180·4	66·2	23·8
		f	230·0	389·9	376·7	219·4	132·2	36·5	24·2	4·6	3·9	0·7	0·2
El Salvador	1950	m	6·6	41·9	48·8	36·0	26·9	21·5	22·1	15·6	14·2	8·0	
		f	34·3	41·0	28·9	23·1	15·6	13·5	10·6		4·2	1·3	
England and Wales	1951	m	6·5	133·0	177·8	130·8	87·7	61·3	47·8	40·2	33·6	23·0	8·4
		f	41·4	220·0	163·1	93·3	54·4	32·5	20·8	13·0	7·2	4·4	1·2
Finland	1950	m	9·5	98·3	160·8	141·6	109·0	73·3	54·4	38·4	27·5	17·7	5·5
		f	35·6	149·3	140·6	83·5	50·4	28·5	17·3	8·6	3·4	1·6	0·3

Country	Year	Sex											
France	1954	m	3·9	108·7	159·3	96·9	64·1	44·0	31·1	24·1	20·4	16·8	4·7
		f	32·3	180·6	143·9	73·5	46·5	27·4	17·8	10·7	6·1	2·8	0·5
Germ. Fed. Rep.	1950	m	3·1	97·6	217·0	255·7	241·6	134·4	106·1	74·8	53·4	9·8	
		f	25·2	154·4	192·6	127·5	71·9	28·0	18·4	8·9	3·9	0·5	
Hungary	1949	m	8·8	122·9	248·0	223·7	160·9	113·9	80·3	69·3	51·1	33·4	9·7
		f	82·7	218·2	180·4	99·3	62·8	35·4	22·4	11·3	6·5	3·0	0·7
Iceland	1950	m	2·4	88·5	120·7	87·3	62·7	35·3	18·7	16·3	8·3	7·4	2·4
		f	36·0	146·1	119·3	59·5	39·1	16·7	15·8	5·4	1·4	0·8	0·2
Italy	1951	m	2·7	42·9	129·5	59·5	102·1	55·9	32·8	23·5	17·9	11·1	3·8
		f	23·8	109·1	124·7	153·5	31·0	16·0	8·6	4·3	2·5	1·3	0·4
Japan	1955	m	0·7	30·6	115·0	66·1	92·8	59·7	37·6	17·7	9·3	4·3	1·3
		f	8·0	96·9	154·5	37·6	13·0	5·1	2·8	1·4	0·7	0·3	0·1
New Zealand	1950	m	6·7	130·5	189·3	126·0	77·4	60·9	47·7	38·3	33·1	27·7	8·8
		f	57·5	285·4	220·4	119·4	74·2	45·6	29·1	20·1	11·3	6·5	1·8
Norway	1950	m	2·3	55·3	139·1	133·9	90·2	55·5	38·0	25·8	17·3	12·0	2·3
		f	21·5	144·6	102·0	112·7	60·5	29·4	16·3	7·4	2·8	1·3	0·3
Poland	1950	m	8·6	145·3	280·0	255·7	210·3	139·8	94·4	59·8		13·5	
		f	48·4	184·4	169·8	90·1	50·1	24·8	13·7	5·1		0·5	
Portugal	1950	m	5·0	80·4	151·5	106·2	64·3	44·9	31·9	25·9	21·4	8·5	
		f	30·0	118·1	105·8	59·1	36·0	20·9	12·2	6·9	3·9	1·0	
Puerto Rico	1950	m	12·3	103·6	125·2	91·3	65·0	53·5	46·0	37·6	37·6	24·5	11·8
		f	67·5	121·5	91·0	62·9	44·7	31·8	25·4	13·0	8·9	4·6	1·6
Sweden	1950	m	4·4	77·2	143·0	109·5	71·7	44·6	31·0	22·6	16·8	9·1	2·2
		f	33·1	161·8	176·4	104·2	59·5	31·6	17·4	9·0	3·8	1·6	0·2
Switzerland	1950	m	1·2	57·0	149·8	131·7	88·9	56·9	42·1	30·9	25·9	16·5	4·2
		f	13·7	116·0	145·7	86·5	48·2	28·3	16·4	9·4	4·8	2·2	0·3
Venezuela	1950	m	5·3	37·8	41·5	32·0	26·2	22·3	13·8	15·7	14·5	8·4	
		f	45·7	38·7	25·9	18·7	15·7	10·3	7·8	3·9	2·9	1·0	
Yugoslavia	1953	m	27·8	126·3	253·9	220·0	144·8	104·6	70·3	46·3	41·6	20·5	7·6
		f	62·6	207·2	144·9	76·9	31·7	20·5	12·4	7·6	5·1	2·1	0·6

The maximum values and the rates of pre-maximum increase and of post-maximum decline in marriage frequencies vary a great deal from country to country. Some typical examples are presented graphically in Fig. 16. It is important to bear in mind here that the statistics are compiled for formal

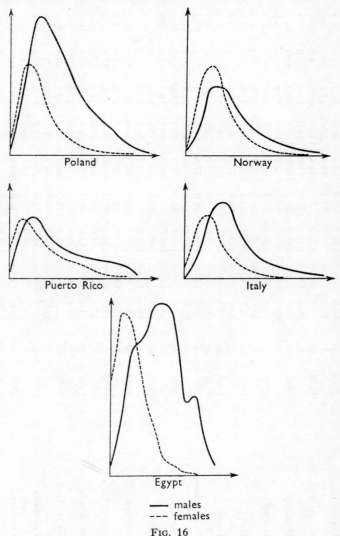

FIG. 16

marriages only. In those countries in which consensual unions prevail, the statistics of marriages contracted are undernumerated and misleading as indicators of the actual rate.

Maximum marriage frequencies fluctuate over a very wide range: from 41·5% to 410·1% among males (in Venezuela and Egypt) and from 38·7% to 389·9% among females (again in Venezuela and Egypt). The maximum among males is usually observed in the 25—29 age group, but in some countries (Austria, German Federal Republic, Italy, Japan) it is noted in the 30—34 age group. Among females, maximum frequencies in most cases are found in the 20—24 age group, but in some countries (Austria, the German Federal Republic, Italy, Japan, and also Sweden and Norway) the next age group, from 25 to 29, has the highest frequencies. In Denmark and Finland marriage frequencies in the 20—24 age group only slightly exceed those in the 25—29 group.

In the countries which were belligerents in World War II, maximum marriage frequency among males is higher than among females, because there are less men than women.

In Japan, more than in any other country, the age at marriage among the two sexes is concentrated within a few birth cohorts.

Just as for marital structure of the population by age, countries can be divided into several typical groups from the point of view of marriage frequencies by age.

The first group comprises Eastern European countries.

The countries listed in our table include Poland, Hungary and Yugoslavia. Early marriages and a high proportion of newly married persons (in ratio to marriageable population) are characteristic for this group.

The second group, which includes Scandinavian countries— Sweden, Norway, Denmark and Iceland—is characterized by much lower marriage rates and relatively late marriages, particularly among women.

The third group, somewhat resembling the second, is composed of Western European countries—France and England. In Canada, Australia and New Zealand the situation is also comparable. In these countries marriages are contracted a little earlier than in Scandinavia.

The fourth group—the Moslem countries—is represented

in our table by Egypt alone. It has very high marriage frequencies and a large number of early and very early marriages.

Data on the fifth group—the Central and South American
countries—vary in proportion to the degree of prevalence
of consensual unions. Consequently, the figures listed in the
table do not reflect the actual situation; they are usually
very low.

Thus far we have examined overall marriage rates of countries as a whole. It is obvious however that marriage frequencies
may also vary within one country. The differences may in
part be the result of variations in the age structure, although
this alone can hardly provide a full explanation of this phenomenon. Table 39 presents the distribution of marriage rates
in 43 counties in England (excluding Wales) in the years
1881—1890 and in 1958.

TABLE 39

Marriage rates per 1000 inhabitants	Number of counties	
	1881—1890	1958
5·00— 5·49	2	—
5·50— 5·99	3	—
6·00— 6·49	9	3
6·50— 6·99	12	14
7·00— 7·49	6	13
7·50— 7·99	8	11
8·00— 8·49	2	1
8·50— 8·99	1	—
9·00— 9·49	—	—
9·50— 9·99	—	—
10·00—10·49	—	1
Total	43	43

The range of difference is quite large: the highest rate
in the two periods specified exceeds one and a half times the
lowest rate. But if we exclude the highest rate in 1958 (for
London), the marriage rates reveal a much higher degree of
concentration than in 1881. A tendency towards equalizing
marriage rates can easily be noticed. In most cases, marriage
rates have increased, but not everywhere. Figure 17 presents
graphically the marriage rates in different counties in the
two periods under examination. A straight line, drawn at
an angle of 45° to the axis, separates the points which rep-

resent the counties where marriage rates have increased
from those where they have declined. The latter are far less
numerous. No regular pattern can be traced in the changes
observed; no interrelation seems to exist between the initial
level of the marriage rates and the degree of their rise.

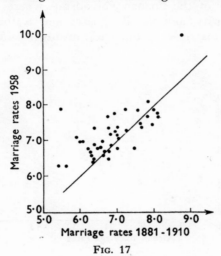

FIG. 17

Marriage frequencies are even more differentiated in Poland.
Taking into account distribution by voivodships, distribution
by towns and urban settlements on the one hand and rural
localities on the other, we can draw up a set of marriage
rates listed in an ascending order (Table 40).

TABLE 40

Marriage rates per 1000 inhabitants	Voivod-ships	Towns and urban settlements	Rural localities
7·0— 7·9	1	—	3
8·0— 8·9	6	4	5
9·0— 9·9	4	5	6
10·0—10·9	4	5	2
11·0—11·9	3	2	1
12·0—12·9	1	2	—
13·0—13·9	—	1	—
Total	19	19	17

Marriage frequencies are more stable in rural than in urban localities. Rural marriage rates fluctuate between 7·6 and 11·2 per thousand population (the range of difference is thus 3·6), and urban—between 8·4 and 13·2 (the range being 4·8). As a rule, urban marriage rates are higher, with the exception of the Poznań voivodship where rural localities have priority, and the Bydgoszcz and Katowice voivodships where marriage frequencies in town and village are the same.

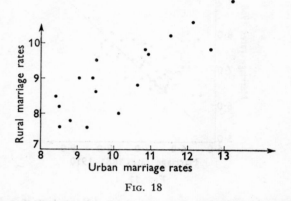

FIG. 18

Figure 18 shows that in those voivodships having higher urban marriage frequencies, rural marriage frequencies in villages are higher too; for the points on the graph are scattered roughly along an ascending line. But the Poznań voivodship shows higher rural and lower urban rates than does the Lublin voivodship. The same correlation exists between the Bydgoszcz and Cracow voivodships and between the Katowice and Białystok voivodships. High marriage rates are noted in Poland's large towns and cities and in the northwestern and western parts of the country (covering the voivodships of Szczecin, Wrocław, Olsztyn, Koszalin, Gdańsk and Zielona Góra). The voivodships of Rzeszów, Lublin, Kielce and Łódź have the lowest marriage frequencies. Differences in marriage rates are to some extent the result of variations in age structures between voivodships. If the influence of age structure were eliminated, the differences would diminish. In the Olsztyn voivodship, for example, the standardized marriage rates would then be 10·5 (the crude rates are 11·1); the corresponding rates for urban settlements on the one hand and for rural localities on the other would equal 10·8 and 10·2 (the respective crude rates are 12·1 and 10·6). These are much closer to the national rates than the crude rates. Similarly, the standardized rates computed for the Łódź voivodship are 9·4, 9·2 and 8·8 respectively (the crude rates are 8·3, 8·5 and 8·2); again, these come nearer to the national rates.

Table 41 presents marriage rates in Poland distributed by age, and classified by urban and rural localities, on the basis of 1956 statistics.

TABLE 41

	Sex	Marriage rates by age									
		—19	20——24	25——29	30——34	35——39	40——44	45——49	50——54	55——59	60 and over
Total	m	11·4	89·3	78·5	23·8	12·6	8·1	6·0	4·8	4·5	3·8
	f	43·7	105·5	40·9	16·5	9·6	6·2	3·6	2·5	1·4	0·8
Urban localities	m	13·5	93·4	73·4	21·7	12·7	9·4	7·8	6·7	7·1	6·0
	f	48·7	101·4	39·4	17·2	10·0	6·7	5·2	3·7	2·1	1·0
Rural localities	m	10·0	83·8	83·7	26·2	12·5	6·8	4·6	3·3	2·9	2·2
	f	40·2	109·5	42·3	15·7	8·4	3·8	2·3	1·5	0·8	0·3

A comparison between the marriage rates in urban and rural localities among persons of the same sex and age reveals the existence of a certain pattern. Thus, towns have the higher marriage rates for the youngest age groups; in the young (but not the youngest) groups they are exceeded by the villages, but in the later ages once again the marriage frequencies in towns are higher than those in villages. Men under 24 and over 35, as well as women under 19 and above 30, marry more frequently in urban than in rural areas. Generally speaking, however, the differences in marriage frequencies by age are not significant.

This means quite an important change in comparison with the situation in the years between the two world wars. Differences between urban and rural areas were then much greater; in the earliest age groups marriages were far more frequent in rural than in urban localities. It was only above the age of 30 among males and 25 among females that towns took first place. The trend towards equality in rural and urban marriage rates may be presumed to have been mainly the result of the vast influx of rural population into the towns.

The marriage rates in some countries where vital statistics have been recorded for a long time, as well as in Poland, are shown in Table 42. The earliest statistics available have been listed, covering a period of varying length dependent upon the availability of reliable data.[1]

TABLE 42

Marriage rates

Year	Sweden	Denmark	France	Germany (Prussia)	England	Poland
1749	8·5	—	—	—	—	—
1750	9·2	—	—	—	—	—
1	9·3	—	—	—	—	—
2	9·3	—	—	—	—	—
3	8·7	—	—	—	—	—
4	9·4	—	—	—	—	—
5	9·2	—	—	—	—	—
6	8·5	—	—	—	—	—
7	8·0	—	—	—	—	—
8	8·1	—	—	—	—	—
9	9·7	—	—	—	—	—
1760	1·8	—	—	—	—	—
1	9·4	—	—	—	—	—
2	9·0	—	—	—	—	—
3	8·6	—	—	—	—	—
4	8·8	—	—	—	—	—
5	8·1	—	—	—	—	—
6	8·3	—	—	—	—	—
7	8·3	—	—	—	—	—
8	8·5	—	—	—	—	—
9	8·1	—	—	—	—	—
1770	8·1	—	—	—	—	—
1	7·8	—	—	—	—	—
2	6·8	—	—	—	—	—
3	7·8	—	—	—	—	—
4	8·8	—	—	—	—	—
5	9·4	—	—	—	—	—
6	9·0	—	—	—	—	—

[1] Sources: Poland—S. Szulc, *Zagadnienia demograficzne Polski, Ruch naturalny w latach 1895—1935* (*Problems of Polish Demography, Natural Movement in 1895—1935*), Warsaw 1939, p. 19, and *Rocznik Statystyczny 1959* (*Statistical Yearbook 1959*); other countries—various demographic yearbooks.

TABLE 42 (cont.)

Marriage rates

Year	Sweden	Denmark	France	Germany (Prussia)	England	Poland
1777	9·1	—	—	—	—	—
8	9·0	—	—	—	—	—
9	8·7	—	—	—	—	—
1780	8·5	—	—	—	—	—
1	7·8	—	—	—	—	—
2	7·7	—	—	—	—	—
3	8·0	—	—	—	—	—
4	7·5	—	—	—	—	—
5	7·8	—	—	—	—	—
6	8·0	—	—	—	—	—
7	7·9	—	—	—	—	—
8	7·9	—	—	—	—	—
9	7·9	—	—	—	—	—
1790	8·2	—	—	—	—	—
1	10·8	—	—	—	—	—
2	10·6	—	—	—	—	—
3	8·9	—	—	—	—	—
4	8·2	—	—	—	—	—
5	7·6	—	—	—	—	—
6	8·4	—	—	—	—	—
7	8·3	—	—	—	—	—
8	8·3	—	—	—	—	—
9	7·3	—	—	—	—	—
1800	7·4	9·4	—	—	—	—
1	7·2	7·9	7·2	—	—	—
2	7·8	9·5	7·3	—	—	—
3	8·2	8·7	7·3	—	—	—
4	8·1	8·8	7·2	—	—	—
5	8·4	7·9	7·5	—	—	—
6	8·0	7·9	7·2	—	—	—
7	8·2	7·3	7·3	—	—	—
8	8·1	8·3	7·6	—	—	—
9	7·8	7·8	9·2	—	—	—
1810	10·8	9·0	7·9	—	—	—
1	10·7	9·5	7·0	—	—	—
2	9·1	8·2	7·5	—	—	—
3	7·7	8·3	13·2	—	—	—
4	7·5	9·5	6·6	—	—	—
5	9·6	10·6	8·3	—	—	—
6	9·3	9·6	8·5	11·5	—	—
7	8·3	7·9	6·9	10·8	—	—
8	8·5	8·7	7·2	10·5	—	—
9	8·1	8·5	7·1	10·3	—	—

TABLE 42 (*cont.*)

Year	Sweden	Denmark	France	Germany (Prussia)	England	Poland
1820	8·4	8·2	6·9	10·0	—	—
1	8·8	8·4	7·3	9·4	—	—
2	9·3	8·7	7·7	9·2	—	—
3	9·0	7·9	8·5	8·8	—	—
4	8·8	8·1	7·6	9·1	—	—
5	8·6	8·3	7·8	9·3	—	—
6	8·1	8·3	7·8	9·3	—	—
7	7·2	7·6	8·0	8·6	—	—
8	7·9	7·9	7·7	8·3	—	—
9	7·9	8·2	7·8	8·5	—	—
1830	7·7	8·4	8·4	8·6	—	—
1	6·9	8·0	7·5	7·6	—	—
2	7·2	8·7	7·4	9·8	—	—
3	7·8	8·7	8·0	9·9	—	—
4	8·0	8·6	8·2	9·8	—	—
5	7·6	8·1	8·3	9·2	—	—
6	7·2	7·6	8·2	9·1	—	—
7	6·9	7·6	7·9	9·2	—	—
8	6·1	7·0	8·1	8·8	7·7	—
9	6·8	6·9	7·9	8·9	8·0	—
1840	7·1	7·3	8·3	9·0	7·8	—
1	7·2	7·6	8·2	9·1	7·7	—
2	7·1	7·7	8·1	9·3	7·3	—
3	7·2	7·8	8·3	9·2	7·6	—
4	7·1	8·1	8·0	9·1	8·0	—
5	7·2	8·2	8·1	9·0	8·6	—
6	6·9	8·1	7·6	8·7	8·6	—
7	6·8	8·0	7·0	7·8	7·9	—
8	7·3	7·5	8·3	8·2	7·9	—
9	7·8	8·0	7·8	9·2	8·1	—
1850	7·6	7·6	8·4	9·5	8·6	—
1	7·4	9·9	8·0	9·2	8·6	—
2	6·8	9·7	7·8	8·5	8·7	—
3	7·2	9·2	7·8	8·6	8·9	—
4	7·7	8·7	7·6	7·9	8·6	—
5	7·5	8·5	7·9	7·7	8·1	—
6	7·4	8·6	7·9	8·2	8·3	—
7	7·7	8·9	8·1	9·4	8·2	—
8	8·1	8·7	8·4	9·5	8·0	—
9	8·3	8·4	8·2	8·5	8·5	—
1860	7·8	8·0	7·9	8·4	8·5	—
1	7·3	7·4	8·1	8·1	8·1	—
2	7·1	7·3	8·1	7·5	8·0	—

TABLE 42 (*cont.*)

Marriage rates						
Year	Sweden	Denmark	France	Germany	England	Poland
1863	7·3	6·4	8·0	8·7	8·4	—
4	7·0	5·6	7·9	8·7	8·6	—
5	7·1	8·8	7·9	9·2	8·7	—
6	6·7	8·3	8·0	7·8	8·7	—
7	6·1	7·6	7·8	9·5	8·2	—
8	5·5	7·3	7·8	8·9	8·0	—
9	5·6	7·3	8·3	9·0	7·9	—
1870	6·0	7·3	3·0	7·5	8·0	—
1	6·5	7·3	7·3	8·2	8·3	—
2	6·9	7·5	9·7	10·3	8·7	—
3	7·3	8·1	8·9	10·0	8·8	—
4	7·3	8·2	8·3	9·5	8·5	—
5	7·0	8·6	8·2	9·1	8·3	—
6	7·1	8·5	7·9	8·5	8·2	—
7	6·8	8·0	7·5	8·0	7·8	—
8	6·5	7·4	7·5	7·7	7·6	—
9	6·3	7·3	7·5	7·5	7·3	—
1880	6·3	7·6	7·5	7·5	7·4	—
1	6·2	6·8	7·5	7·5	7·5	—
2	6·3	7·7	7·4	7·7	7·7	—
3	6·4	7·7	7·5	7·7	7·7	—
4	6·5	7·8	7·6	7·8	7·5	—
5	6·6	7·5	7·5	7·9	7·2	—
6	6·4	7·1	7·4	7·9	7·1	—
7	6·2	6·9	7·2	7·8	7·2	—
8	5·9	7·0	7·2	7·8	7·2	—
9	6·0	7·0	7·1	8·0	7·5	—
1890	6·0	6·9	7·0	8·0	7·7	—
1	5·8	6·8	7·5	8·0	7·8	—
2	5·7	6·8	7·6	7·9	7·7	—
3	5·7	7·1	7·4	7·9	7·3	—
4	5·7	7·0	7·4	7·9	3·5	—
5	5·9	7·1	7·3	8·0	7·5	8·3
6	5·9	7·3	7·6	8·2	7·8	8·1
7	6·1	7·5	7·6	8·4	8·0	8·1
8	6·1	7·5	7·4	8·4	8·1	7·7
9	6·2	7·5	7·6	8·5	8·2	8·4
1900	6·1	7·6	7·7	8·5	8·0	8·2
1	6·1	7·1	7·8	8·2	7·9	8·0
2	6·0	7·1	7·6	7·9	8·9	7·6
3	5·8	7·1	7·6	7·1	7·8	7·7
4	5·8	7·2	7·6	8·0	7·6	7·3
5	5·8	7·2	7·7	8·1	7·6	7·3

TABLE 42 (*cont.*)

			Marriage rates			
Year	Sweden	Denmark	France	Germany	England	Poland
1906	6·1	7·4	7·8	8·2	7·8	8·0
7	6·2	7·6	8·0	8·1	7·9	7·6
8	6·1	7·5	8·0	8·0	7·5	7·3
9	6·0	7·4	7·8	7·8	7·3	7·3
1910	6·0	7·3	7·8	7·7	7·5	(7·3)
1	5·9	7·2	7·8	7·8	7·6	(7·4)
2	5·9	7·3	7·9	7·9	7·8	(7·0)
3	5·9	7·3	7·8	7·7	7·8	(6·5)
4	5·8	6·9	5·1	6·8	8·0	—
5	5·8	6·5	2·2	4·1	9·7	—
6	6·1	7·2	3·3	4·1	7·4	—
7	6·1	7·0	4·9	4·7	6·9	—
8	6·6	7·6	5·4	5·4	7·8	—
9	6·9	8·2	14·0	13·3	9·9	12·7
1920	7·3	8·2	15·9	14·5	10·1	10·6
1	6·7	8·1	11·6	11·9	8·4	11·7
2	6·2	7·9	9·3	11·2	7·8	11·5
3	6·3	8·0	8·9	9·4	7·6	10·0
4	6·2	7·8	8·8	7·1	7·6	9·3
5	6·2	7·5	8·7	7·7	7·6	8·1
6	6·3	7·5	8·4	7·7	7·1	8·6
7	6·4	7·5	8·2	8·5	7·8	8·5
8	6·6	7·8	8·2	9·2	7·7	9·6
9	6·8	7·9	8·1	9·2	7·9	9·6
1930	7·1	8·2	8·2	8·8	7·9	9·4
1	7·0	8·1	7·8	8·0	7·8	8·5
2	6·7	7·8	7·6	7·9	7·6	8·4
3	7·0	8·8	7·6	9·7	7·9	8·4
4	7·7	9·5	7·1	11·1	8·4	8·4
5	8·2	9·3	6·8	9·7	8·6	8·4
6	8·5	9·3	6·7	9·1	8·7	8·4
7	8·9	9·1	6·5	9·1	8·7	8·1
8	9·2	8·9	6·5	9·4	8·8	8·1
9	9·5	9·4	6·2	11·2	10·6	—
1940	9·1	9·2	4·4	8·8	11·2	—
1	9·1	8·7	5·7	7·2	9·3	—
2	9·9	9·2	—	7·4	8·8	—
3	9·7	9·3	—	7·3	7·0	—
4	9·9	9·3	5·4	—	7·1	—
5	9·7	9·0	9·9	—	9·3	—
6	9·5	9·8	12·8	—	9·0	(12·8)
7	8·8	9·6	10·5	—	9·3	(12·4)
8	8·4	9·4	9·0	—	9·1	(12·4)
9	7·9	8·9	8·2	—	8·5	11·2

TABLE 42 (*cont.*)

Marriage rates

Year	Sweden	Denmark	France	Germany	England	Poland
1950	7·7	9·1	7·9	—	8·1	10·8
1	7·7	8·5	7·6	—	8·2	10·7
2	7·5	8·2	7·4	—	7·9	10·4
3	7·4	8·1	7·2	—	7·8	10·0
4	7·3	7·9	7·0	—	7·7	9·8
5	7·2	7·9	7·3	—	8·0	9·5
6	7·1	7·7	6·7	—	7·8	9·4
7	7·1	7·6	5·6	—	7·7	9·1
8	6·8	7·5	7·0	—	7·5	9·2

Note: the rates shown in brackets denote rough estimates only.

Besides the countries specified, statistics of the natural movement of populations have been registered for a long time in the following countries: Ireland (since 1861), Norway (1801), Finland (1750), Austria (1819), the Netherlands (1839), Belgium (1830), Spain (1858), Italy (1863), Greece (1861), various German territories (for different years between 1816 and 1841), etc.[1]

Figure 19 depicts the trends in marriage rates in Sweden, France and Poland.

It is apparent that during the 18th century and the early part of the 19th century annual changes in marriage rates were quite large; this is reflected in the many fluctuations in the corresponding section of the graph. The influence of wars waged by individual countries (the Napoleonic wars, the Franco-Prussian war, the two world wars) is easily seen in the sudden drop in marriage rates at the beginning of the war and compensatory rise after the end of hostilities. However, the Crimean war, for instance, although France took part in it, had no marked influence on marriage frequencies. In addition, a certain parallelism in the pattern of changes in marriage rates is noticed for Sweden and France which can be explained by the influence of business cycles affecting various countries more or less simultaneously. Since

---

[1] For data on these countries brought up to 1905, see *Statistique internationale du mouvement de la population d'après les registres d'état civil*, Paris 1907.

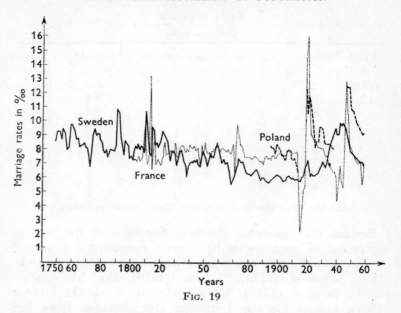

Fig. 19

the mid-19th century approximately, fluctuations in the series are visibly on the decline, and the changes are more and more cyclic. This seems to have been the consequence of the gradual industrialization of the countries concerned and of the growth of a large working class whose material conditions changed with the cyclic variations in the economic situation.

The changing pattern of marriage rates was noticed long ago, and efforts were made to find an explanation for it. These explanations, supplied by statisticians in the earlier years, shed an interesting light, not only on the phenomenon itself but also on the then prevailing opinions. Here are the comments by A. von Fircks, a German statistician whose activities fall within the second half of the 19th century:

"When a marriage takes place it usually denotes the beginning of economic independence; hence, in the civilized countries, where populations no longer increase at a very rapid rate, the number of new conjugal unions is in the long run determined by the number of deaths, unless some extraordinary events, such as an unusual expansion of foreign trade, the establishment of new and highly profitable companies, or exceedingly good crops harvested for several consecutive years, generate a great though temporary increase in the national wealth.

"If the population remained unchanged and the propitious circumstances referred to failed to occur, the number of marriages contracted over a long time ought to be exactly equal to the number of marriages broken by death or divorce; otherwise there would be no room for the establishment of new households.

"If, consequently, as a result of wars or epidemics an excessive number of marriages is disrupted, the possibility of contracting new marriages becomes much greater. Wars and epidemics are therefore followed by increased numbers of new marriages.

"During a war, at the time of an epidemic which takes a heavy toll, in a bad economic period (crop failure, high prices, depression in business, unemployment, internal dissension) there are generally few marriages performed; many persons who intend to marry wait for better times."[1]

Fircks (who wrote in 1875) named 1816, 1865, 1867 and 1872 as war years, and 1832, 1833, 1849, 1850, 1851, 1853, 1856, 1867 and 1874 as years directly following an epidemic of cholera. He also mentions that epidemics of smallpox had been known to have some influence on marriage frequencies in the past.

Of course, we can hardly concur with some of his statements. It is certainly not true that the number of newly contracted marriages is in any way dependent on, or determined by the number of deaths. To be sure, even in Fircks's lifetime the number of existing marriages revealed a steadily rising trend.

The marriage rates listed in Table 40 are rarely above ten per thousand inhabitants. Rates exceeding this limit are noted only in the years after the end of a war, which are characterized by a compensatory post-war rise. However, we know of cases in which much higher marriage rates were observed over a long period. A striking example of this, though dating back to the 17th century, was provided by Canada under French rule. The marriage rates among the French

---

[1] *Preussische Statistik*, XLVIII, Berlin 1876, pp. 135—136.

population in Canada for consecutive decades are presented in Table 43.[1]

TABLE 43

Decades	Marriage rates per 1000 inhabitants
1661—1670	34·5
1671—1680	14·3
1681—1690	20·0
1691—1700	21·3
1701—1710	17·7
1711—1720	20·3
1721—1730	20·0
1731—1740	19·3
1741—1750	22·0
1751—1760	23·4
1761—1770	22·6

In the early days of colonization Canada had very high marriage rates because her population comprised mostly young people (in 1658, 75% of Canada's French population were immigrants from France; only 25% were Canadian--born). Canada's English population was then quite small.

Marriage rates in the various age groups change with the general marriage rates. This is illustrated by French statistics for the years 1856—1955 (Table 44).[2]

The contents of the table are presented graphically in Fig. 20.

The general trend of changes is similar in all age groups. In other words, when marriage frequencies increase among persons of a certain age, an increase is generally also noted

[1] J. HENRIPIN, *La population canadienne au début du XVIII siècle*, Paris. 1954, p. 91.

The statistics in question seem reliable enough, as civil registers were kept most thoroughly even in the 17th century. Data from all Canadian parishes which existed in the 17th and 18th centuries were collected and published by Tanguay in his seven-volume *Dictionnaire généalogique* in which he traced the genealogy of all Canadians of French descent to the end of the 18th century. His work has been brought up to date by the Institut Drouin. (The magnitude of his work is evidenced by the fact that Tanguay incorporated in his work data on 1226 thousand demographic facts to which he dedicated 25 years of his life.)

[2] *Annuaire statistique de la France 1956*, p. 10 (pink).

TABLE 44

Years	Marriage per 1000 marriageable persons						
	total	age groups					
		—19	20—24	25—29	30—39	40—49	50 and over
Males							
1856—1865	6·0	1·3	5·8	11·9	10·9	4·2	1·3
1866—1875	6·2	1·2	6·1	16·1	11·4	4·4	1·1
1876—1885	5·5	1·1	4·9	17·4	9·4	3·6	0·9
1886—1895	5·4	0·9	4·8	14·3	9·2	3·1	0·8
1896—1905	6·0	0·5	5·1	17·9	10·6	3·8	0·8
1906—1913	6·3	0·4	5·4	20·3	10·7	4·0	0·8
1914—1919	4·6	0·5	3·9	14·8	10·0	3·7	0·8
1920—1925	8·6	0·8	12·1	22·3	15·1	6·6	1·3
1926—1930	7·4	0·7	10·8	19·6	11·1	4·8	1·2
1931—1935	6·9	0·7	9·6	16·3	8·9	4·3	1·0
1936	6·6	0·8	8·4	16·5	8·2	4·1	1·0
1937	6·6	0·9	8·3	17·3	8·3	4·1	1·0
1938	6·5	0·9	8·1	17·8	8·7	4·4	1·0
1939	5·8	1·0	6·7	15·1	9·4	5·2	1·0
1940	4·2	1·0	5·8	11·5	6·9	3·8	0·8
1941	5·7	1·0	8·5	20·0	9·3	3·8	0·9
1942	6·6	1·1	10·2	21·9	11·2	4·5	1·0
1943	5·4	1·0	7·9	16·0	10·4	4·4	1·0
1944	5·2	1·1	7·9	14·0	9·8	3·0	0·9
1945	8·8	1·1	10·0	23·9	20·2	6·2	1·4
1946	10·7	1·1	13·0	28·0	18·8	6·7	1·6
1947	8·9	1·2	11·0	21·7	15·3	6·3	1·5
1948	7·6	1·1	9·8	17·9	12·0	5·6	1·4
1949	7·0	1·1	10·1	15·7	9·7	4·7	1·3
1950	6·8	1·1	10·2	14·6	9·1	4·3	1·2
1951	6·6	1·1	9·9	14·4	8·4	4·0	1·2
1952	6·4	1·0	9·6	14·2	7·9	3·8	1·3
1953	6·7	1·0	9·9	16·2	9·0	3·9	1·3
1954	6·8	1·0	10·3	16·8	8·9	3·6	1·2
1955	6·7	1·0	10·0	17·5	8·6	3·5	1·2
Females							
1856—1865	4·8	3·8	10·7	11·2	6·7	2·1	0·3
1866—1875	5·0	4·3	11·3	13·7	6·7	2·0	0·3
1876—1885	4·5	4·1	10·6	13·0	5·5	1·6	0·2
1886—1895	4·3	3·5	11·0	12·0	5·3	1·5	0·2
1896—1905	4·5	3·5	13·8	13·0	5·7	1·5	0·2
1906—1913	4·7	3·3	16·2	14·7	6·0	1·8	0·2
1914—1919	3·1	1·4	9·0	9·5	4·6	1·1	0·2
1920—1925	5·3	3·5	18·6	15·8	6·9	2·3	0·3
1926—1930	4·7	3·6	19·1	11·7	5·1	1·9	0·3
1931—1935	4·5	3·8	19·8	12·5	5·1	1·6	0·2

TABLE 44 (*cont.*)

Years	Marriages per 1000 marriageable persons						
	total	age groups					
		—19	20—24	25—29	30—39	40—49	50 and over
			Females				
1936	4·2	3·9	17·1	14·4	5·3	1·6	0·2
1937	4·0	3·6	17·8	15·2	5·6	1·7	0·2
1938	2·9	3·8	17·8	15·6	6·0	1·9	0·2
1939	3·6	3·2	14·5	13·3	7·2	3·5	0·2
1940	2·4	2·1	9·5	8·2	4·6	1·7	0·2
1941	3·0	2·8	12·3	9·3	4·6	1·6	0·2
1942	3·6	3·1	14·3	10·5	5·4	1·8	0·2
1943	2·9	2·3	10·6	8·6	4·7	1·8	0·2
1944	2·7	2·1	9·4	8·1	4·3	1·6	0·2
1945	5·0	2·8	10·6	20·3	8·9	2·6	0·3
1946	6·8	4·1	25·0	26·5	11·0	3·3	0·3
1947	5·7	3·9	21·5	21·4	9·7	3·2	0·3
1948	5·0	3·6	19·2	18·3	8·4	2·9	0·3
1949	4·6	3·7	18·1	15·9	7·2	2·6	0·3
1950	4·5	3·6	18·3	15·0	6·9	2·4	0·3
1951	4·4	3·5	17·8	14·6	6·6	2·1	0·3
1952	4·3	3·4	17·6	14·3	6·6	2·1	0·3
1953	4·2	3·3	18·1	14·4	6·3	2·2	0·3
1954	4·3	3·3	18·7	15·1	6·5	2·2	0·3
1955	4·3	3·3	18·7	15·7	6·5	2·2	0·3

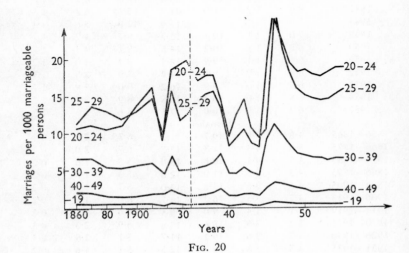

FIG. 20

in other age groups. There are however some exceptions. In the years 1926—1930, the rates in all age groups but one were lower than in the preceding five years; the 20—24 group revealed higher rates. Also, while marriages in the 25—29 age group were initially more frequent than in the 20—24 group, from the turn of the century the reverse was true, though not in all cases. The most striking changes, both in absolute and in relative figures, occurred in the middle age groups; in the two extreme groups, the youngest and the oldest, marriage frequencies changed much less.

Marriage rates among bachelors and spinsters are also important. The more numerous the "never-married" category, the greater the untapped potential of fertility (unless there are many illicit conjugal unions and many children born of such unions). With these considerations in mind, we may proceed to study the proportion of females who remain single until the age of 45 or 50, i.e. are no longer likely to bear children. The corresponding age limit for males should be somewhat higher (e.g. 55 or 60).

Some information on this subject may be derived from the statistics of the distribution of populations by age, sex and marital status. The untapped potential of fertility might be measured by the percentage of spinsters among females aged from 45 to 54 and the percentage of bachelors among males aged from 55 to 64 (the two age groups have been chosen in accordance with the age distribution employed in Demographic Yearbooks). The results of computations made for selected countries are presented in Table 45.

The proportion of bachelors and spinsters in various countries varies strikingly. The percentage of bachelors fluctuates between 0·5% (South Korea) and 28·9% (Ireland) and the proportion of spinsters between 0·2% (South Korea) and 34% (Venezuela). Central and South American countries also have high percentages of single males and females. This is presumably to be explained by the fact that they are mostly individuals who previously cohabited in consensual unions, i.e. were formally single, but since the death of their partners have registered as bachelors or spinsters, because the status of informal widowhood is not recognized in population censuses. Indeed, these countries note the highest proportions

TABLE 45

Country	Year	Percentage of bachelors among males aged 55—64	Percentage of spinsters among females aged 45—54
Algeria:			
— Moslem population . .	1954	2·4	2·6
— European population .	1954	6·0	9·1
Egypt	1947	1·3	0·9
Libya.	1954	2·3	1·3
Mauritius	1952	5·4	5·6
Morocco:			
—indigenous population .	1952	1·6	1·8
—non-indigenous populat-			
ion	1952	6·7	6·4
—Jewish population . .	1952	1·3	2·4
Mozambique	1950	3·6	2·9
Portuguese Guinea	1950	2·6	0·7
South Africa:			
—Bantu population . . .	1946	4·8	3·0
—white population . . .	1946	6·9	8·9
—European population .	1946	9·9	8·6
—Asian population . . .	1946	3·2	1·4
South West Africa	1951	15·3	14·3
Tunisia:			
—indigenous population .	1946	3·6	4·0
—European population .	1946	5·2	9·8
Alaska	1950	22·1	4·7
British Honduras	1946	18·6	20·2
Canada	1951	11·6	11·3
Costa Rica	1950	14·7	17·8
El Salvador	1950	17·6	28·0
Guatemala	1950	11·9	18·6
Nicaragua	1950	15·9	28·5
United States	1950	8·4	7·9
Argentina	1947	19·3	20·6
Bolivia	1950	6·3	11·2
Brazil.	1950	9·5	14·2
Chile	1952	12·1	16·0
Colombia	1951	13·1	22·9
Ecuador	1950	8·3	17·8
Paraguay	1950	16·9	32·7
Venezuela	1950	21·3	34·0
Burma	1954	5·8	6·4
Ceylon	1953	6·7	4·5
India	1951	3·3	1·2
Israel	1948	3·1	4·1

TABLE 45 (cont.)

Country	Year	Percentage of bachelors among males aged 55—64	Percentage of spinsters among females aged 45—54
Japan	1955	0·9	1·5
Pakistan	1951	1·2	1·0
Philippines	1948	2·7	6·7
South Korea	1955	0·5	0·2
Thailand	1947	4·4	2·8
Turkey	1950	3·5	2·2
Austria	1951	8·0	14·3
Belgium	1947	8·0	10·6
Bulgaria	1946	1·8	2·1
Czechoslovakia	1947	4·4	9·6
Denmark	1950	8·0	14·5
England and Wales	1951	7·8	5·1
Finland	1950	10·8	19·0
France	1954	7·4	10·4
Germ. Dem. Rep.	1950	2·7	9·2
Germ. Fed. Rep.	1950	4·7	12·6
Greece	1951	4·9	5·0
Hungary	1949	4·3	8·2
Iceland	1950	15·2	21·7
Ireland	1951	28·9	25·7
Italy	1951	7·3	14·8
Netherlands	1947	8·6	13·3
Norway	1950	13·5	20·7
Portugal	1950	9·0	17·0
Sweden	1950	11·2	19·1
Switzerland	1950	11·9	19·2
Yugoslavia	1953	3·9	5·7
Australia	1954	11·2	10·8
Fiji Islands	1956	6·7	3·6
New Zealand	1956	9·7	10·7

of bachelors and spinsters at the later ages: Venezuela—21·3% bachelors and 34·0% spinsters, and Paraguay—16·9% bachelors and 32·7% spinsters.

If we exclude the countries of Central and South America, the highest percentages of bachelors and spinsters are to be found in Ireland (28·9% and 25·7%) and Iceland (15·2% and 21·7%). Other Scandinavian countries follow very closely. The lowest percentages are observed in South Korea (0·5% and 0·2%), Pakistan (1·2% and 1·0%), Egypt (1·3%

and 0·9%), and Japan (0·9% and 1·5%). Here, too, nearly the same proportion of bachelors and spinsters is noted in countries which are territorially and culturally very close to one another. The inference is that we can try to divide countries into several types, just as we did previously from the point of view of the proportion of married persons and the marriage rates. The various types are: Eastern European, Scandinavian, Western European, South American, and Moslem. The South American type is less distinct because of the above--mentioned statistical shortcomings, as a result of which persons who formerly cohabited in consensual unions have their spinsterhood or bachelorhood restored after the death of their "informal" spouses. The USA and Canada belong to the Western European countries.

The problem may be tackled from another angle. We could construct a table showing the reduction in bachelors and spinsters caused by marriage. The technique of constructing such a table is the same as that used in deriving a life table; the only difference is that the "survivors" are those males or females who remain unmarried at each age, and the probabilities of death in consecutive age groups are replaced by the probabilities of marriage. Calculations are made beginning with the earliest age at which marriage is allowed by law. The results obtained in the table may be somewhat different than those yielded by computing the proportion of single males or single females in the various age groups; for such a table is constructed for a definite time and assumes that the current marriage frequencies among bachelors and spinsters at each age remain unchanged. Actually the proportion of single males or females is to some extent the function of circumstances which may change in the long run. If marriage rates diminish with time, the actual proportion of single males or females to the total population at a certain time will be smaller than is indicated in the table; conversely, if marriage rates increase with time, the true proportion of bachelors and spinsters will be higher than that shown in the table. To put it briefly, the table is constructed for a definite time, while the true rates mirror the fate of generations.

Marriage rates among bachelors and spinsters (i.e. the

probability that a bachelor or spinster in each age group
will marry within one year) and the rates computed on this
basis showing how each group of bachelors or spinsters
decreases annually due to marriage, are listed in Table 46.

TABLE 46

Age groups	Egypt 1947		Finland 1950		Denmark 1950		Japan 1955	
	m	f	m	f	m	f	m	f
	Marriage rates							
—19	0·014	0·228	0·009	0·036	0·004	0·044	0·001	0·008
20—24	0·133	0·317	0·094	0·140	0·102	0·206	0·031	0·094
25—34	0·226	0·157	0·150	0·126	0·181	0·100	0·153	0·110
35—44	0·137	0·045	0·104	0·057	0·107	0·075	0·141	0·048
45—54	0·058	0·022	0·062	0·024	0·068	0·030	0·124	0·032
Age	Decreasing number of bachelors (spinsters)							
15	1000	1000	1000	1000	1000	1000	1000	1000
20	932	274	956	833	981	799	995	960
25	457	41	583	392	573	252	850	590
35	35	7	115	102	78	31	162	184
45	8	5	38	57	25	14	35	112
55	4	4	20	44	12	10	9	81

The distribution of marriage rates by age among bachelors
and spinsters follows a trend comparable to that prevailing
in general marriage rates: initially small, the rate increases
rapidly until it reaches a maximum (at a later age among
men than among women), following which it gradually declines.

The numbers of bachelors (spinsters) per thousand aged
15, shown in Table 46, provide information on how many
15 year-old bachelors (spinsters) per thousand will remain
single at the age of 20, 25, 35 and so on, on the assumption
that none of them dies. The values listed may also be regarded
as the number of bachelors (spinsters) per 1000 population
at each age; such an interpretation eliminates the necessity
of assuming that there is no mortality. For example, 4 in
the first column (Egypt, males) indicates that if the marriage rates remained unchanged for a long time and equalled
the values listed above, the proportion of bachelors among
55-year-old males in Egypt would be exactly 0·4% (0·4% = 4
out of the initial group of 1000 15-year-old males). As the
reader can easily see, the data contained in Table 46 in most

cases do not correspond to the true rates presented in Table 45.

Marriage rates among bachelors and spinsters, like general marriage rates, are subject to changes with time. There is no uniformity in these changes; the rates decline in some age groups and rise in others. To illustrate this, the marriage rates in Sweden for selected periods are presented in Table 47.

TABLE 47

Years	Marriages per 1000 population by age groups							
	15—19	20—24	25—29	30—34	35—39	40—44	45—49	50 and over
Bachelors								
1861—1870	0·08	42·3	104·4	106·2	72·1	48·9	26·4	6·35
1901—1910	0·27	42·5	100·2	88·9	60·7	37·4	21·7	5·31
1957	5·3	94·3	157·6	100·4	54·6	26·6	15·3	4·0
Spinsters								
1861—1870	8·40	65·8	98·1	83·1	53·4	29·6	14·5	—
1901—1910	10·10	73·1	92·5	62·5	31·9	19·4	10·7	1·68
1957	34·4	187·1	189·7	95·4	46·4	23·0	12·5	2·3

Among bachelors, marriage rates show a steady rise in the earliest age groups, a decline followed by a rise in middle age groups, and a constant decline in the later age groups. Among spinsters, marriage rates reveal a constant rise among the earliest age groups and an initial decline followed by a rise in the middle and later groups.

The order of decrease in single males and females, computed on the basis of this table, is shown in Table 48.

TABLE 48

Age	Bachelors			Spinsters		
	1861—1870	1901—1910	1957	1861—1870	1901—1910	1957
15	1000	1000	1000	1000	1000	1000
20	1000	999	974	958	951	841
25	807	980	607	689	664	330
30	479	594	376	420	415	127
35	282	381	167	277	304	79
40	187	281	127	212	256	62
45	147	233	112	183	233	55
50	129	209	104	152	221	52

These tables show (even more distinctly than do the marriage rates alone) that the changes are large and quite rapid. In 1861—1879 the proportion of females who remained single during the reproductive period was some 15%; by 1901—1910 it rose to more than 22% and dropped again to 5% in 1957. The example is perhaps not very illustrative; in Sweden the percentage of illegitimate births happens to be quite high and, hence, the decrease in the proportion of single females in the later age groups may be just as well caused by a stronger tendency to have conjugal unions legitimized.

England, on the contrary, noted no large fluctuations in the period specified; this is borne out by Table 49 which shows the decrease in spinsters.[1] A noticeable change occurred only after World War II.

TABLE 49

Age	Spinsters									
	1851– –1852	1860– –1862	1870– –1872	1880– –1882	1890– –1892	1900– –1902	1910– –1912	1921	1930– –1932	1950– –1952
15	1000	1000	1000	1000	1000	1000	1000	1000	1000	1000
20	900	886	875	898	922	938	945	929	919	816
25	474	456	436	478	517	548	574	516	534	272
30	293	287	273	290	295	310	328	278	283	—
35	218	211	196	204	207	211	213	202	216	78
40	180	179	164	175	175	175	209	172	188	—
45	160	162	146	156	158	164	192	158	175	57
50	149	152	135	146	148	155	182	150	167	—

Figure 21 illustrates the trends in marriage rates by age among bachelors (for ages under 34 the rates used in constructing the graph relate to individual year cohorts) in Germany in 1910—1911 and in 1938. Apart from a few generations (from 22 to 24), the marriage rates increased to a varying extent, the highest relative rise being observed among the

---

[1] Statistics up to 1930—1932 inclusive have been taken from "Changes in Fertility in England and Wales 1856 to 1931" by D. V. GLASS, *Political Arithmetic*, London 1938, p. 168. The rates for 1950/1952 have been computed on the basis of the data contained in the *Annual Abstract of Statistics 1954*.

older cohorts. At the same time, the age at maximum marriage frequency has climbed from 27 to 28. Thus, in 1938 the marriage rates were generally higher than in 1910—1911, but the proportion of marriages contracted by single males at the older ages was also higher.

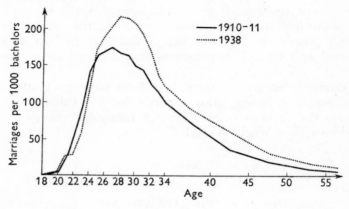

FIG. 21

A study of marriage must of necessity involve an examination of death and divorce as factors causing the dissolution of marriage.

Widowhood data can be obtained from mortality statistics by marital status; deaths of wives indicate the number of widowers, and deaths of married men give the number of new widows. Information on widowhood rates by age can be obtained only when death certificates give the ages of the surviving spouses. Pertinent statistics for France in 1952 are listed in Table 50.[1]

The corresponding graph is shown in Fig. 22.

The probability of widowhood among women is always higher than among men of the same age, because the husband is usually somewhat older than the wife and also because of the higher mortality rate among men.

Interesting results can be obtained by collating the proba-

---

[1] *Statistique du mouvement de la population.* Année 1952, Paris 1958, p. 83.

TABLE 50

Age	Probability of widowhood (⁰/₀₀)		Age	Probability of widowhood (⁰/₀₀)	
	m	f		m	f
20	0·6	0·9	56	8·1	22·2
25	0·9	1·3	57	7·6	21·9
30	1·1	1·8	58	7·7	23·5
35	1·4	3·2	59	9·1	26·5
36	1·3	2·6	60	9·4	27·8
37	1·1	2·4	61	9·9	31·2
38	1·7	3·8	62	10·5	33·2
39	1·9	4·0	63	11·6	37·5
40	2·1	4·9	64	12·3	40·2
41	2·3	4·6	65	14·6	44·6
42	2·4	5·8	66	14·9	45·9
43	2·4	6·1	67	17·3	51·6
44	2·8	7·2	68	18·2	57·2
45	2·9	7·3	69	20·1	61·2
46	3·3	8·0	70	21·5	67·9
47	3·4	9·0	71	23·7	73·0
48	3·7	10·4	72	25·6	83·9
49	3·9	10·9	73	29·2	87·2
50	4·6	12·3	74	31·2	93·7
51	5·1	14·2	75	32·5	97·2
52	5·6	15·2	76	39·2	107·1
53	6·2	16·1	77	44·5	117·4
54	6·2	17·5	78	47·2	121·6
55	7·1	18·9	79	49·7	128·1

bilities of widowhood and the probabilities of death as given in life tables for the same period (Table 51).

The widowhood statistics contained in the table relate to 1952; the French life table used covers the years 1952—1956. We have made the collation in the following way: given a certain probability of widowhood among males, we find in the life table an analogous probability of death among females and we note the age which corresponds to such a probability of death. The probability of widowhood for a man aged 30 is, for example, $1·1\%_{00}$; this equals the probability of death for a woman aged 26. Similarly, we select the probability of death among males equal to the probability of widowhood among females and note the corresponding age of the male.

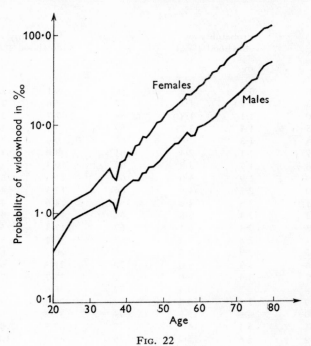

Fig. 22

TABLE 51

Age	Males		Females	
	Widowhoods per 1000 husbands	Female age corresponding to given widowhood rates	Widowhoods per 1000 wives	Male age corresponding to given widowhood rates
20	0·6	18	0·9	—
25	0·9	23	1·3	17
30	1·1	26	1·8	25
35	1·4	31	3·2	37
40	2·1	37	4·9	42
45	2·9	42	7·3	46
50	4·6	47	12·3	52
55	7·1	53	18·9	57
60	9·4	57	27·8	63
65	14·6	62	44·6	68
70	21·5	66	67·9	73
75	32·5	70	97·2	77

The table reveals that in most cases the age of new widowers has an equivalent in a female age some two to three years younger; and, *vice versa*, the age of widows has an equivalent in a male age some two to three years older. Visible deviations from this rule are noted in the younger groups (among females) and in the oldest (among both sexes). Two to three years is the average age difference between spouses at marriage; it is not subject to significant changes over time. It can thus be estimated, very approximately, that the probability of widowhood equals the probability of death of an individual of the opposite sex, younger or older by a given number of years.

In Poland, the average age difference between spouses is almost exactly three years; the median age at marriage for the whole population is 25·4 years among men and 22·4 years among women; the respective figures for the urban population are 25·4 and 22·5, and for the rural population, 25·4 and 22·2.[1] Accordingly, information on the probability of widowhood among males can be obtained by finding from the life table the probability of death among females three years younger. Similarly, we obtain the probability of widowhood among females from the probability of death among males three years older, as given by the life table. In view of the deviations observed in the youngest age groups, the probability for females aged 20 has not been taken into account (Table 52).[2]

Since the probability of widowhood for females is in most cases more than twice the probability of widowhood for males at the same age, it is to be expected that cases of widowhood among females in general will also be more than twice as numerous as among males. In fact, in 1956 the ratio between the two was 2·2 : 1.

Divorce frequencies per 1000 population in selected countries about the year 1957 are listed in Table 53.[3]

It should be added that divorces do not exist in the following countries: Argentina, Brazil, Chile, Colombia, Paraguay, Ireland, Italy, Spain and the Philippines.

---

[1] *Rocznik Statystyczny (Statistical Yearbook) 1959*, p. 27.

[2] *Ibid.*, pp. 34—35.

[3] *Demographic Yearbook 1958.*

TABLE 52

Age	Probability of widowhood per 1000 married persons	
	m	f
20	0·80	—
25	1·23	2·47
30	1·42	2·70
35	1·78	3·51
40	2·37	4·57
45	2·89	7·25
50	4·12	11·99
55	6·40	19·52
60	9·92	30·23
65	17·14	45·83
70	27·96	70·09
75	45·45	101·76
80	70·12	140·22

The rates contained in Table 53 fluctuate within a very wide range: from 0 to 4·54 per 1000 population. This is mainly a reflection of the laws relating to divorce in different countries, but it is partly also a function of the greater or smaller prevalence of consensual unions (countries where consensual unions are frequent obviously note fewer divorces).

Divorce rates computed per 1000 inhabitants are not a precise measure as they do not take into account the distribution of population by age and by marital status. The ratio of divorces to the number of married couples would be much more revealing. The values of these rates in selected countries, along with the divorce rates per 1000 population listed for comparative purposes, are presented in Table 54.[1]

The higher the divorce rates per 1000 married couples the higher also in most cases the divorce rates per 1000 population. The close correlation between the two rates is illustrated in Fig. 23 which represents graphically the values of these rates in each of the countries enumerated in Table 54.

The correlation is almost exactly linear. With a few exceptions, the points are scattered within a very narrow strip.

Demographic Yearbook 1958.

TABLE 53

Divorce rates per 1000 population

under 0·49		0·50—0·99		1·00—1·49		1·50—1·99		2·00 and over	
Bahamas	0·03	Algeria —European population	0·67	Algeria —Moslem population	1·02	Hawaii	1·91	Alaska	2·62
British Guiana	0·18	Australia	0·65	Austria	1·17	Hungary	1·82	Egypt	2·30
British Honduras	0·12	Belgium	0·54	Bermuda	1·32	Rumania	1·86	Puerto Rico	2·04
Canada	0·40	Bulgaria	0·60	Czechoslovakia	1·07			United States	2·22
Ceylon	0·22	England and Wales	0·52	Denmark	1·46			Zanzibar and Pemba	4·54
Costa Rica	0·16	Finland	0·81	Germ. Dem. Rep.	1·25				
Dominican Rep.	0·32	France	0·66	Israel	1·14				
				Iran	1·37				
Ecuador	0·27	Germ. Fed. Rep.	0·81	Jordania	1·20				
El Salvador	0·19	Iceland	0·82	South Africa —white population	1·32				
Guatemala	0·16	Japan	0·78						
Guadeloupe	0·29	Monaco	0·59	Sweden	1·23				

TABLE 53 (cont.)

Divorce rates per 1000 population

under 0·49		0·50—0·99		1·00—1·49		1·50—1·99	2·00 and over
Honduras	0·12	Norway	0·58	Yugoslavia	1·10		
Iraq	0·37	Poland	0·55				
Libya	0·45	Syria	0·60				
Korea South	0·14	Switzerland	0·89				
Luxembourg	0·29	USSR	0·8				
Martinique	0·15	Uruguay	0·63				
Mauritius	0·24	New Zealand	0·62				
Mexico	0·30						
Nicaragua	0·15						
Portugal	0·09						
Taiwan	0·46						
Thailand	0·15						
Turkey	0·43						
Venezuela	0·16						

TABLE 54

Country	Years	Divorces per 1000	
		married couples	population
Algeria			
—Moslem population . . .	1953—1955	9·1	1·64
Alaska	1949—1951	16·3	3·10
Austria	1950—1952	6·7	1·47
Australia	1953—1955	3·3	0·78
Bermuda	1949—1951	4·9	0·94
Canada	1955—1957	1·7	0·38
Ceylon.	1952—1954	2·9	0·22
Costa Rica	1949—1951	1·9	0·22
Dominican Republic . . .	1949—1951	5·0	0·39
Denmark.	1949—1951	6·8	1·60
Ecuador	1949	1·7	0·22
Egypt	1946—1948	16·9	3·27
El Salvador	1949—1951	2·5	0·18
England and Wales	1950—1952	2·8	0·69
Finland	1949—1951	4·6	0·91
France	1953—1955	2·9	0·68
Guadeloupe	1953—1955	1·9	0·21
Guatemala	1949—1951	1·8	0·10
Germ. Dem. Rep.	1949—1951	9·5	2·24
Germ. Fed. Rep.	1949—1951	6·4	1·48
Hawaii.	1949—1951	11·2	2·20
Honduras	1951	1·3	0·09
Iceland	1949—1951	3·8	0·65
Israel	1947—1949	7·6	1·76
Japan	1954—1956	4·4	0·84
Martinique	1953—1955	2·0	0·21
Mexico	1949—1951	2·1	0·29
Nicaragua	1949—1951	1·8	0·15
Norway	1949—1951	3·2	0·70
Poland	1950—1951	2·2	0·44
Portugal	1949—1951	0·7	0·12
Puerto Rico	1949—1951	12·8	1·61
South Africa			
—white population . . .	1950—1952	6·2	1·38
Sweden	1949—1951	4·9	1·14
Switzerland	1949—1951	4·2	0·90
Thailand	1946—1948	0·8	0·14
Turkey	1954—1955	2·0	0·43
United States	1949—1951	10·4	2·57
Venezuela	1949—1951	1·8	0·15
Yugoslavia	1952—1953	4·0	0·84

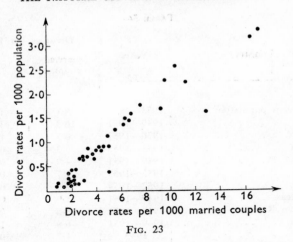

Fig. 23

The incidence of divorce is largely influenced by the age of the spouses; the divorce rates are higher in the earlier and lower in the later ages (Table 55).

TABLE 55

| Age | Divorce rates per 1000 married population | | | | | |
| | Egypt 1947 | | Finland 1950 | | Japan 1955 | |
	m	f	m	f	m	f
15—19	12·7	32·4	14·0	0·7	1·1	13·1
20—24	37·1	38·8	11·3	3·8	11·3	8·2
25—34	36·4	24·9	7·7	5·7	4·8	3·7
35—44	19·3	11·8	5·2	5·7	1·8	1·5
45—54	11·9	7·1	2·9	4·4	1·0	0·6
55—64	7·4	4·0	1·3	2·1	0·6	0·3
65 and over	5·1	2·4	0·7	1·2	0·4	0·2

While the incidence of divorce in some countries has a strong bearing on the number of existing conjugal unions, marriage annulments have little if any numerical effect; this is borne out by the contents of Table 56.[1]

---

[1] *Demographic Yearbook 1958.*

TABLE 56

Country	Annulments of marriage per 1000 population
Alaska	0·05
Austria	0·01
Bahamas	
England and Wales . . .	0·01
Germ. Fed. Rep.	0·01
Guam	0·32
Hawaii.	0·02
New Zealand	0·01
United States	0·05
Yugoslavia	0·01

The choice of the countries listed is explained by the fact that all other countries reported 0·00 annulments. The countries enumerated in Table 56 have thus the highest relative proportions of marriage annulments.

CHAPTER 5

BIRTHS

BIRTHS usually form the largest numerical component of the natural movement of population, as in most cases they exceed deaths and certainly marriages.

The number of births depends on demographic factors such as the sex and age structure of the population, the marriage rate and its distribution by age, the duration of marriage and the number of children in a family unit; but it is also determined by many other economic and social factors. To isolate each of these factors and measure their values would be somewhat difficult because they are closely linked and inter-related. We might facilitate our task by classifying the available statistics as far as possible by various characteristics. This calls, however, for very precise birth registration. Births recorded in registers are nearly always fewer than the actual number of births, if only for the reason that in some cases the births of children who died in the post-natal period are never registered. Thus, in United States statistics for instance, in addition to the data on births obtained from vital records, revised data are also issued which in recent years were some 1·5% higher. The time-limit set in some countries for the registration of births is so long that some births are never entered in vital records. Moreover, there are differences in the interpretation of live births and still births.

Comparisons between the birth levels in different countries and at different times are made in most cases on the basis of crude rates which show the number of births per 1000 population. However, these rates are not a very accurate measure of reproduction, since they are affected not only by fertility but also by the age structure of the population and by other factors. Naturally, given a certain fertility rate, the greater the ratio of females of childbearing age to the total population, the higher the birth rate. Since the age structure

of the population in individual countries changes with time
(it may change very rapidly, e.g. as a result of wars), birth
rates over a prolonged period are not completely comparable
even in the same country, and even less so between different
countries. Here are some examples.

In France, both the crude birth rate and the standardized
birth rate are calculated on the basis of a constant age and
sex structure of the population. Table 57[1] presents the values
of the two rates for several past decades.

TABLE 57

| Years | Birth rate | | Difference |
	crude	standardized	
1910—1912	19·1	19·3	+0·2
1923—1925	18·6	18·3	−0·3
1935—1937	15·0	16·3	+1·3
1939	14·7	17·2	+2·5
1940	13·6	15·7	+2·1
1941	13·1	14·4	+1·3
1942	14·5	15·9	+1·4
1943	15·7	16·9	+1·2
1944	16·1	17·5	+1·4
1945	16·2	18·0	+1·8
1947	20·7	23·2	+2·5
1952	19·3	21·8	+2·5

The standardized rates have been computed on the basis
of the structure of population obtained in 1901. No wonder,
therefore, that in time the difference between the crude and
standardized rates increased. But this increase was neither
regular nor constant. Some periods were even marked by
a significant decrease in the difference between the two rates.
In the last year named in Table 57 the difference equaled 13%
of the crude rate. It should be noted that the rates changed
in different directions. Thus, judging from the crude rate
the level of natality in 1939 was somewhat lower than in
1935—1937, but according to the standardized rate the opposite was true.

A comparison between the crude rates in 1910—1912 and
1952 seems to indicate that natality in the two periods was

---

[1] *Statistique du mouvement de la population*, Année 1952, Première
partie, p. 57.

more or less the same, but the standardized rates show that it was distinctly higher in 1952.

Similar differences may be observed when comparing the birth rates in various countries. Table 58 gives the crude rates in selected countries in 1952, along with the standardized rates calculated on the basis of an age and sex structure of the population analogous to that in Poland in 1960.

TABLE 58

Country	Birth rates	
	crude	standardized
Australia	23·3	23·7
Canada	27·9	27·2
England and Wales . . .	15·7	16·2
France	19·3	20·3
Israel	33·0	29·5
Japan	23·5	22·5
Netherlands	22·4	23·1
Poland	29·7	26·6
Portugal	24·7	23·3
Sweden	17·4	17·6
United States	24·6	23·6

In a few cases the difference between the crude and standardized rates is quite large (Israel, Poland). The great difference in Poland's rates can be explained by the fact that between 1952 and 1960 the age structure of the Polish population experienced changes because the less numerous cohorts born during World War II entered the reproductive period and also due to the shifts in the gaps caused by the two world wars.

Table 58 indicates that the crude rates are higher in some countries and the standardized rates are higher in others. Hence, the order of populations classified by the two rates will be entirely different. Thus, in Canada the crude birth rate is lower than in Poland, but for standardized rates the relation between the two countries is reversed. A similar reversal of order occurs in the case of the Netherlands and Japan.

The same remarks can be made in regard to the fertility rate for women of childbearing age (Table 59).

TABLE 59

Country	Fertility rates	
	crude	standardized
Australia	83·9	99·5
Canada	97·3	114·3
England and Wales . . .	54·2	67·9
France	70·9	85·5
Israel	105·2	124·0
Japan	75·8	94·6
Netherlands	78·4	97·2
Poland	109·0	114·0
Portugal	79·7	98·1
Sweden	60·4	74·1
United States	84·1	99·4

Here, the standardized rate is invariably higher than the crude rate. In every country, except Poland, the difference between the two rates is even higher than in the case of birth rates. As far as the crude fertility rate is concerned, Poland takes first place among the countries listed in the table, but for the standardized rate occupies the third place, following Israel and Canada.

It is noteworthy that the order of the standardized rates remains the same whether births are counted per thousand population or per thousand females of reproductive age. Some disparity between the two rates seems to appear only as an exception, i.e. only in an exceptional case is the standardized birth rate in a given country higher but the standardized fertility rate lower than in another country. Hence, to establish the order of countries by frequency of births it is sufficient to standardize the birth rate computed per 1000 population. All this calls for utmost caution when making direct comparisons between the crude rates. They are comparable only when the countries studied have similar age structures. If the age structures differ a great deal, any conclusions based on the crude rates may be misleading.

Birth rates (per 1000 population) about the year 1957 in selected countries are listed in Table 60.[1]

Some of the rates listed seem to be strikingly at variance

---

[1] *Demographic Yearbook 1958.*

TABLE 60

Birth rates per 1000 population

under 20		20—29·9		30—39·9		40—49·9		50 and over	
Mozambique	7·6	Finland	20·1	French Guiana	32·2	Martinique	40·1	Nine	50·8
East Berlin	8·0	Ireland	21·1	Puerto Rico	32·6	Panama	40·4	Sudan	51·7
Korea, South	10·0	Netherlands	21·2	Pacific Islands	32·7	Dominican Republic	40·9	French West Africa	54·3
Uruguay	11·4	Pakistan	21·2	Peru	33·4	Taiwan	41·4	Guinea	60·0
Spanish Guinea	11·6	Spain	21·9	Thailand	35·0	Nicaragua	41·8	Guam	64·3
Norfolk Islands	13·2	Faroe Islands	21·9	Tonga	35·0	Fiji Islands	41·9		
Monaco	14·2	Angola	22·7	Dutch Antilles	35·3	Colombia	42·6		
Sweden	14·6	Philippines	22·7	Ghana	35·3	Singapore	42·9		
Channel Islands	15·3	Rumania	22·9	Lebanon	35·4	Brazil	43·0		
Luxembourg	15·7	Australia	22·9	Chile	36·2	Honduras	43·1		
Germ. Dem. Rep.	15·9	Bolivia	23·2	Ceylon	36·5	Mauritius	43·1		
England and Wales	16·5	Liechtenstein	23·2	Madagascar	36·6	British Honduras	43·2		
Iraq	16·6	Argentina	23·3	Borneo, North	37·0	Greenland	44·1		
Andorra	16·7	Portugal	23·7	China	37·0	British Guiana	44·5		
		Yugoslavia	23·7						
		Sarawak	24·0						
		Syria	24·3						

Country	Rate	Country	Rate	Country	Rate	Country	Rate
Denmark	16·7	Riu-Kiu Islands	24·6	Alaska	37·0	Nepal	45·0
Germ. Dem. Rep.	17·0	United States	25·0	Tunisia	37·0	Brunei	45·5
Hungary	17·0	USSR	25·3	Antilles	37·3	Venezuela	45·8
Austria	17·0	Bahama Islands	25·4	Ifni	37·4	Federation of Malaya	46·2
Belgium	17·0	Bermuda	25·6	American Samoa	37·5	Mexico	46·9
Japan	17·2	New Zealand	26·2	Iran	37·8	Ecuador	47·0
Switzerland	17·7	Cyprus	26·3	Albania	39·1	Cape Verde Islands	47·2
Falkland Islands	18·0	Portuguese India	26·7	Egypt	39·2	Surinam	47·3
San Marino	18·0	Poland	27·5	Costa Rica	39·2	Takelau Islands	47·4
Italy	18·2	Hawaii	27·8	Guadeloupe	39·5	El Salvador	48·9
Norway	18·2	Israel	28·2	Jordan	39·7	Paraguay	49·0
Zanzibar and Pemba	18·3	Canada	28·3	Western Samoa	39·8	Nigeria	49·2
France	18·6	Iceland	28·7	India	39·9	Guatemala	49·4
Czechoslovakia	18·9	Indonesia	29·1				
Greece	19·3						
Bulgaria	19·5						

with what we imagined to be the birth levels in certain countries.

Mozambique shows the lowest birth rate (7·6). But in other African countries at approximately the same stage of economic development, the rates are much higher; the inference is that birth registration in Mozambique is far from complete. Birth registers in Spanish Guinea and Zanzibar too are probably incomplete. We may safely assume that in economically backward countries the birth rate should not be less than 30 per 1000 population. If a lower rate is recorded, it is evidence of incomplete birth registration.

For example, according to Table 60, Indonesia's birth rate is 29·1; but estimates based on an intimate knowledge of local habits give a rate of nearly 40 per 1000. The true birth rate would thus be one third higher than the rate given by the official index.

It is interesting to compare the birth rates for different sections of the population. Unfortunately, there is no uniformity in dealing with sub-populations. Statistical coverage for some segments of the population is relatively complete, while the rates relating to other segments are obviously unreliable. In the Congo, for example, the 1955 birth rates were:

> white population   — 41·6
> indigenous population — 33·1.

The white population would thus have higher natality than the indigenous population, which runs counter to what we know of the demographic development of African countries. An opposite phenomenon is observed in other countries: high natality among the indigenous population and low natality among the white population. In Northern Rhodesia, the 1950 birth rate for the indigenous population was 56·8 and for the European population, 31·4. In Southern Rhodesia the corresponding rates (in 1953) were 41·8 and 27·8; in Ruanda-Urundi, 44·6 and 34·4. In New Zealand, the birth rate of the Maori population was 46·8 and that of the white population, 24·9. It can be safely assumed, therefore, that the birth rate among the indigenous population in the Congo in actual fact far exceeds the official index and probably is far above 40‰, i.e. it is higher than among the white population.

The differences are even more striking in South Africa where the 1956 birth rates were:

Bantu population — 17·3
European population — 24·2
Asian population — 31·2
Coloured (mixed) population — 45·7

A mere glance at these data shows that the birth rate of the Bantu population is certainly understated; it should be at least twice as high.

We have said before that the fertility rate, or the number of births per 1000 females of reproductive age, is a much better measure of the frequency of births. The reproductive period is usually assumed to cover the ages from 15 to 49. Fertility rates in selected countries are given in Table 61.[1]

TABLE 61

Country	Year	Births per 1000 females aged 15—49
Alaska	1950	136
Canada	1953	114
Dominican Republic	1950	190
Mexico	1950	185
Puerto Rico	1950	169
United States	1953	99
Venezuela	1950	177
India	1951	79
Israel		
—Jewish population	1953	116
Japan	1952	91
Austria	1953	56
Belgium	1952	68
Denmark	1950	75
England and Wales	1953	73
Finland	1952	89
France	1953	81
Germ. Dem. Rep.	1952	58

[1] *Demographic Yearbook 1958.*

TABLE 61 (*cont.*)

Country	Year	Births per 1000 females aged 15—49
Iceland	1950	118
Italy	1951	70
Netherlands	1953	90
Norway	1952	76
Poland	1955	111
Portugal	1952	93
Sweden	1950	66
Switzerland	1952	68
Yugoslavia	1953	105
Australia	1953	95
Fiji Islands	1953	184
Hawaii	1950	115

To compute the birth rate (per 1000 population) and the fertility rate (per 1000 women of childbearing age) we must have data on population statistics and on the number of births. But there is also a way of measuring the birth level solely on the basis of population statistics; this is the child-women ratio, which usually gives the number of children under 5 per 1000 women of childbearing age (Table 62).[1]

The advantage of these rates is that they are not subject to large errors, as the age statistics yielded by population censuses are usually quite accurate.

They present, however, the drawback that they can only be computed at longer intervals of time (in census years) and not every year, and with considerable delay since they depend on statistics which take time to process. It is to be expected that the rates thus obtained will be somewhat less than five times the birth rates per 1000 females of childbearing age; for the former take into account five cohorts of children and the latter, only one, usually the largest.

We shall now examine the relations between the three rates which characterize the single phenomenon of the frequency of births. Figure 24 illustrates the relation between the rates computed per 1000 population and per 1000 females of childbearing age.

---

[1] *Demographic Yearbook 1954.*

TABLE 62

Country	Year	Children under 5 per 1000 females aged 15—49
Algeria		
—Moslem population	1948	633
—European population	1948	341
Basutoland	1946	403
Egypt	1947	546
Mauritius	1952	742
Mozambique	1940	777
Tunisia		
—Moslem population	1946	622
—European population	1946	374
Alaska	1950	566
Canada	1951	498
Costa Rica	1950	686
Dominican Republic	1950	749
El Salvador	1950	623
Greenland	1945	662
Guatemala	1940	666
Haiti	1950	452
Honduras	1950	666
Mexico	1950	626
Nicaragua	1950	650
Puerto Rico	1950	725
United States	1950	417
Argentina	1947	423
British Guiana	1946	565
Ecuador	1950	705
Paraguay	1950	694
Peru	1940	655
Venezuela	1950	711
Ceylon	1946	543
Federation of Malaya	1947	565
India	1951	549
Israel		
—Jewish population	1948	434
Japan	1950	527
Korea, South	1952	527
Philippines	1948	650
Thailand	1947	626
Turkey	1950	609
Austria	1951	293
Belgium	1947	293
Czechoslovakia	1947	343

TABLE 62 (*cont.*)

Country	Year	Children under 5 per 1000 females aged 15—49
Denmark	1950	393
England and Wales	1951	335
Finland	1950	474
France	1946	278
Germ. Dem. Rep.	1946	236
Germ. Fed. Rep.	1950	257
Iceland	1950	527
Ireland	1951	467
Monaco	1951	186
Netherlands	1947	472
Norway	1950	387
Poland	1955	496
Portugal	1950	398
Sweden	1950	348
Switzerland	1950	335
Yugoslavia	1948	391
Australia	1947	395
Cook Islands	1951	813
Fiji Islands	1946	814
Guam	1950	776
Hawaii	1950	524
New Zealand		
—white population	1951	491
—Maori population	1951	839

The relationship is roughly linear, as the points are fairly widely scattered. The points which represent the birth rates in India and Alaska deviate most from the line. In the case of India, the large deviation is probably to be explained by the incompleteness of population statistics, as a result of which the information on the number of births and on the age structure of the population may be subject to large errors. We have already noted the unusual sex structure of the Alaskan population, where males are in the great majority; in view of this, the rate computed for the total population is bound to differ very much from the rate computed for females only. The United Nations publication points out that data on the Dominican Republic and Puerto Rico are unreliable. If we exclude from our considerations the rates relating to

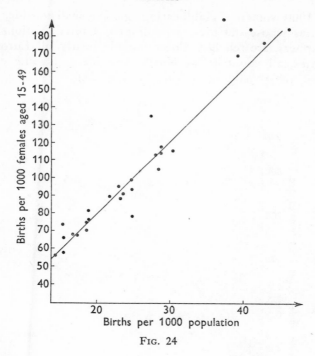

FIG. 24

these four countries, the relation is much more regular, so much so that we may venture to find the formula for the regression line. It is:

$$b_f = 4{\cdot}17b_p - 1{\cdot}0$$

where:

b_f = birth rate related to the number of females of child-bearing age, and

b_p = birth rate computed per 1000 population.

The constant term in the equation of the regression line is small, as was to be expected (the values of b_f and b_p must be zero simultaneously, when the number of births is zero; hence, the constant term must be zero).

Let us now compare the relation between the birth rate per 1000 population as a measure of the current frequency of births in selected countries, and the index which we have found to be the most exact—the number of children under

5 per 1000 women of childbearing age. We shall consider only countries whose statistics, according to United Nations demographers, are reliable. These include nearly all European countries, all countries of North America and some countries of the remaining continents (Fig. 25).

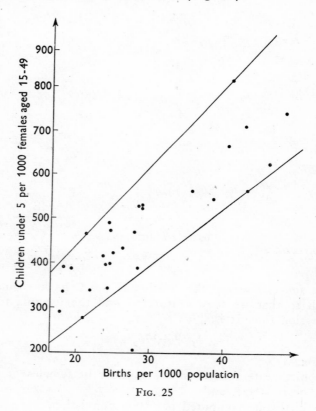

FIG. 25

The points in Fig. 25 denote the values of the two rates in individual countries. The lines drawn between the two extreme couples of points—the lowest and the highest—bound the strip within which all the points lie. We may venture to state that all points without exception should lie within the strip bounded by the two lines—i.e. not only the points denoting the countries which have reliable statistics on the natural movement of population but also those where the statistics are certainly incomplete. Knowing the age and sex structure of populations in the latter countries, i.e. knowing the number of children under 5 per 1000 females of child-bearing age, we can calculate the lower and upper limits within which the birth rates per 1000 population can lie. The two limits are the lines which bound the strip; their equations are:

$$b_p = 0.077b_c - 0.5$$
$$b_p = 0.0565b_c - 5.2$$

where:

b_p = birth rate per 1000 population, and
b_c = number of children under 5 per 1000 females aged 15—49.

By substituting the given values of b_c in the two equations we can find the limits within which the actual value of the b_p index should lie. The b_c values can be obtained from the results of population censuses and, hence, may be regarded to be quite accurate, although not all of them are equally reliable.

The results of our computations are presented in Table 63.

The actual rates for Mozambique, Paraguay, Peru, India, Thailand and the Cook Islands are under the lower limit. According to our criterion, this means that births registration in these countries is understated. In Mozambique, current registration covers, at best, $8.9 \div 38.6 = 23\%$, and in the worst event, $8.9 \div 65.5 = 14\%$ of all births. The official rate should thus be multiplied by 4 to 7 to obtain the actual rate. In Paraguay, birth statistics cover at least 38% but not more than 66% of all births; in Peru—from 48 to 84%; in India—from 54 to 89%; in Thailand—from 45 to 79%; and in the Cook Islands—from 57 to 96%.

The results obtained for other countries seem to prove that there too the records are incomplete. Thus, in several countries the actual birth rate is only slightly above or even exactly equal the lower boundary value. These include the Dominican Republic, Puerto Rico, the Philippines, and the Maori population of New Zealand. Birth registration in these countries is presumably also incomplete.

If we want to make a more detailed study of the birth

TABLE 63

Country	Year	Birth rates per 1000 population b_p		
		limits		actual
		lower	upper	
Algeria				
—Moslem population . . .	1948	30·6	53·2	44·3
Egypt	1947	25·6	45·7	43·6
Mozambique	1940	38·6	65·5	8·9
Tunisia				
—Moslem population . . .	1946	30·0	52·3	40·3
Costa Rica	1950	33·2	57·7	46·5
Dominican Republic	1950	37·1	63·1	37·2
El Salvador	1950	30·0	52·3	48·5
Greenland	1945	32·4	55·7	39·5
Guatemala	1940	32·4	45·0	48·2
Nicaragua	1950	32·3	53·6	41·2
Puerto Rico	1950	37·7	61·1	39·0
Ecuador	1950	34·6	59·4	47·3
Paraguay	1950	34·0	58·4	22·4
Peru.	1940	31·8	55·1	26·7
India	1951	27·9	46·1	24·9
Philippines	1948	31·5	53·6	31·5
Thailand	1947	30·2	52·6	23·7
Cook Islands	1951	40·7	68·6	39·2
Guam	1950	38·6	65·4	62·7
New Zealand				
—Maori population	1951	42·2	70·8	45·0

rate, we must pass from statistics of the total population to data on different groups of the population classified by various characteristics. The most basic of them is age. Age strongly affects fertility; age also has an important bearing on the proportion of married females which, in its turn, influences the birth rate. But we must always remember that statistical coverage of births is not equally complete for all countries, which detracts from the comparability of the resulting data.

Fertility rates by age in selected countries are listed in Table 64.[1]

---

[1] Poland — *Statystyka ludności (Population Statistics) 1955*; other countries—*Demographic Yearbook 1954.*

TABLE 64

Country	Year	Total	Age group							
			—14	15—19	20—24	25—29	30—34	35—39	40—44	45 and over
Alaska	1950	119·1	0·3	109·2	267·4	207·7	130·5	83·3	24·3	5·7
Canada	1952	97·3	0·2	50·4	201·4	204·0	151·5	87·3	30·7	2·8
Dominican Republic . .	1950	172·2	0·8	115·2	285·2	326·1	299·5	211·0	120·4	75·7
El Salvador . .	1950	157·1	59·9		296·0	320·3	249·4	146·0	58·4	18·3
Nicaragua . . .	1940	108·4		36·7	221·4	224·0	171·9	138·2	21·3	6·2
Panama	1950	114·2	1·4	123·6	244·2	211·3	139·3	82·1	26·2	8·3
Puerto Rico . .	1950	135·0	0·4	99·2	279·7	260·3	200·0	142·1	53·1	11·7
United States . .	1951	84·1	0·9	84·6	208·5	171·6	106·4	52·7	14·8	1·1
Chile	1940	104·2	27·6		166·3	194·7	187·6	138·8	73·1	26·4
Peru	1940	91·3	0·3	51·0	168·3	175·8	146·3	109·0	52·2	23·7
Venezuela . . .	1950	144·4	53·8		276·4	277·5	217·3	144·7	52·4	20·1
Israel	1952	105·2	0·5	82·2	223·0	212·3	162·5	84·6	25·5	5·8
Japan	1952	75·8	0·0	8·8	130·8	206·1	149·0	77·4	23·0	1·4
Taiwan	1953	155·5	0·1	48·0	265·3	335·5	291·9	217·5	108·1	27·2
Austria	1951	49·7	0·1	33·9	117·3	115·1	84·2	44·0	15·5	1·3
Belgium	1952	60·4	0·0	20·7	125·8	144·5	102·9	57·3	19·3	1·3

TABLE 64 (cont.)

Country	Year	Total	—14	15—19	20—24	25—29	30—34	35—39	40—44	45 and over
Denmark . . .	1952	62·9		19·4	155·6	150·6	95·0	49·0	15·4	1·1
England and Wales . . .	1952	54·2	0·0	21·0	128·6	135·6	88·9	44·3	13·1	1·0
Finland . . .	1952	77·0	0·0	26·4	159·8	168·4	131·2	83·7	36·8	5·6
France . . .	1952	70·9	0·0	22·3	152·6	166·4	118·1	62·0	22·2	2·0
Germ. Fed. Rep.	1952	49·9	0·1	31·3	121·4	125·6	82·7	44·5	12·1	0·8
Iceland . . .	1950	101·9	—	68·6	192·6	195·8	162·0	105·2	45·9	2·4
Netherlands .	1953	76·8	0·0	13·4	99·1	184·4	161·2	104·8	42·5	3·7
Norway . . .	1952	67·3	—	20·1	122·6	148·8	117·8	74·4	29·4	3·0
Poland . . .	1955—56	110·0	—	43·0	210·0	198·0	140·0	87·0	31·0	3·0
Portugal . . .	1952	79·7	0·1	23·5	137·6	168·9	138·5	107·6	51·8	8·4
Spain . . .	1940	75·6	0·0	8·6	89·7	185·3	166·2	109·5	45·0	8·2
Sweden . . .	1951	55·7	0·1	38·0	122·8	124·0	88·5	49·1	16·7	1·5
Switzerland .	1952	60·4	0·0	13·6	107·5	153·7	113·5	60·3	19·4	1·8
Yugoslavia .	1952	93·0	0·0	38·7	199·5	201·5	151·8	82·1	40·2	10·6
Australia . .	1952	83·9	0·1	39·0	188·9	192·8	125·9	66·5	20·1	1·6
Fiji Islands .	1953	145·7	0·2	113·1	298·7	276·9	202·9	160·1	64·0	24·0
Hawaii . . .	1950	98·8	0·8	57·9	200·6	195·5	125·8	64·4	17·3	1·0

The general trend in fertility rates by age is as follows: in the youngest group the rate is low, after a rapid rise it reaches a maximum about the age of 25, following which it begins to decline, first slowly and then increasingly faster.

The trends in fertility rates in various countries seem to follow an individual pattern in each case and in this respect it is impossible to distinguish types of countries, as we did in the case of marriages. For instance, the countries of South and Central America, which obviously belong to the same category in regard to the frequency of marriage, reveal differences in the ages at maximum fertility rate. In the Dominican Republic, El Salvador, Nicaragua, Chile and Peru, the maximum is reached in the 25—29 age group; in Panama and Puerto Rico in the 20—24 age group. The rate of decline in fertility rates at older ages also varies: in the Dominican Republic the fertility rate at the age of 40—44 is 37% of the maximum, in El Salvador, 18%, in Nicaragua, less than 10%, in Panama, 11%, in Puerto Rico, 19%, in Chile, 38%, in Peru, 30%, and in Venezuela, 19%.

Knowing the fertility rate per 1000 females at each age, we can compute the gross birth rate, i.e. the average number of children born to each female at the existing fertility rate for various age groups, on the assumption that there is no mortality. In other words, it is the average number of children born to each female who have reached the end of the reproductive period, i.e. who have survived at least to the age of 50.

The gross birth rate is the sum of all fertility rates by age during the whole reproductive period. The rate can be split into two components—for the younger cohorts (up to 29 years inclusive) and for the older cohorts (30 years and over). Table 65 presents the results of such computations based on the contents of Table 64.

The first component, for the younger cohorts of mothers, is usually the greater of the two. Only Chile, the Netherlands and Spain note more births among the older mothers.
i Male fertility rates by age and birth rates can be computed n a similar manner (Tables 66 and 67).

Among males, maximum fertility rates are observed in the 25—29 or 30—34 age groups, i.e. somewhat later than among females. The general trend of fertility rates by age among men is similar to that among women, but there is a shift towards the later ages.

TABLE 65

Country	Year	Gross birth rates		
		total	to 29	30 and over
Alaska	1950	4·14	2·92	1·22
Canada	1952	3·64	2·28	1·36
Dominican Republic	1950	7·22	3·69	3·53
El Salvador	1950	5·94	3·68	2·26
Nicaragua . . . /	1940	4·28	2·59	1·69
Panama	1950	4·18	2·90	1·28
Puerto Rico	1950	5·23	3·20	2·03
United States	1951	3·21	2·33	0·88
Chile	1940	4·21	2·08	2·13
Peru.	1940	3·64	1·98	1·68
Venezuela	1950	5·48	3·31	2·17
Israel	1952	3·98	2·59	1·39
Japan	1952	3·38	2·13	1·25
Taiwan	1953	6·46	3·24	3·22
Austria	1951	2·06	1·33	0·73
Belgium	1952	2·36	1·46	0·90
Denmark.	1952	2·53	1·73	0·80
England and Wales	1952	2·17	1·43	0·74
Finland	1952	3·06	1·77	1·29
France	1952	2·73	1·71	1·02
Germ. Fed. Rep..	1952	2·09	1·39	0·70
Iceland	1950	3·87	2·29	1·58
Italy.	1951	2·38	1·28	1·10
Netherlands	1953	3·04	1·48	1·56
Norway	1952	2·58	1·46	1·12
Poland	1955—56	3·56	2·26	1·30
Portugal	1952	3·18	1·65	1·53
Spain	1940	3·06	1·42	1·64
Sweden	1951	2·20	1·42	0·78
Switzerland	1952	2·34	1·37	0·97
Yugoslavia	1952	3·62	2·20	1·42
Australia	1952	3·17	2·10	1·07
Fiji Islands	1953	5·70	3·44	2·26
Hawaii.	1950	3·31	2·27	1·04

TABLE 66

Country	Year	Total	—19	20—24	25—29	30—34	35—39	40—44	45—49	50 and over
Canada	1951	86·5	5·8	102·9	198·7	182·2	127·2	75·0	34·3	6·5
United States. .	1951	77·5	14·2	154·2	197·6	148·6	88·9	45·0	18·9	4·3
Venezuela . . .	1950	63·1	1·9	44·4	96·4	116·1	105·1	87·5	63·4	28·8
Israel	1952	96·0	10·1	110·3	186·4	197·4	148·1	92·4	46·4	16·0
Japan	1952	78·6	1·1	48·2	189·0	222·9	152·4	83·0	33·2	5·2
Taiwan . . .	1953	154·8	11·3	152·8	289·9	299·4	252·3	174·7	46·0	
Belgium . . .	1952	48·4	3·6	67·0	134·1	115·7	75·7	37·6	11·9	1·4
Finland . . .	1952	73·7	5·0	90·0	164·6	152·6	111·5	71·0	34·1	8·4
France . . .	1951	56·1	2·0	68·6	149·6	137·1	91·7	47·9	16·4	2·4
Netherlands . .	1953	70·1	1·5	43·0	153·1	181·9	136·2	78·5	28·7	3·9
Sweden . . .	1951	42·8	2·1	52·4	103·2	97·6	65·2	35·7	15·2	2·7
Australia . . .	1952	68·0	3·8	85·0	167·6	142·8	92·2	49·3	21·2	3·9
Fiji Islands . .	1953	149·6	28·2	203·7	267·6	227·9	238·3	148·0	53·4	
Hawaii. . . .	1940	55·4	3·5	47·2	105·1	101·6	81·0	56·0	30·2	13·0

Age group

Of course, the total gross birth rate must be approximately the same among males and among females, since the number of men in the age groups accounted for here is nearly the same as that of women. The only exception is Venezuela, where statistics give the number of mothers and not of fathers cohabiting in consensual unions. In Hawaii, the data relate to various years, which accounts for their discrepancies.

TABLE 67

Country	Year	Gross birth rates		
		total	to 29	30 and over
Canada	1951	3·67	1·54	2·13
United States	1951	3·36	1·83	1·53
Venezuela	1950	2·72	0·71	2·01
Israel	1952	4·03	1·53	2·50
Japan	1952	3·67	1·19	2·48
Taiwan	1953	6·36	2·27	4·09
Belgium	1952	2·23	1·02	1·21
Finland	1952	2·19	1·30	1·89
France	1951	2·58	1·10	1·48
Netherlands	1953	3·14	0·99	2·15
Sweden	1951	1·87	0·79	1·08
Australia	1952	2·33	0·78	1·55
Hawaii.	1940	2·19	0·78	1·41
Fiji Islands	1953	6·10	2·50	3·60

Apart from the United States, higher rates are noted among the older cohorts, which have a larger share in the total gross birth rate.

Analogies exist not only in the values of the gross birth rate among males and females; they can also be found in the rates at various ages. This is illustrated by the two graphs, for Canada and the Fiji Islands, presented in Fig. 26.

The general course of the two sets of curves is similar, with the male fertility curve in both cases shifted to the right, i.e. towards the later ages, by a distance which increases with time. This becomes still more evident when using cumulative instead of individual values (before cumulation, the data for the Fiji Islands have been so computed as to bring the female gross birth rate to the same level as the male rate; to this end, female fertility rates for each age group have been multiplied by the same coefficient). Cumulative values are useful because

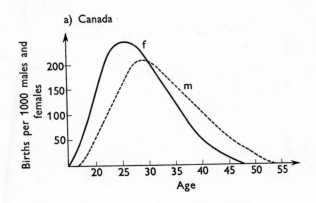

a) Canada

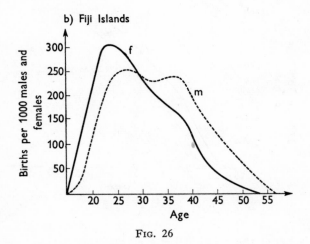

b) Fiji Islands

FIG. 26

cumulation results in levelling out the random deviations, which in the case of Fiji Islands, for instance, are obvious enough particularly among males; this is revealed in the rather "capricious" shape of the curve.

A comparison of the graphs of the cumulative values shows that in the earlier ages the distance between the two curves is small, some 2 years; it then gradually increases up to about the age of 35, to reach some 5 years, and subsequently remains virtually unchanged.

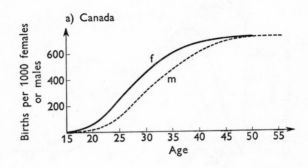

a) Canada

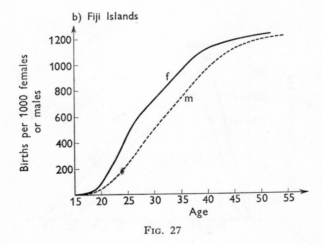

b) Fiji Islands

FIG. 27

This being the relation between the two curves, we might endeavour to estimate roughly male fertility rates by age on the basis of female fertility rates by age. For, while data on female fertility by age are common enough, births classified by the age of the father are computed in very few countries. Poland, too, publishes statistics on females only.

We shall calculate the male rates for Poland in 1955. We assume that the ratio of children born to fathers aged 55 and over is so small that such births can be disregarded in our considerations.

A graphic method appears the best in this case. We begin by drawing the curve of cumulative fertility rates (solid curve in Fig. 28). From the point on the curve which denotes the age of 20 we go to the right and mark a distance corresponding to two years on the horizontal axis; similarly, from the point denoting the age of 25 we mark a segment equal to three years, and so on; from the points denoting the ages of 35, 40, 45 and 50 years we mark a distance of 5 years. We join the points thus obtained (dotted curve in Fig. 28), and

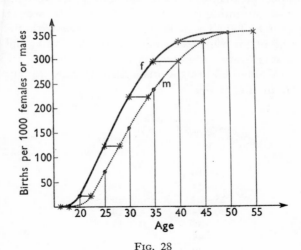

FIG. 28

from the resulting curve we read the values corresponding to the ages of 20, 25, 30 ... 55 years. They are the cumulative values; by subtracting them, one after another, we arrive back at the individual values. The results thus obtained are presented in Table 68.

The male fertility rates at various ages must be proportional to the individual values (may equal them by chance); related to the male age structure in 1955, they must furnish a number of births equal to that in 1955, i.e. 789,800. By multiplying

TABLE 68

Age	Cumulative values according to graph	Individual values	Age group
20	4	4	15—19
25	138	134	20—24
30	317	179	25—29
35	376	159	30—34
40	591	115	35—39
45	678	87	40—44
50	709	31	45—49
55	712	3	50—54

the number of males in each age group by the individual values and summing the resulting products we arrive at the figure 690,000. To make this sum agree with the actual number of births we must multiply all the individual values by a constant ratio which equals $779 \cdot 8 \div 690 = 1 \cdot 13$. The values thus obtained are the male fertility rates by age. They are listed in Table 69.

TABLE 69

Age	Births per 1000 males
15—19	5
20—24	151
25—29	202
30—34	180
35—39	130
40—44	98
45—49	35
50—54	3

The gross male birth rate, computed on this basis, is $4 \cdot 02$, i.e. considerably higher than the corresponding female rate of $3 \cdot 56$.

Figure 29 illustrates separately for men and women the relation between fertility and age in Poland in 1955.

The gross birth rate is directly related to a value, sometimes recorded in census results, which shows the average number of live births among females at various ages. In the case of older women, above 50, this is simply the value of the crude birth rate for a given female age group. The birth rates listed in Tables 65, 66 and 67 refer to the current fertility and not to the completed fertility of an age group. If fertility de-

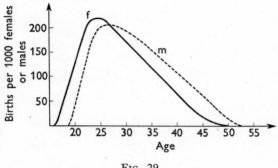

Fig. 29

creases with time, the average number of births among older women will be higher than the gross birth rate which refers to current fertility; if, on the other hand, fertility increases the birth rate will be higher. Table 70 contains a list of the two indices in selected countries.

The gross birth rate in Canada. Peru, Japan, Norway, Portugal and Australia is smaller than the average number of children born to one female aged 50 and over; this shows that the level of fertility in these countries has decreased during the last few decades. In the United States, on the contrary, the birth rate is higher; this is the result of the rapid rise in fertility in the post-war years. In Switzerland and in England and Wales the two values are almost exactly equal, which shows that fertility in these countries has not been subject to any marked changes.

The gross reproduction rate is obtained by computing the gross birth rate in relation to one sex. The gross female reproduction rate is defined as the average number of daughters that would be born to one female during the reproductive period, or the average number of daughters born to one woman who has reached the end of the reproductive age. In other words, the gross reproduction rate is the ratio of

TABLE 70

Country	Year	Average number of live births per female aged 50 and over	Gross birth rate
Angola	1940	4·068	—
Australia	1947	3·419	3·17
Brazil	1940	6·220	—
British Honduras	1946	5·064	—
Canada	1941	4·594	3·64
Egypt	1947	5·680	—
England and Wales	1951	2·026	2·17
Japan	1952	4·692	3·38
Norway	1950	3·253	2·58
Peru	1940	6·596	3·64
Portugal	1950	3·576	3·18
Sarawak	1947	4·084	—
Switzerland	1951	2·308	2·34
United States	1950	2·822	3·21

daughters to mothers, computed on the assumption that none of the mothers die before the end of the reproductive age. If the ratio is less than 1, then even assuming the lowest possible mortality, daughters cannot numerically replace mothers, and the population is bound to diminish in future generations. The population can increase only if the gross reproduction rate exceeds 1, to compensate for the decrease due to mortality.

The gross male reproduction rate can be computed similarly.

The gross reproduction rate is a function only of fertilities by cohort or age group. If the influence of mortality is also taken into account, we obtain the net reproduction rate. It is the ratio of daughters to mothers (or sons to fathers), computed on the assumption that fertility and mortality rates will remain stable over a long period of time, i.e. at least over one generation. A net reproduction rate greater than 1 ensures that, if the current mortality rates prevail, the present generation will be more than replaced by the next generation. A net reproduction rate less than 1 means that the next genera-

tion will be smaller than the preceding, i.e. it may be anticipated that sooner or later the population will diminish.

The quotient of the net reproduction rate to the gross reproduction rate corresponds almost exactly to the probability of survival from infancy to an age equal to the length
of a generation (female or male). Usually, the length of a
generation, or the mean interval between the birth of the
mother and the birth of the daughter (or the birth of the
father and the birth of the son) is some 28—30 years for
females and some 35—37 years for males.

Knowing the net reproduction rate and the length of a
generation we can compute the annual rate of increase of
the population, on the assumption that the population is stable,
i.e. that its age and sex distribution is constant and only its
total number increases or decreases. If the net female reproduction rate is N_f and the length of a female generation
is g_f, the annual rate of increase will be

$$\sqrt[g_f]{N_f}$$

The annual percentage increase (or decrease) of the population is

$$100 \times \left(\sqrt[g_f]{N_f} - 1 \right).$$

It is clear that the annual rate of increase must be the
same, irrespective as to whether computed for males or females; hence, if the length of a male generation and the
male net reproduction rate are represented by g_m and N_m
respectively, then

$$\sqrt[g_f]{N_f} = \sqrt[g_m]{N_m}.$$

Taking the logarithm of both sides of the equation we obtain

$$\frac{1}{g_f} \log N_f = \frac{1}{g_m} \log N_m$$

or

$$g_m \log N_f = g_f \log N_m.$$

Hence, if we know one of the two net reproduction rates (computed either for females or for males) and the length of a female and a male generation, we can find the second net reproduction rate.

Table 71 presents the gross and net female reproduction rates in selected countries.

TABLE 71

Country	Year	Female reproduction rate	
		gross	net
Canada	1952	1·765	—
Jamaica	1952	2·283	1·742
United States	1951	1·591	1·519
Ceylon.	1952	3·66	1·987
Cyprus	1953	1·744	1·562
Israel	1952	1·931	1·794
Japan	1952	1·444	1·292
Thailand	1951	2·028	1·513
Austria	1951	0·986	0·911
Belgium	1952	1·128	1·029
Denmark	1953	1·252	1·142
England and Wales	1952	1·052	1·009
Finland	1952	1·490	1·387
France	1952	1·330	1·249
Germ. Fed. Rep.	1952	1·005	0·927
Iceland	1947—1948	1·806	1·381
Ireland	1950—1952	1·600	1·381
Netherlands	1953	1·462	1·386
Norway	1952	1·240	1·174
Poland	1956	1·695	1·478
Portugal	1951	1·488	1·086
Sweden	1951	1·067	1·021
Switzerland	1952	1·250	1·145
Yugoslavia	1953	1·983	1·421
Australia	1952	1·547	1·468
Fiji Islands	1952	2·18	—
New Zealand —white population	1953	1·696	1·632

The gross female reproduction rates in selected countries, computed by multiplying the gross birth rates (see Table 63) by the proportion of female births, are listed in Table 72.

TABLE 72

Country	Year	Gross female reproduction rates
Alaska	1950	2·03
Chile	1940	2·05
Dominican Republic	1950	3·53
El Salvador	1950	2·90
Italy.	1951	1·16
Nicaragua	1940	2·09
Panama	1950	2·04
Puerto Rico	1950	2·54
Taiwan	1952	3·12
Venezuela	1950	2·67

Table 73 gives the computed gross reproduction rates for males in selected countries.

TABLE 73

Country	Year	Gross male reproduction rates
Australia	1952	1·19
Belgium	1952	1·14
Canada	1951	1·89
Fiji Islands	1953	3·12
Finland	1952	1·64
France	1951	1·32
Hawaii	1940	1·12
Israel	1952	2·06
Japan	1952	1·88
Netherlands	1953	1·61
Sweden	1951	0·95
Taiwan	1953	3·25
United States	1951	1·72
Venezuela	1950	1·39

The Swedish rate listed in Table 73 is questionable because it is less than 1, while the corresponding female rate, shown in Table 71, is slightly more than 1. According to the equation on page 147, log N_m must always have the same sign as log N_f, i.e. both must be either positive or negative. This, in turn, means that the values of the two rates must either both be lower than 1 or both be higher than 1. Since, as a rule, data on the age of the mother are usually more reliable, the error is presumably to be sought in the male reproduction rate in Sweden.

Figure 30 shows the relation between net and gross reproduction rates in some countries. The relation is particularly close for the lower rates; for higher rates the dispersion becomes quite large. Moreover, the relation is certainly not linear, as witnessed by the position of the last point which denotes a very high value of the gross reproduction rate.

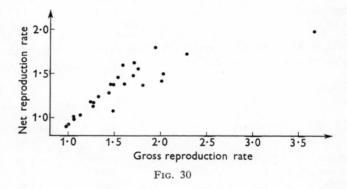

Fig. 30

Naturally, we can examine cohort as well as current fertility and reproduction rates. Examples and comparative lists of cohort rates collated with current rates will be given later.

Higher or lower fertility brings us to the problem of childless women. The percentage of such women, obviously very high at the earlier ages, decreases with time, and after the end of the reproduction period it is no longer subject to appreciable changes. A question pertaining to infertility is sometimes included in population censuses; it makes it possible to analyse fertility from another angle. However, the processing of the data thus obtained does not follow a uniform pattern; the age groups considered vary (the 50 and over age group, in which we are most interested, is commonly taken into account, but sometimes the information is related to other groups, such as 55 and over, 45 and over; in some cases the 45—49 age group is the oldest considered); the

TABLE 74

Country	Year	Percentage of childless females aged 50 and over
Angola	1940	13·5
Egypt	1947	7·0
Morocco		
—Jewish population	1951	8·3
Mauritius	1952	13·3
Mozambique	1940	16·3
Portuguese Guinea	1950	8·0
Barbados	1946	20·0
British Honduras	1946	12·9
Canada	1941	13·0
Mexico	1950	21·3
Panama	1950	11·8
United States	1950	18·0
Brazil	1940	16·0
Japan	1950	10·7
Federation of Malaya	1947	12·0
Philippines	1948	3·1
Singapore	1947	19·5
England and Wales	1951	20·5
France	1946	11·2
Germ. Fed. Rep.	1950	24·1
Norway	1950	14·1
Portugal	1950	9·5
Switzerland	1940	19·5
Yugoslavia	1953	12·6
Australia	1947	10·9
Fiji Islands	1946	17·9

cohorts among which infertility is examined also differ (in most cases all females of a given age are taken into account, but sometimes the cohort considered includes married women only, or even married women minus those whose husbands are in captivity or reported to be missing, etc.). Since the reliability of census returns also varies from country to country, the inevitable conclusion is that the comparability of statistics is dubious and that they must be regarded merely as tentative data indicating the order of magnitude of the phenomenon of infertility.

There is so little uniformity in these statistics that we shall refrain from trying to collate them with other rates.

The next problem to consider are the births of legitimate and illegitimate children. Judging from Table 75, in some countries illegitimate births form a high percentage of the total number of births (we have not listed in the table the percentage of illegitimate births in the countries where consensual unions are prevalent).[1]

Among the countries named in Table 75 the largest percentage of illegitimate births was recorded in Austria (one-sixth of all births), followed by Portugal, Sweden and West Germany. Poland is in the middle of the list (illegitimate births constitute one-eighteenth of all births in Poland). The Netherlands had the lowest relative proportion of illegitimate births.

TABLE 75

Country	Percentage of illegitimate births
Canada	3·8
United States	4·1
Austria	16·8
Belgium	2·3
Denmark	7·0
Finland	4·7
France	6·8
Germany	9·0
Iceland	2·3
Italy	3·3
Netherlands	1·4
Norway	3·8
Poland	5·6
Portugal	11·4
Sweden	9·7
Switzerland	3·6
England and Wales	4·8
Australia	3·9
New Zealand	4·3

[1] Data on Poland have been taken from *Małżeństwa, urodzenia, zgony (Marriages, Births, Deaths) 1956*. Warsaw 1957; on other countries from *Recent Trends in Fertility in Industrialized Countries*. United Nations, New York 1958; they refer to the years 1950—1954.

The distribution of illegitimate births by the age of the mother differs noticeably from that of all births. Illegitimate births are relatively more frequent in the earlier than in the later ages; hence, the average age of the mother of an illegitimate child is lower than the average age of the mother of a legitimate child. In 1956 in Poland, the average age of all mothers giving birth was 27·7, giving birth to a legitimate child was 27·8, and to an illegitimate child, 25·7 years.

The frequencies of legitimate and illegitimate births per 1000 females at various ages are enumerated in Table 76.

TABLE 76

Type	Age groups						
	15—19	20—24	25—29	30—34	35—39	40—44	45—49
Legitimate births . .	35·5	193·2	188·0	129·3	79·5	28·4	2·8
Illegitimate births . .	6·9	13·0	8·5	5·6	3·7	1·1	0·1

These data are presented graphically in Fig. 31; the frequencies of illegitimate births are multiplied by a factor of ten, in order to render the graph more legible.

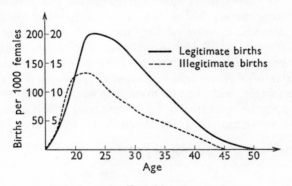

FIG. 31

As can be clearly seen on the graph, the maximum frequency of illegitimate births is noted at an earlier age than the maximum frequency of legitimate births.

Gross and net reproduction rates can be computed separa-

tely for legitimate and illegitimate births. The results of
such computations for Poland are shown in Table 77.

TABLE 77

	Reproduction rate	
	gross	net
Legitimate births	1·605	1·452
Illegitimate births . . .	0·095	0·086
Total	1·700	1·538

It is noteworthy that the proportion of illegitimate births
in the gross reproduction rate is almost exactly the same
as in the net reproduction rate, and equals the proportion
of illegitimate births in all births. This is not a coincidence;
it results from the fact that the probability of survival from
infancy to the age of 27·8 (the length of a generation relating
to legitimate births) is only a little smaller than the probability
of survival to the age of 25·7 (the length of a generation relating
to illegitimate births).

In other countries too, the difference between the two
indices is quite small. Hence, in order to compute the reproduction rate (gross or net) separately for legitimate and
illegitimate births, it is sufficient to divide the reproduction
rate relating to all births into two component parts, proportional to the number of legitimate and illegitimate births.

The frequency of legitimate and illegitimate births can
also be computed in another way—by relating births, not to
all females of a given age, but separately to married and unmarried (single, widowed or divorced) women. This produces
a more precise picture of legitimate and illegitimate fertility. The pertinent data for Sweden in 1956 are shown in
Table 78.[1]

TABLE 78

	Age groups						
	15—19	20—24	25—29	30—34	35—39	40—44	45—49
Births per 1000 married females .	556	272	172	102	52	16	1·2
unmarried females	19·5	31·4	25·8	18·2	10·2	3·6	0·2

[1] *Arsbok för Sverige 1958.*

The picture is different here. To begin with, the fertility rate among married women is the highest in the earliest age group; in the subsequent groups it consistently drops steeply. Among unmarried women, on the other hand, maximum fertility is reached only in the 20—24 age group, following which the rate declines, but at a much slower pace than in the case of married women.

We shall now proceed to demonstrate that, based on fertility rates among married women, the general level of fertility in Poland in 1955 was lower than in 1931 (within the territorial frontiers at the time). The line of reasoning is as follows.

We have the fertility rates by age among married women in 1931—1932 (i.e. we know the number of legitimate births per 100 married females at various ages). True, we do not have the corresponding data for the post-war years, but this is a difficulty we can overcome. We know the distribution of females by age and marital status in 1954. On this basis we calculate for each age group the number of legitimate births per 100 females (married and unmarried) in 1954, assuming the fertility rate among married women equals the rate in 1931—1932. By transferring these rates to the known female age structure in 1955 (the change which occurred in this respect among females of childbearing age between 1954 and 1955 was relatively insignificant), we can ascertain the number of legitimate births in 1955 if marital fertility remained the same as in 1931—1932. We add to the result obtained the estimated number of illegitimate births, on the assumption that in relation to the total number of births their proportion equalled the 1956 index i.e. 5·6%.

All these calculations are presented in Table 79.

If we assume that illegitimate births constituted 5·6% of all births we obtain a hypothetical total number of births equalling 794,000 ÷ 0·944 (= 100% — 5·6%) = 841,000. The actual number of births in 1955 was 794,000, or 5·6% less than the hypothetical total. Thus, fertility in 1955 was 5·6% lower than in 1931—1932.

Births are sometimes registered in vital records by birth order. For the purpose of analysis, the most revealing is the classification of births by age of the mother and by birth

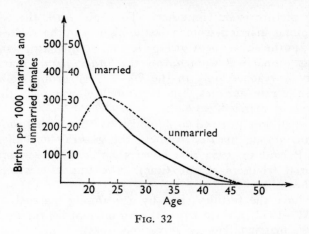

Fɪɢ. 32

Tᴀʙʟᴇ 79

Age groups	Legitimate births per 100 married females 1931—1932	Percentage of married females 1954	Hypothetical number of legitimate births per 100 females 1954	Number of females in thous. 1955	Hypothetical number of legitimate births in thous. 1955
15—19	34·4	6·3	2·2	1140	25
20—24	34·0	50·0	17·5	1193	209
25—29	26·8	76·3	20·5	1195	245
30—34	20·1	80·1	16·1	1093	176
35—39	14·3	} 74·2	11·5	720	83
40—44	6·7		5·0	938	47
45—49	1·4		1·0	921	9
					794

order, computed per 1000 females at corresponding ages. Data processed on this basis are presented in Table 80.[1]

The older the age the greater the frequency of higher order births. This can be seen quite distinctly on Fig. 33 which presents curves drawn on the basis of the frequency of births of various orders, classified by age groups for 1956.

---

[1] *Demographic Yearbook 1954.*

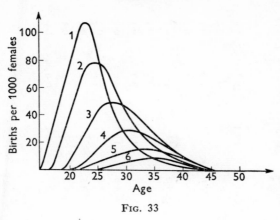

FIG. 33

The distribution by order of births (if not classified by the age of the mother) usually relates births to 1000 women of childbearing age. Such data indicate not only the relative frequency of first births, second births etc., but also the general fertility level (Table 81).

In principle, the frequency of births should decline on passing from first to subsequent births. For, after the birth of the first child some marriages are dissolved by the death of one of the spouses or by divorce, and the number of married couples who can have a second child diminishes; the number of couples who can have a third, fourth and more children is even smaller. Moreover, female fertility decreases with age. Exceptions to this rule are to be expected when the age structure of a population is very irregular and when, for instance in the aftermath of war, the cohorts reaching the reproductive period are very small, much smaller than the cohorts of women who have already borne one child. A large and rapid decline in fertility may have a similar effect.

This phenomenon was observed in Japan, where fertility in the post-war years dropped to almost one-half; as a consequence, in 1952 there were more second births than first births. A similar configuration of the order of births in Cyprus was probably caused by external strife.

If no birth control methods are applied, the frequency of births by order is solely a function of the diminishing number

TABLE 80

Birth order	Total	—14	15—19	20—24	25—29	30—34	35—39	40—44	45—49
Japan 1951	81·9	0·0	10·7	141·0	216·4	161·1	89·4	28·7	1·6
1	20·4	0·0	9·3	77·1	41·9	10·7	2·9	0·5	0·0
2	22·8	0·0	1·3	49·5	84·3	27·6	6·2	1·0	0·1
3	15·7	—	0·1	12·6	61·2	40·7	9·8	1·4	0·1
4	9·1	—	0·0	1·4	21·7	39·0	14·4	2·0	0·1
5	5·5	—	0·0	0·2	5·5	24·6	16·6	3·0	0·1
6	3·4	—	—	0·0	1·3	11·7	15·2	3·9	0·1
7	2·2	—	—	0·0	0·2	4·6	11·5	4·6	0·2
8	1·4	—	—	0·0	0·1	1·5	7·1	4·5	0·2
9	0·8	—	—	0·0	0·0	0·5	3·5	3·5	0·2
10 and subsequent	0·7	—	—	—	0·0	0·2	2·2	4·2	0·4
unknown	0·1	—	0·0	0·1	0·2	0·1	0·1	0·0	0·0
Switzerland 1951	60·0	0·0	13·0	105·7	153·0	113·7	61·2	20·3	1·9
1	22·3	0·0	11·7	66·6	60·0	24·6	9·4	2·4	0·2
2	16·1	—	1·2	28·1	50·3	31·8	11·5	2·6	0·1
3	9·7	—	0·1	8·6	25·7	25·7	12·4	3·1	0·2

Birth frequencies by age

4	0·3	3·3	10·4	15·8	10·9	1·9	—	—	5·4
5	0·2	2·5	6·7	7·9	3·8	0·4	—	—	2·7
6	0·1	1·8	4·2	4·0	1·6	0·0	—	—	1·5
7	0·1	1·3	2·6	2·1	0·5	—	—	—	0·9
8	0·1	1·1	1·6	0·9	0·2	—	—	—	0·5
9	0·2	0·8	0·9	0·4	0·0	—	—	—	0·3
10 and subsequent	0·3	1·5	1·5	0·4	0·0	—	—	—	0·5
unknown	—	—	—	—	—	—	—	—	—
Poland 1956	2·9	29·6	83·2	133·8	197·5	207·2	42·5	—	107·2
1	0·2	1·6	5·0	14·6	44·5	106·9	36·3	—	33·3
2	0·2	2·6	10·8	27·4	63·8	69·3	5·7	—	28·5
3	0·4	4·6	17·5	35·4	49·6	23·5	0·5	—	20·4
4	0·5	5·4	17·4	26·8	25·0	6·0	0·0	—	12·0
5	0·4	4·5	12·6	15·5	9·8	1·2	—	—	6·3
6	0·4	3·5	8·2	8·0	3·4	0·2	—	—	3·3
7	0·3	2·6	5·1	3·6	1·0	—	—	—	1·7
8	0·2	1·8	2·9	1·5	0·3	—	—	—	0·8
9	0·1	1·2	1·4	0·6	0·0	—	—	—	0·4
10 and subsequent	0·2	1·7	1·4	0·3	—	—	—	—	0·4
unknown	0·0	0·1	0·1	0·1	0·1	0·1	0·0	—	0·1

TABLE 81

Country	Year	Total	Frequency by order of births										
			1	2	3	4	5	6	7	8	9	10 and subsequent	unknown
Canada	1952	97·3	27·8	22·8	17·0	10·5	6·1	3·9	2·5	1·8	1·2	2·7	0·0
Puerto Rico	1950	135·0	27·4	22·9	20·4	15·2	11·7	9·7	7·5	6·0	4·3	9·4	0·5
United States . . .	1951	84·1	25·7	23·9	14·7	7·5	3·8	2·2	1·4	0·9	1·6	1·0	2·4
Cyprus	1953	87·8	19·9	20·6	15·6	11·3	7·7	5·7	3·1	1·0	1·0	0·8	—
Israel	1952	105·2	31·6	30·9	15·3	8·2	5·2	3·6	2·7	1·9	1·3	2·1	2·4
Japan	1952	75·8	19·9	20·2	16·0	8·5	4·8	2·8	1·7	1·0	0·5	0·5	0·0
Austria	1952	42·3	16·7	12·6	6·4	3·0	1·5	0·8	0·5	0·3	0·2	0·3	0·0
Belgium	1952	58·5	22·7	14·9	8·8	5·1	2·8	1·6	1·0	0·6			0·0
Denmark	1952	62·9	20·6	18·8	11·2	5·8	3·0	1·5	0·8	0·4		0·9	—
England and Wales . .	1952	50·4	19·9	15·2	7·9	3·6	1·8	0·9	0·5	0·3		0·7	0·0
Finland	1952	77·0	24·0	19·3	13·1	8·3	4·9	2·8	1·7	1·1	0·2	0·3	0·0
France	1952	66·2	20·1	18·1	12·3	6·9	3·7	2·0	1·1	0·7	0·7	1·0	0·2
Germ. Fed. Rep. . .	1952	45·5	20·4	13·4	6·3	2·8	1·3	0·6	0·3	0·2	0·4	0·7	0·0
Italy	1951	57·6	19·6	14·7	8·4	5·0	3·2	2·2	1·5	1·0		0·3	0·6
Netherlands . . .	1953	76·8	22·1	18·7	12·7	8·3	5·4	3·5	2·1	1·4	0·6	0·8	—
Norway	1952	64·8	24·9	19·0	10·7	5·2	2·4	1·2	0·6	0·3	1·0	1·5	0·0
Poland	1945	107·2	33·3	28·5	20·4	12·0	6·3	3·3	1·7	0·8	0·2	0·2	0·1
Portugal	1952	70·5	20·2	14·3	10·6	7·7	5·7	3·9	2·8	2·1	0·4	0·4	0·0
Switzerland . . .	1952	60·4	22·5	16·3	9·9	5·4	2·8	1·5	0·8	0·3	1·3	2·0	—
Yugoslavia . . .	1952	93·0	28·5	24·6	15·3	8·6	5·5	3·7	2·5	1·7	0·3	0·4	0·1
Australia	1952	79·8	27·2	23·2	14·9	7·5	3·4	1·7	0·9	0·5	0·3	1·6	—
Fiji Islands . . .	1953	145·7	28·9	24·2	19·8	17·4	14·7	12·0	9·3	7·7	3·9	6·1	1·7
Hawaii	1950	98·8	29·5	26·7	18·1	10·4	5·9	3·1	2·0	1·2	0·8	1·2	0·0

of marriages and the declining fertility. The result is a gradual decrease in the number of successive births and a high relative prevalence of large families. Puerto Rico and the Fiji Islands are examples of this.

Countries in which the size of family is successfully planned, show a sharp drop in the frequency of consecutive births. Here the typical examples are Belgium and Switzerland.

Figure 34 presents the curves of successive birth frequencies for Puerto Rico, Belgium and Poland.

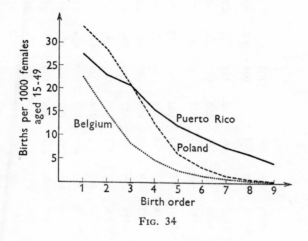

FIG. 34

Earlier in this chapter, we split the reproduction rate into two components, representing the respective proportions of legitimate and illegitimate births. We can also divide the rate into components representing births of different orders. Knowing the frequency of births distributed by age and by birth order (Table 80), we compute the distribution of the gross reproduction rate by summing the frequencies relating to successive births and multiplying them by the proportion of female births. The results thus obtained for selected countries are listed in Table 82.

In order to split the gross reproduction rate into components corresponding to births of various orders it is necessary to classify births by birth order and by age of the mother. The

TABLE 82

Country	Year	Gross reproduction rates by birth order									
		1	2	3	4	5	6	7	8	9	10 and subsequent
Canada · · · · · · ·	1951	0·468	416	284	169	104	068	047	033	024	056
United States · · · ·	1951	0·513	466	282	143	074	040	025	017	011	020
Cyprus · · · · ·	1951	0·405	399	346	258	182	127	080	052	021	023
Israel · · · · ·	1951	0·639	572	290	153	093	066	045	033	022	034
Japan · · · · ·	1951	0·349	414	307	191	122	078	052	033	019	017
Belgium · · · · ·	1951	0·440	295	169	092	049	028	016	009	012	
Denmark · · · · ·	1951	0·414	361	214	096	056	030	015	009	013	
England and Wales · ·	1951	0·422	319	160	070	033	017	010	006	003	005
Finland · · · ·	1951	0·450	368	256	157	089	054	033	022	015	022
France · · · · ·	1951	0·406	371	253	140	073	041	024	015	010	017
Italy · · · · ·	1951	0·363	285	171	106	069	047	030	021	013	016
Netherlands · · · ·	1951	0·410	358	261	172	109	074	048	048	032	021
Norway · · · ·	1951	0·466	344	187	092	044	024	011	007	003	003
Poland · · · ·	1956	0·519	420	325	200	108	059	031	016	008	009
Portugal · · · ·	1951	0·376	290	171	126	093	070	049	034	034	050
Switzerland · · ·	1951	0·452	326	197	112	055	030	017	010	006	009
Yugoslavia · · · ·	1951	0·542	480	313	199	147	105	072	048	032	045
Australia · · · ·	1951	0·510	449	269	129	061	030	017	009	006	005

calculations involved are rather complex as we must first find the frequency of births relating to various combinations of age and birth order, then derive certain sums of these frequencies. Having obtained the data on total births, we then proceed to compute the data on female births. This method is exact. A simpler and less exact one, although often sufficient for the purpose of analysis, consists in splitting the gross reproduction rate proportionally into frequencies of birth by order. The results of such computations for several countries are shown in Table 83.

TABLE 83

Birth order	Canada 1951		Cyprus 1951		Poland 1956	
	Distribution of gross reproduction rate					
	approx-imate	exact	approx-imate	exact	approx-imate	exact
1	0·472	0·468	0·446	0·405	0·528	0·519
2	0·422	0·416	0·420	0·399	0·451	0.420
3	0·287	0·284	0.349	0·346	0·322	0·325
4	0·176	0·169	0·249	0·259	0·190	0·200
5	0·103	0·104	0·178	0·167	0·100	0·108
6	0·066	0·068	0·112	0·127	0·052	0·059
7	0·044	0·047	0·069	0·080	0·027	0·031
8	0·030	0·033	0·043	0·052	0·013	0·016
9	0·021	0·024	0·018	0·021	0·006	0·008
10 and subsequent	0·048	0·056	0·020	0·023	0·006	0·009
Total	1·669		1·893		1·695	

The rates agree quite well even in the case of Cyprus and Poland, where the growth of population was by no means free from perturbations, and even more so for Canada, a country far from the theatre of war. In each of the three countries the approximate rate of first and second births is higher and that of subsequent births, lower than the exact rate.

By constructing a cumulative set of values for birth frequencies by order we may arrive at interesting conclusions. Table 84 presents such a series, computed on the basis of data contained in Table 82.

The table makes it possible to determine which successive births result in a gross reproduction rate equal to or higher

TABLE 84

Country	Year	Cumulative values of birth frequency by birth order									Total
		1	1—2	1—3	1—4	1—5	1—6	1—7	1—8	1—9	
Australia	1951	0·510	0·959	1·228	1·357	1·418	1·448	1·465	1·474	1·480	1·485
Belgium	1951	0·440	0·735	0·904	0·996	1·045	1·073	1·089	1·089	—	1·110
Canada	1951	0·468	0·884	1·168	1·337	1·441	1·509	1·556	1·589	1·613	1·569
Cyprus	1951	0·405	0·804	1·150	1·408	1·590	1·717	1·797	1·849	1·870	1·893
Denmark	1951	0·414	0·775	0·989	1·085	1·141	1·171	1·186	1·195	—	1·208
England and Wales	1951	0·422	0·741	0·901	0·971	1·004	1·021	1·031	1·037	1·040	1·045
Finland	1951	0·450	0·818	1·074	1·231	1·320	1·374	1·407	1·429	1·444	1·466
France	1951	0·406	0·777	1·030	1·170	1·243	1·284	1·308	1·323	1·333	1·350
Israel	1951	0·639	1·211	1·501	1·654	1·747	1·813	1·858	1·891	1·913	1·947
Italy	1951	0·363	0·648	0·819	0·925	0·994	1·041	1·071	1·092	1·105	1·121
Japan	1951	0·349	0·763	1·070	1·261	1·383	1·461	1·513	1·546	1·565	1·582
Netherlands	1951	0·410	0·768	1·029	1·201	1·310	1·384	1·432	1·480	1·512	1·533
Norway	1951	0·466	0·810	0·997	1·059	1·133	1·157	1·168	1·175	1·178	1·181
Poland	1956	0·619	0·939	1·264	1·464	1·572	1·631	1·662	1·678	1·686	1·695
Portugal	1951	0·376	0·666	0·895	1·066	1·192	1·285	1·355	1·404	1·438	1·488
Switzerland	1951	0·452	0·778	0·975	1·087	1·142	1·178	1·189	1·199	1·205	1·214
United States	1951	0·513	0·979	1·261	1·404	1·478	1·518	1·603	1·620	1·631	0·651
Yugoslavia	1951	0·542	1·022	1·335	1·534	1·681	1·786	1·858	1·906	1·938	1·983

than 1. The table thus indicates the minimum of births which ensures that a generation of daughters will replace or even outnumber that of mothers, on the assumption that mortality is zero during the whole course of the reproductive period.

Even if mortality is the lowest possible, such replacement clearly cannot be ensured at second births, since two births denote on the average a little more than one male child and a little less than one female child, which of course is not enough to replace one mother. Hence, the fact that in Israel and Yugoslavia the sum of first and second births gives a reproduction rate higher than 1 can only be evidence of erroneous information on the order of births.

Apart from these two countries, Table 84 indicates that in most cases a rate slightly higher than 1 is already attained at third births. This means that if the current level of fertility remains unchanged, first, second and third births, taken together, will ensure replacement or over-replacement of the mothers, provided that the level of mortality remains sufficiently low. In some countries, however, even third births do not suffice as the sum of rates exceeds 1 only at higher order births. In Belgium, for example, it is at the fifth birth only that the generation of daughters will exceed that of the mothers, unless mortality eliminates the small surplus attained at the fifth birth. In other words, if there are no fifth and subsequent births, even assuming the lowest mortality, the generation of mothers cannot be replaced by the generation of daughters and, after a certain time, a decline of population will ensue.

In Norway, a rate somewhat larger than 1 can be attained at the fourth birth, in England and Wales, at the fifth birth only. However, in the latter case the surplus is so small that it is completely eliminated by mortality in the reproductive period. In other words, if England had no families with more than five children and the current fertility rate continued to prevail, gradual depopulation would be inevitable even if the mortality were very low.

Poland is in a better situation in this respect, because already at the third birth the number of daughters exceeds the number of mothers.

Like the gross reproduction rate, the net reproduction rate can also be distributed by birth order. Such rates computed for selected countries are listed in Table 85.

The range of rates relating to various countries is wide, irrespective of the order of births. But here, too, a certain regular pattern prevails. First births give the lowest rate (0·304) in Portugal and the highest (0·478) in the United States. The ratio of these two extreme rates is 1 : 1·58. The extreme rates attained at second births are 0·222 and 0·444 (in the two countries named); their ratio is 1 : 2. Third births give extreme rates of 0·126 and 0·133, i.e. a ratio of 1 : 2·49; tenth and subsequent births result in extreme rates having a ratio of 1 : 15.

The situation can be explained as follows. In those countries where some measure of family planning is in operation, the larger the family the more stringent the restriction on further births. Parents want to have several children, but with each successive child the problem of sustaining the family, housing conditions, etc. grow more and more difficult and troublesome. This is why subsequent births are more affected by birth control measures. Hence, the higher the birth order the larger the gap between countries in which limitation of births is nonexistent and those where family planning is widespread. This is also the reason for the increasing difference between the extreme values of the rates.

Cumulative values constructed on the basis of the contents of Table 85 are presented in Table 86.

From these data it is possible to ascertain which births produce a growing trend of the population within a given country. For Canada they are the first, second and third births taken together, since the cumulative sum of the first three births is already greater than 1. The situation is similar in the United States, Cyprus, Finland, Poland, and Australia. In all these countries the first three births are sufficient to ensure that the generation of daughters will be at least as numerous as that of the mothers, assuming an unchanged level of mortality. In Japan, France and the Netherlands this can be attained at the fourth births only, since only then can the cumulative sum exceed 1. In Denmark, Norway and Switzerland, the fifth births are also necessary. To reach this goal, Portugal

TABLE 85

Country	Year	Net reproduction rate by birth order									
		1	2	3	4	5	6	7	8	9	10 and subsequent
Canada	1951	0·445	400	270	164	097	062	042	028	020	045
United States . . .	1951	0·478	444	273	140	071	041	026	017	011	019
Chile	1940	0·355	229	169	125			273			043
Cyprus	1951	0·400	376	313	223	159	100	062	039	016	018
Japan	1951	0·343	384	264	154	093	057	037	024	014	012
Austria	1951	0·364	271	130	064	033	018	011	007	004	009
Belgium	1951	0·397	260	140	084	047	029	018	011	018 [9 & subs.]	
Denmark	1951	0·365	323	194	102	051	028	014	009	012 [9 & subs.]	
England and Wales .	1951	0·378	314	160	071	035	017	010	006	004	006
Finland	1951	0·427	344	238	143	081	048	030	020	014	020
France	1951	0·392	352	231	123	064	037	012	013	008	015
German Fed. Rep. .	1951	0·418	266	126	055	025	012	008	004	006 [9 & subs.]	
Netherlands . . .	1951	0·396	338	236	154	098	065	042	029	018	029
Norway	1951	0·413	318	175	087	042	023	010	007	003	003
Poland	1956	0·461	395	282	161	087	146	023	011	006	006
Portugal	1951	0·304	222	166	119	085	061	045	031	002	031
Switzerland . . .	1951	0·414	299	180	100	050	028	017	009	006	009
Australia	1951	0·477	430	257	123	058	029	014	009	005	007

TABLE 86

Country	Year	Cumulative values of birth frequency by birth order									
		1	1—2	1—3	1—4	1—5	1—6	1—7	1—8	1—9	Total
Canada	1951	0·445	0·845	1·115	1·279	1·376	1·438	1·480	1·508	1·528	1·573
United States . .	1951	0·478	0·922	1·194	1·334	1·405	1·446	1·472	1·489	1·500	1·519
Chile	1940	0·355	0·584	0·753	0·878	—	—	—	—	1·151	1·194
Cyprus . . .	1951	0·400	0·776	1·089	1·312	1·461	1·561	1·623	1·662	1·178	1·695
Japan . . .	1951	0·343	0·727	0·991	1·145	1·238	1·295	1·332	1·356	1·370	1·382
Austria . .	1951	0·364	0·635	0·765	0·829	0·862	0·880	0·891	0·898	0·902	0·911
Belgium . .	1951	0·397	0·657	0·806	0·890	0·937	0·966	0·984	0·995	—	1·013
Denmark . .	1951	0·365	0·688	0·822	0·984	1·035	1·063	1·077	1·086	—	1·098
England and Wales .	1951	0·378	0·692	0·852	0·923	0·958	0·975	0·985	0·991	0·995	1·001
Finland . .	1951	0·427	0·771	1·009	1·152	1·233	1·281	1·311	1·331	1·345	1·365
France . .	1951	0·392	0·744	0·975	1·098	1·162	1·199	1·220	1·233	1·241	1·256
Germ. Fed. Rep. . .	1951	0·418	0·684	0·810	0·865	0·890	0·902	0·910	0·914	—	0·920
Netherlands . .	1951	0·396	0·734	0·970	1·124	1·222	1·287	1·328	1·358	1·376	1·405
Norway . .	1951	0·413	0·731	0·906	0·993	1·035	1·058	1·068	1·075	1·078	1·081
Poland . .	1951	0·461	0·856	1·138	1·299	1·386	1·432	1·455	1·466	1·472	1·478
Portugal . .	1951	0·304	0·526	0·692	0·811	0·896	0·957	1·002	1·033	1·055	1·086
Switzerland . .	1951	0·414	0·713	0·893	0·993	1·043	1·071	1·088	1·097	1·103	1·112
Australia . .	1951	0·477	0·907	1·164	1·287	1·345	1·374	1·388	1·307	1·402	1·409

needs seven births and England as many as ten, because in the case of England the first nine births cannot yield a rate higher than 1. In Austria and the German Federal Republic where the net reproduction rate is less than 1, all births taken together cannot compensate for the decrease in the previous generation.

It can be generally assumed that if the net reproduction rate is 1·4 or more, the first three births are sufficient to ensure that the generation of daughters will be as numerous as the generation of mothers. If the net reproduction rate is from 1·2 to 1·4, this can be attained at the fourth births only; if the rate is from 1·1 to 1·2, at the fifth births; and, if the rate is between 1 and 1·1, at a still higher order of births.

An approximate distribution of the net reproduction rate by order of births can also be obtained by splitting the rate into components proportional to the actual number of births by order. A comparison between the approximate and exact distributions of the net rate by birth order for Poland in 1956, is presented in Table 87.

TABLE 87

Birth order	Poland 1956	
	Distribution of net reproduction rate	
	approximate	exact
1	0·461	0·447
2	0·395	0·382
3	0·282	0·279
4	0·161	0·171
5	0·087	0·093
6	0·046	0·050
7	0·023	0·027
8	0·011	0·014
9	0·006	0·007
10 and subsequent	0·006	0·008
Total	1·478	

The table reveals that, similarly to the gross reproduction rates, the approximate net rates are somewhat overstated at lower order births and somewhat understated at higher order births.

Generally speaking, however, the values of the approximate and exact rates are closer to each other in the case of the net reproduction rate. They would be identical for a stationary population structure. However, even then, the gross reproduction rates distributed proportionally to the numbers of births by order would differ from the rates obtained by accurate calculation. The results of such a distribution of the gross reproduction rate would be accurate only if all cohorts within the reproductive age were equally numerous, which is certainly not the case for a stationary population structure.

We have applied the same approximate method to find the distribution of the net reproduction rate in Chile. But Table 83, which presents the distribution of the gross reproduction rate, does not include Chile, as the incidence of error in the distribution would be too large.

Births can also be classified by duration of marriage. Most births occur within the first years after marriage; in subsequent years the frequency of births is gradually reduced, although sometimes a child may be born after twenty and more years of marital life. If we want to find the distribution of the gross or net reproduction rate by duration of marriage, we must have data on births classified by the interval of time since marriage and the age of the mother. As such data are not available, we shall confine ourselves to finding only the approximate distribution of the net reproduction rates in proportion to the number of births for particular years of married life. Just as in the case of birth order, the distribution of the net reproduction rate will presumably contain a smaller error than the distribution of the gross reproduction rate.

It should be noted that the data contained in Table 88 are strongly affected by the method of measuring the interval between marriage and the birth of a child. The correct procedure is to take the exact dates of the two demographic facts and calculate the interval between them. This method is accurate but rather complicated; for this reason some countries take into consideration the calendar year in which the marriage was contracted and the calendar year in which the birth occurred. However, by this method births from marriages of under 1 year include only those which occurred

TABLE 88

Distribution of net reproduction rate

Duration of marriage in years	Australia 1951	Sweden 1951	Switzerland 1951	Germ. Fed. Rep. 1951	Norway 1951	Yugoslavia 1951	Netherlands 1951	France 1951	Finland 1951	Denmark 1951	Belgium 1951	England and Wales 1951	Japan 1951	Israel 1951	Egypt 1947
Under 1	0·184	0·216	0·204	0·114	0·103	0·172	0·067	0·208	0·248	0·217	0·172	0·124	0·147	0·176	0·003
1	0·180	0·113	0·153	0·207	0·194	0·227	0·203	0·167	0·153	0·138	0·137	0·139	0·156	0·294	0·157
2	0·163	0·099	0·134	0·124	0·119	0·145	0·148	0·139	0·137	0·116	0·114	0·113	0·114	0·166	0·125
3	0·151	0·094	0·121	0·096	0·106	0·165	0·142	0·132	0·127	0·106	0·104	0·104	0·141	0·151	0·128
4	0·138	0·085	0·100	0·073	0·095	0·154	0·143	0·137	0·124	0·091	0·094	0·091	0·134	0·162	0·112
5	0·108	0·075	0·078	0·053	0·082	0·116	0·138	0·114	0·111	0·077	0·080	0·077	0·131	0·165	
6	0·079	0·061	0·060	0·025	0·063	0·077	0·084	0·059	0·068	0·063	0·049	0·053	0·079	0·109	
7	0·068	0·053	0·050	0·032	0·049	0·046	0·052	0·038	0·057	0·050	0·036	0·038	0·047	0·073	0·506
8	0·065	0·042	0·044	0·031	0·042	0·037	0·059	0·041	0·044	0·041	0·038	0·037	0·054	0·069	
9	0·059	0·035	0·034	0·026	0·039	0·053	0·068	0·034	0·045	0·034	0·030	0·039	0·047	0·054	
10—14	0·152	0·105	0·094	0·093	0·134	0·131	0·195	0·108	0·156		0·094	0·126	0·150	0·232	0·288
15—19	0·048	0·035	0·033	0·037	0·043	0·092	0·082	0·060	0·070	0·165	0·051	0·039	0·067	0·109	0·122
20 and more	0·014	0·008	0·007	0·009	0·012	0·052	0·024	0·019	0·025		0·014	0·011	0·025	0·054	0·048

in the same calendar year in which the parents married. Hence, the only births recorded by this method are those which took place in the last months of a given year, to parents who had married in the first months of the same year. Marriages registered in the second half of each calendar year, as a rule, are no longer listed in the group in question but in the next, labelled "1 year" etc., even though the child may have actually been born before the first anniversary of the marriage. Consequently, earlier births are understated and later births are overstated. This is of little significance in the later years of marital life, but it completely distorts the configuration of birth frequency in the first years of marriage.

The pattern is comparable to that for a birth classification by order. The relative range of rates, which is the smallest in the initial years of marriage, gradually increases with the duration of marriage. After one year of marriage the lowest rate is 0·113 (Sweden) and the highest, 0·294 (Israel); the ratio between the two is 1 : 2·6 (Israel's rate is certainly overstated at the expense of the rate relating to marriages under 1 year's duration). The extreme rates for marriages lasting from 10 to 14 years, are 0·093 (German Federal Republic) and 0·288 (Egypt); their ratio is 1 : 3·1. In the case of marriages lasting 20 years and more the two extreme rates are 0·0007 (Switzerland) and 0·054 (Israel), and their ratio is 1 : 7·7.

As before, we may ask ourselves how many years a marriage must last to ensure a net reproduction rate equal to at least 1, i.e. how many years of marriage are needed to ensure that the generation of daughters will replace the generation of mothers. To find the answer to this question we shall compute the cumulative values of birth frequencies and ascertain the duration of marriage for which the cumulative sum exceeds 1.

The cumulative values, based on the contents of Table 88, are presented in Table 89.

Hence, if the generation of mothers is to be at least replaced by the generation of daughters (assuming that there are no illegitimate births), the duration of marriage must be:

TABLE 89

Duration of marriage in years	Egypt 1947	Israel 1951	Japan 1951	Belgium 1951	Denmark 1951	England and Wales 1951	Finland 1951	France 1951
	Cumulative values of birth frequencies							
Under 1	0·003	0·176	0·147	0·172	0·217	0·134	0·248	0·208
,, 2	0·160	0·470	0·303	0·309	0·355	0·273	0·401	0·375
,, 3	0·285	0·636	0·417	0·423	0·471	0·386	0·538	0·514
,, 4	0·413	0·787	0·558	0·527	0·577	0·490	0·666	0·646
,, 5	0·525	0·949	0·692	0·621	0·568	0·581	0·789	0·783
,, 6	.	1·114	0·823	0·701	0·745	0·658	0·900	0·897
,, 7	.	1·223	0·902	0·750	0·808	0·711	0·968	0·956
,, 8	.	1·296	0·949	0·786	0·858	0·749	1·025	0·994
,, 9	.	1·365	1·003	0·824	0·899	0·786	1·069	1·035
,, 10	1·031	1·419	1·056	0·854	0·933	0·825	1·114	1·069
,, 15	1·319	1·651	1·200	0·948	.	0·951	1·270	1·177
,, 20	1·441	1·760	1·267	0·999	.	0·990	1·340	1·237
Total	1·490	1·814	1·292	1·013	1·098	1·001	1·365	1·256

Duration of marriage in years	Germ. Fed. Rep. 1951	Netherlands 1951	Norway 1951	Sweden 1951	Switzerland 1951	Yugoslavia 1951	Australia 1951
	Cumulative values of birth frequencies						
Under 1	0·114	0·067	0·103	0·216	0·204	0·172	0·184
,, 2	0·321	0·270	0·297	0·329	0·357	0·399	0·364
,, 3	0·445	0·418	0·416	0·428	0·491	0·555	0·527
,, 4	0·541	0·560	0·522	0·522	0·612	0·720	0·678
,, 5	0·614	0·703	0·617	0·607	0·712	0·874	0·816
,, 6	0·667	0·841	0·699	0·682	0·790	0·990	0·924
,, 7	0·692	0·925	0·762	0·743	0·850	1·067	1·003
,, 8	0·724	0·977	0·811	0·796	0·900	1·113	1·071
,, 9	0·755	1·036	0·853	0·838	0·944	1·150	1·136
,, 10	0·781	1·104	0·892	0·873	0·978	1·203	1·195
,, 15	0·874	1·299	1·026	0·978	1·072	1·334	1·347
,, 20	0·911	1·381	1·069	1·013	1·105	1·426	1·395
Total	0·920	1·405	1·081	1·021	1·112	1·478	1·409

in Israel	6 years
in Yugoslavia and Australia	7 years
in Finland	8 years
in the Netherlands, France and Japan	9 years
in Egypt	10 years
in Norway, Switzerland (and probably Denmark)	about 15 years
in Belgium, England and Sweden	about 20 years

Since the birth frequency within one country varies a great deal, birth rates also vary. This is illustrated by Table 90 which contains the birth rates for various voivodships in Poland in 1956, listing separately urban and rural areas.

TABLE 90

Birth rate per 1000 population	Number of voivodships		
	jointly	urban	rural
20—	2	2	—
22—	1	1	—
24—	4	4	5
26—	4	3	5
28—	2	4	—
30—	—	—	1
32—	1	1	—
34—	1	1	1
36—	2	2	2
38—	2	1	1
40—	—	—	1
42—	—	—	1
Total	19	19	17

The lowest rate is recorded for the city of Łódź (20·9) and the highest for the rural districts of the Szczecin voivodship (42·9); the latter is more than twice as high as the former.

As previously mentioned, the birth rate per 1000 population is affected not only by birth frequency but also by the age structure of the population. The ratio of the number of children under 5 to the number of women of childbearing age (i.e. from 15 to 49) is a more precise measure. The distribution of this ratio by different voivodships, listed separately for urban and rural areas, is shown in Table 91.

TABLE 91

Births per 1000 females	Number of voivodships		
	jointly	urban	rural
350—	1	1	—
375—	1	2	—
400—	1	1	—
425—	2	2	2
450—	2	5	1
475—	3	2	3
500—	2	1	3
525—	1	1	1
550—	1	1	—
575—	1	1	—
600—	2	2	1
625—	—	—	1
650—	2	—	3
675—	—	—	—
700—	—	—	1
725—	—	—	—
750—774	—	—	1
Total	19	19	17

The difference between the lowest and highest values of the rates is still quite significant, the latter being more than double the former. This proves that even after the influence of various age structures is eliminated, differences in natality within one country remain very large. Here, too, the city of Łódź and the Szczecin voivodship reveal the lowest and the highest natality respectively.

The values of the two rates (births per 1000 population and children under 5 per 1000 women of childbearing age), classified by voivodships in 1956, listed separately for urban and rural areas, are collated in Table 92.

As a rule, the patterns of the two rates agree; the higher the values of the first rate, the higher the values of the second, and *vice versa*. But there are exceptions to this rule. The Białystok voivodship has more births per 1000 population but less children per 1000 women of childbearing age than the Kielce voivodship. Judging from the first rate, the Opole voivodship has a higher natality than the Lublin voivodship,

TABLE 92

Voivodships	Births per 1000 population			Children under 5 per 1000 females aged 15—49		
	jointly	urban	rural	jointly	urban	rural
1	2	3	4	5	6	7
Poland	27·8	26·7	28·7	495	452	530
Białystok	27·9	29·8	27·2	488	462	499
Bydgoszcz	29·8	27·8	31·5	532	481	602
Gdańsk	32·2	29·9	36·4	567	522	662
Katowice.	23·3	22·5	25·6	407	386	467
Kielce	26·9	28·7	25·4	499	483	507
Koszalin	39·2	38·0	40·1	668	605	717
Kraków	25·3	24·4	25·9	465	410	501
Lublin	25·1	26·8	24·7	448	455	446
City of Łódź . .	20·9	20·9	—	363	363	—
Łódź	24·7	24·9	24·7	471	452	480
Opole	28·3	29·1	27·9	447	447	447
Olsztyn	37·6	35·3	38·7	619	561	651
Poznań	26·3	24·6	27·7	502	451	548
Rzeszów	25·8	26·7	25·6	484	456	494
Szczecin	38·9	36·1	42·9	660	600	756
City of Warsaw .	21·9	21·9	—	376	376	—
Warsaw	26·9	24·3	27·9	501	448	523
Wrocław	34·2	33·2	35·5	582	525	666
Zielona Góra . . .	36·6	36·4	36·8	614	589	638

but the second rate seems to prove that natality is the same in both voivodships. In the Białystok voivodship natality in urban areas exceeds that in rural areas according to the first rate, but the reverse is true according to the second; an analogous situation exists in the Kielce voivodship. There are other such examples.

All this goes to prove that differences in the age structure may lead to incomparability of the crude birth rates even within one country.

Natality in villages is commonly higher than in towns. The two exceptions are the Lublin voivodship where births are somewhat more frequent in urban than in rural areas, and the Opole voivodship where the number of children in both is the same. If we were to operate with crude birth rates there would be more exceptions (voivodships of Łódź, Kielce, Lublin, Białystok, Rzeszów, Opole).

TABLE 93

Voivodship j—jointly u—urban r—rural		Live births per 100 females by age groups							
		15–49	15–19	20–24	25–29	30–34	35–39	40–44	45–49
Poland	j	11·0	4·3	21·0	19·8	14·0	8·7	3·1	0·3
	u	10·0	4·7	20·4	17·5	11·3	6·5	2·1	0·2
	r	11·8	4·1	21·5	22·1	16·7	10·8	4·1	0·5
Białystok	j	11·4	3·1	20·2	19·9	15·8	10·3	2·7	0·7
	u	11·0	3·1	21·1	22·2	13·7	8·2	4·1	0·5
	r	11·5	3·0	19·7	24·7	16·7	11·2	4·5	0·3
Bydgoszcz	j	12·1	4·2	23·0	19·7	16·5	11·1	3·6	0·3
	u	10·6	4·4	21·5	26·1	13·2	8·3	2·3	0·1
	r	13·4	4·1	24·6	16·8	20·0	13·6	4·9	0·4
Gdańsk	j	12·7	5·0	23·1	18·8	15·3	10·0	2·7	0·3
	u	11·3	5·0	21·6	28·7	12·6	7·7	6·3	0·7
	r	15·4	5·0	25·8	25·5	22·0	14·6	4·3	0·6
Katowice	j	8·8	4·3	19·4	16·5	10·5	5·9	1·8	0·1
	u	8·4	4·6	19·3	15·7	9·8	5·2	1·5	0·1
	r	9·8	3·6	19·7	18·7	12·7	8·1	2·5	0·3
Kielce	j	11·1	3·8	21·1	19·2	15·3	9·5	2·6	0·6
	u	11·1	4·6	21·6	21·2	13·4	7·7	3·9	0·3
	r	11·1	3·5	20·9	18·8	16·0	10·1	2·3	0·2
Koszalin	j	15·8	7·6	27·3	23·7	18·5	12·8	3·1	0·5
	u	14·5	7·3	26·2	26·9	15·5	9·7	5·1	0·3
	r	16·7	7·7	28·3	21·9	21·4	14·9	3·8	0·8
City of Kraków	j,u	8·2	3·5	17·1	14·5	9·8	5·8	1·6	0·1
Kraków	j	10·5	3·0	17·5	19·9	15·4	10·0	4·3	0·6
	u	9·9	3·7	18·7	18·5	11·9	7·2	3·0	0·3
	r	10·7	2·8	17·1	20·4	16·7	11·6	4·8	0·6
Lublin	j	10·1	4·1	20·7	18·2	13·4	7·6	2·7	0·3
	u	10·5	4·7	21·9	18·9	12·4	6·6	2·8	0·6
	r	10·0	3·9	28·1	21·5	13·6	7·8	3·8	0·3

TABLE 93 *(cont.)*

Voivodship j—jointly u—urban r—rural		Live births per 100 females by age groups							
		15–49	15–19	20–24	25–29	30–34	35–39	40–44	45–49
City of Łódź	j,u	7·4	3·7	16·6	19·8	7·9	4·4	2·8	0·2
Łódź	j	10·2	3·7	20·6	17·8	13·6	8·6	2·0	0·3
	u	9·6	4·4	20·2	20·8	10·8	6·6	3·1	0·5
	r	10·4	3·4	20·7	20·7	15·1	9·4	3·6	0·3
Opole	j	10·3	3·4	18·0	19·5	13·6	6·1	4·2	0·3
	u	10·3	4·2	19·2	17·8	11·3	6·4	2·2	0·2
	r	10·3	3·1	17·3	20·6	14·9	6·0	5·2	0·3
Olsztyn	j	15·0	6·1	26·7	20·9	18·8	12·4	3·0	0·6
	u	13·4	6·1	23·6	27·2	14·1	8·8	5·3	6·4
	r	15·9	6·2	28·7	21·7	21·7	14·3	3·9	0·3
City of Poznań	j,u	8·3	3·3	17·8	22·3	10·0	6·1	1·8	0·2
Poznań	j	11·2	3·6	21·6	20·2	16·7	10·8	3·5	0·4
	u	10·7	3·5	20·8	23·6	14·2	8·4	4·1	0·1
	r	11·8	3·6	22·1	13·2	18·2	12·1	1·2	0·3
Rzeszów	j	10·3	2·8	17·6	19·6	14·9	10·1	4·0	0·5
	u	10·1	3·6	19·6	18·7	11·8	6·9	2·6	0·3
	r	10·3	2·6	17·0	19·8	16·0	11·2	4·4	0·6
Szczecin	j	15·1	9·0	27·1	3·6	15·3	10·4	3·9	0·5
	u	13·5	7·8	24·6	19·0	12·9	8·0	2·9	0·3
	r	17·8	10·5	31·3	27·4	19·9	14·1	5·0	0·8
City of Warsaw	j,u	8·1	4·8	18·4	22·1	8·7	4·3	1·3	0·2
Warsaw	j	11·0	3·9	21·3	16·7	14·7	9·1	3·3	0·4
	u	9·3	4·0	19·6	22·1	11·2	6·1	2·1	0·2
	r	11·7	3·8	22·0	22·9	16·2	10·1	3·7	0·5
City of Wrocław	j,u	10·7	5·6	19·2	16·5	10·2	5·8	2·1	0·2
Wrocław	j	13·8	6·8	24·2	21·2	14·9	9·6	3·4	0·4
	u	12·6	6·6	22·5	19·4	12·7	7·6	2·3	0·2
	r	14·5	7·0	26·1	23·4	17·2	11·6	4·3	0·6
Zielona Góra	j	14·7	7·6	26·1	23·4	16·6	11·0	3·9	0·5
	u	13·7	7·4	25·5	21·0	13·8	8·5	2·8	0·3
	r	15·5	7·8	26·7	25·6	19·2	13·2	4·8	0·6

Figure 35 illustrates the relation between the two rates. It is approximately linear, but the large dispersal of points proves that the relationship is not very close.

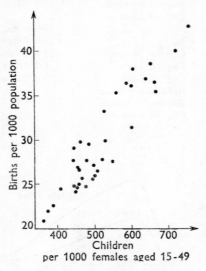

FIG. 35

Table 93 presents birth rates in Poland by age of the mother, classified by voivodships, listing separately urban and rural areas, for the years 1955—1956.[1]

The rates reveal a different pattern in urban and rural areas. In urban areas, the maximum number of births is usually noted in the 20—24 age group, and in rural areas in the 25—29 age group. The city of Łodź has the lowest fertility, but not all rates by age are the lowest in Łodź. Nor are all rural rates the highest in the Szczecin voivodship (Table 94).

The gap between the extreme rates is very large, the highest rate being two or three times as great as the lowest (the ratio is even lower for the later ages). The two curves drawn on Figure 36 bound the zone within which lie the rates for the various voivodships.

---

[1] *Małżeństwa, urodzenia i zgony (Marriages, Births and Deaths) 1955,* supplement: Płodność kobiet w latach 1950—1951 i 1955—1956. (Female Fertility in the Years 1950—1951 and 1955—1956).

TABLE 94

Age groups	Lowest rate	Highest rate
15—19	3·0 Białystok—rural	10·5 Szczecin—rural
20—24	16·6 City of Łódź	31·3 ,, ,,
25—29	13·2 ,, ,, ,,	27·4 ,, ,,
30—34	7·9 ,, ,, ,,	22·0 Gdańsk—rural
35—39	4·3 City of Warsaw	14·9 Koszalin— ,,
40—44	1·2 City of Łódź	6·3 Gdańsk— ,,
45—49	0·1 City of Łódź Bydgoszcz—urban Katowice—urban City of Cracow	0·8 Szczecin— ,,

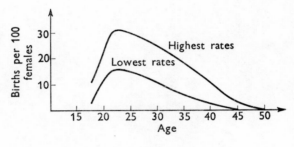

FIG. 36

Given the fertility rates for various age groups, we can compute the net reproduction rate on the basis of the life tables for 1955—1956. The gross reproduction rate can be obtained directly from fertility statistics (Table 95).

The values of the reproduction rates also vary very much from voivodship to voivodship. This is only to be expected, since the gross reproduction rate is almost exactly proportional to the number of children under 5 years of age per 1000 women of childbearing age (such proportionality renders it possible to estimate the net reproduction rate where statistics of female fertility by age are not available). The city of Łódź has the lowest rate and the rural areas of the Szczecin voivodship have the highest; the difference between these rates is more than twofold. The reproduction rate for the city of Łódź is barely sufficient to ensure that the generation of daughters

TABLE 95

Voivodships	Reproduction rate					
	gross			net		
	jointly	urban	rural	jointly	urban	rural
Poland	1·72	1·52	1·93	1·56	1·38	1·72
City of Warsaw. .	1·26	1·26	—	1·14	1·14	—
Warsaw	1·77	1·70	1·90	1·60	1·49	1·70
Bydgoszcz	1·97	1·68	2·26	1·77	1·53	2·02
City of Łódź . .	1·14	1·14	—	1·03	1·03	—
Łódź	1·67	1·50	1·76	1·50	1·37	1·57
Kielce	1·79	1·67	1·84	1·61	1·52	1·64
Lublin	1·63	1·60	1·82	1·47	1·46	1·62
City of Poznań . .	1·35	1·35	—	1·22	1·22	—
Poznań	1·90	1·69	2·02	1·71	1·54	1·80
Białystok	1·82	1·67	1·87	1·64	1·52	1·67
City of Cracow .	1·27	1·27	—	1·15	1·15	—
Cracow	1·71	1·53	1·79	1·54	1·39	1·60
City of Wrocław .	1·44	1·44	—	1·30	1·30	—
Wrocław	1·95	1·72	2·18	1·76	1·60	1·95
Gdańsk	1·92	1·67	2·50	1·73	1·52	2·23
Katowice.	1·41	1·36	1·58	1·27	1·24	1·41
Koszalin	2·34	2·06	2·54	2·11	1·88	2·26
Olsztyn	2·27	1·86	2·52	2·05	1·69	2·25
Opole	1·57	1·48	1·63	1·42	1·35	1·45
Rzeszów	1·68	1·54	1·73	1·51	1·40	1·54
Szczecin	2·13	1·83	2·64	1·92	1·67	2·36
Zielona Góra . . .	2·15	1·92	2·37	1·94	1·75	2·11

will replace the generation of mothers; in the case of the Szczecin voivodship, if the current reproduction rate continues, the population will double within 25 to 26 years. The urban rate of population growth is distinctly slower than the rural.

Table 96 presents the distribution of reproduction rates by voivodship, listed in an ascending order.

The range of rates is quite large. The net reproduction rates show some downward shifts in comparison to the gross reproduction rates. The pattern of the rural reproduction rate is less consistent than the urban; the lowest and the highest rates for the town are 1·03 and 1·88, the difference between the two being 0·85, while the respective rates for the country are 1·41 and 2·36, with a difference of 0·95.

TABLE 96

Rates	Reproduction rate					
	gross			net		
	Number of voivodships					
	jointly	urban	rural	jointly	urban	rural
1·0—1·19	1	1	—	3	3	—
1·2—1·39	3	4	—	3	6	—
1·4—1·59	3	5	1	5	8	4
1·6—1·79	6	7	5	7	4	5
1·8—1·99	5	4	3	2	1	2
2·0—2·19	2	1	2	2	—	2
2·2—2·39	2	—	2	—	—	4
2·4—2·59	—	—	3	—	—	—
2·6—2·79	—	—	1	—	—	—
	22	22	17	22	22	17

Trends in the crude birth rate over longer periods of time in selected countries are shown in Table 97 (the countries listed are the same as in Table 42 which illustrates trends in the marriage rate; the sources of the data are also the same).

TABLE 97

Year	Sweden	Denmark	France	Germany (Prussia)	England	Poland
1721	33·3	—	—	—	—	—
2	32·3	—	—	—	—	—
3	32·2	—	—	—	—	—
4	31·9	—	—	—	—	—
5	32·4	—	—	—	—	—
6	30·2	—	—	—	—	—
7	28·2	—	—	—	—	—
8	26·6	—	—	—	—	—
9	31·3	—	—	—	—	—
1730	30·1	—	—	—	—	—
1	30·1	—	—	—	—	—
2	31·0	—	—	—	—	—
3	30·4	—	—	—	—	—
4	31·4	—	—	—	—	—
5	31·4	—	—	—	—	—
6	9·8	—	—	—	—	—
7	30·5	—	—	—	—	—
8	33·6	—	—	—	—	—
9	36·4	—	—	—	—	—

TABLE 97 *(cont.)*

Year	Sweden	Denmark	France	Germany (Prussia)	England	Poland
1740	32·0	—	—	—	—	—
1	31·9	—	—	—	—	—
2	31·5	—	—	—	—	—
3	30·1	—	—	—	—	—
4	35·1	—	—	—	—	—
5	36·9	—	—	—	—	—
6	34·8	—	—	—	—	—
7	34·6	—	—	—	—	—
8	33·5	—	—	—	—	—
9	33·8	—	—	—	—	—
1750	36·4	—	—	—	—	—
1	38·7	—	—	—	—	—
2	35·9	—	—	—	—	—
3	36·1	—	—	—	—	—
4	37·2	—	—	—	—	—
5	37·5	—	—	—	—	—
6	36·1	—	—	—	—	—
7	32·6	—	—	—	—	—
8	33·4	—	—	—	—	—
9	33·6	—	—	—	—	—
1760	35·7	—	—	—	—	—
1	34·8	—	—	—	—	—
2	35·1	—	—	—	—	—
3	35·0	—	—	—	—	—
4	34·7	—	—	—	—	—
5	33·4	—	—	—	—	—
6	33·8	—	—	—	—	—
7	35·4	—	—	—	—	—
8	33·6	—	—	—	—	—
9	33·1	—	—	—	—	—
1770	33·0	—	—	—	—	—
1	32·2	—	—	—	—	—
2	28·9	—	—	—	—	—
3	25·5	—	—	—	—	—
4	34·4	—	—	—	—	—
5	35·6	—	—	—	—	—
6	32·9	—	—	—	—	—
7	33·0	—	—	—	—	—
8	34·0	—	—	—	—	—
9	36·7	—	—	—	—	—
1780	35·7	—	—	—	—	—
1	33·5	—	—	—	—	—
2	32·0	—	—	—	—	—
3	30·3	—	—	—	—	—

TABLE 97 *(cont.)*

Year	Sweden	Denmark	France	Germany (Prussia)	England	Poland
1784	31·5	—	—	—	—	—
5	31·4	—	—	—	—	—
6	32·9	—	—	—	—	—
7	31·5	—	—	—	—	—
8	33·9	—	—	—	—	—
9	32·0	—	—	—	—	—
1790	30·5	—	—	—	—	—
1	32·6	—	—	—	—	—
2	36·6	—	—	—	—	—
3	34·4	—	—	—	—	—
4	33·8	—	—	—	—	—
5	32·0	—	—	—	—	—
6	34·7	—	—	—	—	—
7	34·8	—	—	—	—	—
8	33·7	—	—	—	—	—
9	32·0	—	—	—	—	—
1800	28·7	29·9	—	—	—	—
1	30·0	31·1	32·9	—	—	—
2	31·7	32·2	33·0	—	—	—
3	31·4	33·1	32·5	—	—	—
4	31·9	32·2	31·3	—	—	—
5	31·7	32·8	31·6	—	—	—
6	30·7	30·2	31·4	—	—	—
7	31·2	31·0	31·8	—	—	—
8	30·4	30·6	31·3	—	—	—
9	26·7	29·3	32·0	—	—	—
1810	32·9	30·3	31·8	—	—	—
1	35·3	30·5	31·6	—	—	—
2	33·6	29·8	30·1	—	—	—
3	29·7	29·1	30·5	—	—	—
4	31·2	30·4	33·9	—	—	—
5	34·8	34·1	32·5	—	—	—
6	35·3	32·9	32·9	43·2	—	—
7	33·4	32·8	31·8	43·1	—	—
8	33·8	32·1	30·6	43·0	—	—
9	33·0	32·5	32·9	44·9	—	—
1820	33·0	31·5	31·7	43·1	—	—
1	35·4	32·1	31·7	44·0	—	—
2	35·9	33·7	31·7	43·8	—	—
3	36·8	32·6	31·2	42·8	—	—
4	34·6	31·3	31·6	42·7	—	—
5	36·5	31·3	31·0	42·5	—	—
6	34·8	31·4	31·4	42·9	—	—
7	31·3	29·2	30·8	39·5	—	—

TABLE 97 (*cont.*)

Year	Sweden	Denmark	France	Germany (Prussia)	England	Poland
1828	33·6	30·3	30·5	39·8	—	—
9	34·8	29·6	30·0	38·9	—	—
1830	32·9	28·9	29·9	38·7	—	—
1	30·5	29·7	30·3	37·8	—	—
2	30·9	27·0	28·6	37·0	—	—
3	34·1	32·2	29·5	40·9	—	—
4	33·7	33·0	29·8	41·7	—	—
5	32·7	31·7	29·9	39·5	—	—
6	31·8	30·5	29·2	40·2	—	—
7	30·8	30·0	28·0	40·0	—	—
8	29·4	29·8	28·5	40·2	30·3	—
9	29·5	29·0	28·2	40·0	31·7	—
1840	31·4	30·4	27·9	40·1	31·8	—
1	30·3	29·7	28·5	39·6	32·2	—
2	31·6	30·1	28·5	41·3	32·1	—
3	30·8	29·8	28·2	39·5	32·3	—
4	32·1	30·3	27·5	40·3	32·6	—
5	31·4	30·6	27·9	41·2	32·5	—
6	29·9	30·1	27·3	39·3	33·8	—
7	29·6	30·6	25·4	36·2	31·5	—
8	30·3	30·6	26·5	35·7	32·4	—
9	32·8	31·0	27·7	42·8	32·9	—
1850	31·9	31·4	26·8	41·5	33·4	—
1	31·7	30·1	27·1	40·8	34·2	—
2	30·7	33·2	26·8	40·0	34·2	—
3	31·4	31·6	26·0	38·9	33·3	—
4	33·5	32·7	25·5	38·1	34·1	—
5	31·7	31·9	25·0	36·0	33·7	—
6	31·5	32·4	26·3	36·4	34·4	—
7	32·4	32·9	25·9	40·6	34·4	—
8	34·7	33·2	26·7	41·7	33·7	—
9	35·0	33·6	27·9	42·1	35·0	—
1860	34·8	32·6	26·2	40·6	34·3	—
1	32·6	31·6	26·9	39·6	34·6	—
2	33·4	30·8	26·5	39·1	35·0	—
3	33·6	30·9	26·9	41·5	35·3	—
4	33·6	30·1	26·6	41·7	35·4	—
5	32·8	31·1	26·5	41·2	35·4	—
6	33·1	42·0	26·4	41·1	35·2	—
7	30·8	0·3	26·4	38·6	35·4	—
8	27·5	31·0	25·7	38·3	35·8	—
9	28·2	29·3	25·7	39·5	34·8	—
1870	28·8	30·3	25·5	39·9	35·2	—
1	30·4	30·1	22·9	34·5	35·0	—

TABLE 97 (cont.)

Year	Sweden	Denmark	France	Germany	England	Poland
1872	30·0	30·3	26·7	39·5	35·6	—
3	30·8	30·8	26·0	39·7	35·4	—
4	30·8	30·9	26·2	40·1	36·0	—
5	31·2	31·9	25·9	40·6	35·4	—
6	30·8	32·6	26·2	40·9	36·3	—
7	31·1	32·3	25·5	40·0	36·0	—
8	31·1	32·3	25·5	40·0	36·0	—
9	30·5	31·9	25·1	38·9	34·7	—
1880	29·4	31·7	24·6	37·6	34·2	—
1	29·1	32·2	24·9	37·0	33·9	—
2	29·3	32·3	24·8	37·2	33·8	—
3	28·9	31·8	24·8	36·5	33·5	—
4	30·0	33·3	24·7	37·2	33·6	—
5	29·4	32·5	24·3	37·0	32·9	—
6	29·8	32·4	23·9	37·1	32·8	—
7	29·7	31·7	23·5	36·9	31·9	—
8	28·8	31·5	23·0	36·6	31·2	—
9	27·7	31·2	23·0	36·4	31·1	—
1890	27·9	30·5	21·8	35·7	30·2	—
1	28·3	31·0	22·6	37·0	31·4	—
2	27·0	29·6	22·3	35·7	30·4	—
3	27·4	30·8	22·8	36·8	30·7	—
4	27·1	30·4	22·3	35·9	29·6	—
5	27·5	30·3	21·7	36·1	30·3	44·6
6	27·2	30·5	22·5	36·3	29·6	44·2
7	26·7	29·8	22·3	36·0	29·6	43·5
8	27·1	30·2	21·8	36·1	29·3	42·6
9	26·3	29·7	21·9	35·8	29·1	43·9
1900	27·0	29·7	21·4	35·6	28·7	44·0
1	27·0	29·7	22·0	35·7	28·5	43·2
2	27·0	29·7	22·0	35·7	28·5	43·2
3	25·7	28·7	21·1	33·8	28·5	41·8
4	25·7	28·9	20·9	34·1	28·0	41·8
5	25·7	28·4	20·6	32·9	27·3	41·1
6	25·7	28·5	20·5	33·1	27·2	40·9
7	25·5	28·2	19·7	32·4	26·5	40·4
8	25·7	28·6	20·1	32·1	26·7	39·5
9	25·6	28·2	19·5	31·0	25·8	39·7
1910	24·7	27·5	19·6	29·8	25·1	38·5
1	24·0	26·7	18·7	28·6	24·4	37·8
2	23·8	26·6	18·9	28·3	23·9	(37·8)
3	23·2	25·6	18·8	27·5	24·1	(35·4)
4	22·9	25·9	17·9	26·8	23·8	—
5	21·6	24·2	11·6	20·4	21·8	—

TABLE 97 (*cont.*)

Year	Sweden	Denmark	France	Germany	England	Poland
1916	21·2	24·4	9·5	15·2	21·0	—
7	20·9	23·7	10·5	13·9	17·8	—
8	20·3	24·1	12·2	14·3	17·7	—
9	19·8	22·6	12·6	20·0	18·5	30·5
1920	23·6	24·0	21·3	25·9	25·5	31·2
1	21·5	24·0	20·7	25·3	22·4	32·8
2	19·6	22·2	19·3	23·0	20·4	35·3
3	18·9	22·3	19·1	21·2	19·7	35·6
4	18·1	21·8	18·7	20·6	18·8	34·5
5	17·6	21·0	18·0	20·8	18·3	35·2
6	16·8	20·5	18·8	19·6	17·8	33·1
7	16·1	19·6	18·2	18·4	16·7	31·6
8	16·0	19·6	18·3	18·6	16·7	32·3
9	15·2	18·6	17·7	18·0	16·3	32·0
1930	15·4	18·7	18·0	17·6	16·3	32·5
1	14·8	18·0	17·5	16·0	15·8	30·2
2	14·5	18·0	17·3	15·1	15·3	29·1
3	13·7	17·3	16·2	14·7	14·4	26·6
4	13·7	17·8	16·2	18·0	14·8	26·7
5	13·8	17·7	15·3	18·9	14·7	26·2
6	14·2	17·8	15·0	19·0	14·8	26·4
7	14·4	18·0	14·7	18·8	14·9	25·0
8	14·9	18·1	14·6	19·6	15·1	24·6
9	15·3	17·8	14·6	20·4	14·8	—
1940	15·1	18·3	13·8	20·0	14·1	—
1	15·5	18·5	13·1	18·6	13·9	—
2	17·7	20·4	14·5	14·9	15·6	—
3	19·3	21·4	15·8	16·0	16·2	—
4	20·6	22·6	16·5	—	17·7	—
5	20·4	23·5	16·4	—	15·9	—
6	19·7	23·4	20·8	—	19·2	22·8
7	18·9	22·1	21·3	—	20·5	26·2
8	18·4	20·3	21·0	—	17·8	29·3
9	17·4	18·9	20·9	—	16·7	29·7
1950	16·4	18·7	20·5	—	15·8	30·7
1	15·6	17·8	19·6	—	15·4	31·0
2	15·5	17·8	19·3	—	15·3	30·2
3	15·4	17·9	18·8	—	15·4	29·7
4	15·6	17·3	18·8	—	15·1	29·1
5	14·8	17·3	18·5	—	15·0	29·1
6	14·8	17·2	18·1	—	15·6	28·1
7	14·5	16·8	18·1	—	16·1	27·6
8	14·2	16·5	18·1	—	16·4	26·3

Note: data in brackets denote very rough estimates.

Figure 37 represents the trends in birth rates in Sweden, France and Poland.

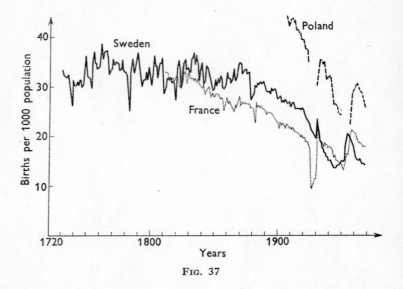

Fig. 37

The birth curve is, in general, similar to the marriage rate curve, both showing a marked drop during the war years and a compensatory rise directly after the war. The birth rate curve which is rather irregular in the sections representing the eighteenth and early nineteenth centuries, runs much more smoothly in subsequent periods, revealing a cyclic rhythm similar to that in the marriage curve. However, the general downward trend in the course of the last century or so is much more pronounced in the case of the birth rate curve. In Poland, while the marriage rate shows a slight increase over a longer period of time, the birth rate distinctly declines. It is the highest prior to World War I, much lower between the two world wars, with a strong downward trend since the economic crisis of the 1930s, and after World War II it never regained its level of the years immediately following World War I, although now it is somewhat higher than in the last interwar years. In Sweden, the marriage rate is at present higher than at the beginning of the twentieth century, but natality has diminished almost continually. In France, natality has decreased but the birth rate is higher than it was by the end of the interwar period.

The remaining countries listed in Table 97 also reveal a decreasing trend in recent years. However, this trend is not universal as is evidenced by the data in Table 98.

In recent years, the birth rate has risen or remained unchanged in the following countries listed in Table 98: South Africa (European and coloured population; the birth rate of the Asiatic population has decreased), Austria, Australia, Belgium, British Honduras, El Salvador, the Federation of

TABLE 98

Year	Birth rate						
	Argen-tina	Austra-lia	Austria	Belgium	British Hondu-ras	Bulgaria	Canada
1948	25·3	23·1	17·7	17·6	39·9	24·6	27·3
9	25·1	22·9	16·3	17·2	39·0	24·7	27·3
1950	25·5	23·3	15·6	16·9	39·4	25·1	27·1
1	25·2	23·0	14·8	16·4	41·7	21·0	27·2
2	24·7	23·3	14·8	16·7	42·1	21·1	27·9
3	25·0	22·9	14·8	16·6	40·0	20·7	28·7
4	24·4	22·5	14·9	16·8	42·0	20·1	28·5
5	24·1	22·6	15·6	16·8	43·4	20·0	28·2
6	23·9	22·5	16·6	16·8	45·5	20·0	28·0
7	23·3	22·9	17·0	17·0	43·2	18·4	28·3

Year	Czecho-slovakia	El Sal-vador	Federa-tion of Malaya	Germ. Dem. Rep.	Germ. Fed. Rep.	Guate-mala	Hawaii
1948	23·4	44·6	40·4	13·0	17·0	51·9	28·0
9	22·4	46·2	43·8	14·8	17·2	51·6	27·7
1950	23·3	48·5	42·0	16·9	16·5	50·9	28·6
1	22·8	48·8	43·6	17·4	16·0	52·3	28·1
2	22·2	48·7	44·4	17·1	16·0	50·9	29·8
3	21·2	47·9	43·7	16·8	15·8	51·1	30·8
4	20·6	48·1	43·8	16·6	16·1	51·5	31·0
5	20·3	47·9	43·0	16·7	16·0	48·8	29·1
6	19·8	47·0	45·5	16·2	16·5	48·8	29·3
7	18·9	48·9	46·2	15·9	17·0	49·4	27·8

TABLE 98 (*cont.*)

Year	Hungary	Iceland	Ireland	Israel	Italy	Japan	Mexico
1948	21·0	27·8	22·1	26·3	21·9	33·7	44·6
9	20·6	27·8	22·5	29·9	20·3	32·8	44·7
1950	21·0	28·7	22·3	33·0	19·6	28·2	45·5
1	20·2	27·5	22·3	32·7	18·4	25·4	44·6
2	19·6	27·6	22·9	31·6	17·9	23·5	43·8
3	21·6	28·2	22·2	30·2	17·5	21·5	45·0
4	23·0	27·8	22·3	27·4	18·2	20·1	46·4
5	21·5	28·4	22·1	27·2	18·1	19·4	46·4
6	19·6	28·3	22·0	26·7	18·1	18·5	46·9
7	17·0	28·7	22·2	25·9	18·2	17·2	

Year	New Zealand population		Norway	Portugal	Rumania	Spain	Swit-zerland
	white	Maori					
1948	25·6	46·0	20·5	26·7	23·9	23·3	19·2
9	25·0	44·5	19·5	25·5	27·6	21·7	18·4
1950	24·7	45·1	19·1	24·4	26·2	20·2	18·1
1	24·4	45·0	18·4	24·5	25·1	20·1	17·2
2	24·8	45·4	18·8	24·7	24·8	20·8	17·4
3	24·1	44·6	18·7	23·4	23·8	20·6	17·0
4	24·7	44·4	18·5	22·7	24·8	20·0	17·0
5	24·9	43·6	18·5	23·9	25·6	20·6	17·1
6	24·7	44·6	18·5	23·9	24·2	10·2	17·4
7	24·9	46·3	18·2	23·7	23·7	20·6	17·7

Year	South African population			United States	U.S.S.R.	Yugo-slavia	Venezu-ela
	Euro-pean	coloured	Asian				
1948	26·5	47·1	39·1	24·2	—	28·1	39·2
9	25·6	47·6	36·8	23·9	—	30·0	41·2
1950	25·1	46·9	37·9	23·5	26·5	30·2	42·6
1	25·0	47·9	35·5	24·5	26·8	27·0	43·8
2	25·2	47·7	34·8	24·7	26·4	29·7	43·7
3	25·1	47·6	35·0	24·5	25·1	28·4	46·1
4	24·6	47·5	34·8	24·9	26·6	28·5	46·7
5	24·6	46·3	34·6	24·6	25·7	26·8	47·2
6	24·2	45·7	31·2	24·9	25·2	25·9	46·7
7	25·6	49·0	32·8	25·0	25·4	23·7	45·8

Malaya, the German Democratic Republic, Hawaii, Iceland, Ireland, New Zealand (white and Maori population), Mexico, Rumania, the United States, the U.S.S.R. and Venezuela.

A decreasing birth rate usually reflects a decrease in fertility, i.e. a declining birth rate is the result of lower birth frequencies among females at all ages. Sometimes, however, the reduced birth rate may be the result of a gradual change in the age structure of the population. If in a given population the younger cohorts, i.e. those taking the most active part in the reproductive process are very numerous, then as these cohorts grow older and are replaced by less numerous cohorts, the birth rate will diminish even though female fertility remains unchanged. This may happen in countries which, having absorbed large numbers of immigrants, subsequently stopped the influx of newcomers.

Canada is an example of a country which has had a very high birth rate for a long time (Table 99).[1]

TABLE 99

Years	Birth rate
1661—1670	50·6
1671—1680	52·5
1681—1690	47·3
1691—1700	54·2
1701—1710	56·4
1711—1720	56·9
1721—1730	54·2
1731—1740	58·1
1741—1750	59·0
1751—1760	61·8
1761—1770	65·2

The birth rate can be so high only in the event of very high fertility at various ages. The fertility rates by age within the same period are listed in Table 100.

---

[1] Data on the demographic situation in Canada in the seventeenth and eighteenth centuries are based on J. HENRIPIN's *La population canadienne au début du XVIII siècle*, Paris 1954, pp. 73 and 60. The reliability of these data is corroborated by the fact that they are only slightly higher than the corresponding data relating to the province of Quebec about the year 1850, by which time Canada already had complete records on the movement of population.

TABLE 100

Females	Births per 1000 females by age groups						
	15—19	20—24	25—29	30—34	35—39	40—44	45—49
Total . . .	74	306	397	436	370	203	25
Married. . .	493	509	496	484	420	231	30

It may be assumed that the rates shown in the table are close to the physiological maximum for fertility. They are all the more interesting as they are based on reliable statistics.

A change in the birth rate is usually linked with a change in fertility in particular groups. Table 101 contains data on the change in fertility in France and Norway over a longer period of time.

Figure 38 illustrates the pattern of change in fertility rates for various age groups in France.

TABLE 101

Years	Births per 1000 females by age groups						
	15—19	20—24	25—29	30—34	35—39	40—44	45—49
France							
1851—1855	25	135	182	156	114	51	13
1856—1860	26	140	187	159	115	52	13
1861—1865	27	144	190	161	115	51	12
1866—1870	27	146	191	160	113	50	12
1871—1875	27	145	188	152	109	48	11
1876—1880	28	148	191	156	108	48	10
1881—1885	28	148	188	152	105	46	9
1886—1890	27	139	175	140	95	41	7
1891—1895	26	132	169	134	88	38	6
1896—1900	26	137	162	128	86	35	6
1901—1905	27	135	161	119	78	33	5
1906—1910	27	135	147	111	69	27	3
1911—1915	24	119	129	92	61	23	2
1916—1920	14	72	93	75	52	22	2
1921—1925	26	131	142	102	59	22	2
1926—1928	28	130	132	94	54	20	2
1929—1930	30	126	123	85	48	17	2
1936	27	120	119	79	44	16	1
1939	26	138	130	83	44	14	1
1942	20	103	121	88	52	17	1
1948	23	161	184	126	75	26	2
1952	22	153	166	118	62	22	2

TABLE 101 (*cont.*)

Years	Births per 1000 females by age groups						
	15—19	20—24	25—29	30—34	35—39	40—44	45—49
Norway							
1889—1892	7·3	97·8	199·6	224·2	203·5	123·6	—
1899—1900	11·0	115·5	203·8	220·5	192·2	14·3	—
1910—1911	10·6	105·6	186·2	188·7	165·4	93·2	—
1920—1921	12·6	109·4	175·8	166·8	138·4	75·5	—
1930—1931	8·2	70·9	112·2	105·8	79·9	42·3	—
1932—1935	7·6	63·3	101·9	94·3	67·8	34·7	—
1936—1940	8·2	67·8	107·9	96·3	62·7	28·3	—
1941—1945	11·3	83·9	127·4	113·3	75·5	29·9	—
1946—1950	15·3	99·5	125·7	133·4	89·9	36·3	—
1951—1955	21·8	129·5	152·1	116·8	72·4	28·5	—
1957	27·5	157·1	169·4	115·6	68·3	24·8	—

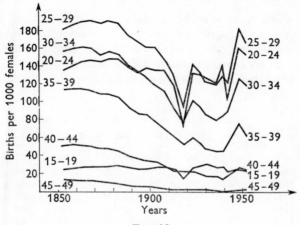

FIG. 38

The pattern is far from uniform. True, the periods of decline and rise are generally the same for all the rates (except for the fertility rate in the 45—49 age group, which drops continually), but there are large differences in the extent of change. Thus, the frequency of births among women between 30 and 34 is initially higher than among those between 20 and 24, but after the end of the nineteenth century this relation is reversed. Similarly, the frequency of births among women aged from 40 to 44 is sometimes higher and sometimes lower than among women aged 15 to 19. Consequently, the

trends in the crude birth rate cannot be taken as a basis for
any conclusions as to fertility by age. Indeed, a situation
may well arise in which fertility in certain age groups changes
inversely to the birth rate.

The rates for Norway reveal a similar disparity in the
direction of change. While the fertility rate in the 40—44
age group almost constantly decreases, other rates by age
show both periods of decline and periods of rise. Thus, in
the last year under study, the fertility rate in the 40—44 age
group is below that in the 20—24 and even in the 15—19
age groups. The level of fertility in the 35—39 age group,
originally higher, is now lower than in the 20—24 and 25—29
age groups. In 1950, the highest fertility is recorded for the
25—29 age group and not, as formerly, for the 30—34 age
group.

The pattern is somewhat more consistent when, instead
of fertility at a particular time, we consider the fertility of
particular generations. The results of such computations available for France are given in Table 102.[1]

Fertility rates in various age groups change more "smoothly",

TABLE 102

Generations	Female births in France per 1000 women by age groups						
	15—19	20—24	25—29	30—34	35—39	40—44	45—49
1826—1830	13	68	88	77	56	25	5
1831—1835	12	66	91	78	55	24	5
1836—1840	12	68	93	78	53	23	5
1841—1845	13	70	93	76	53	22	3·5
1846—1850	13	71	92	76	51	20	3
1851—1855	13	71	93	74	47	18	2·7
1856—1860	13	73	92	69	43	17	2·5
1861—1865	14	72	86	66	42	16	1·6
1866—1870	14	68	82	67	38	14	1·1
1871—1875	13	65	79	58	34	14	1·0
1876—1880	13	67	79	54	30	11	1·0
1881—1885	12	66	72	45	26	11	0·9
1886—1890	13	66	61	37	29	10	0·7
1891—1895	13	58	40	50	27	8	0·6
1896—1900	12	35	70	45	24	7	0·5
1901—1905	7	64	64	42	22	7	0·4

[1] *Reproduction nette en Europe depuis l'origine des statistiques de l'état
civil*, Paris 1941, p. 14.

but certain trends also reappear in the pattern of fertility within a generation.

Fertility continually dicreases in the three oldest groups, from 35 years upwards, irrespective as to whether the fertility rates in other age groups increase or decrease. World War I left its mark in a sharp fall in some rates followed by a rise to nearly the previous level in the 15—19 age group of the 1901—1905 generation, in the 20—24 age group of the 1896—1900 generation, in the 25—29 age group of the 1891—1895 generation and so on, moving diagonally from the lower lefthand corner to the upper righthand corner of the graph.

The pattern of fertility rates relating separately to married and single women is shown in the example of Sweden (Table 103[1]).

TABLE 103

Years	Births per 1000 married women in Sweden by age groups						
	15—19	20—24	25—29	30—34	35—39	40—44	45—49
1751—1755	—	483	416	363	246	134	31
1801—1805	—	466	379	314	226	120	26
1851—1855	—	457	373	320	247	141	22
1896—1900	620	453	350	278	212	113	14·7
1911—1920	595	398	287	220	166	87	10·7
1921—1930	588	332	220	158	114	57	7·2
1931—1940	524	266	171	119	75	32	3·6
1940	499	256	166	113	70	28	2·9
1950	556	270	170	112	65	22	2·0
1956	—	272	172	102	52	16	1·2

Years	Births per 1000 single, widowed and divorced women in Sweden by age groups						
	15—19	20—24	25—29	30—34	35—39	40—44	45—49
1871—1880	4·14	31·4	49·1	47·3	36·7	16·7	1·71
1881—1890	5·06	31·7	43·3	39·3	30·3	14·5	1·62
1891—1900	7·18	35·1	41·0	35·9	27·8	13·2	1·39
1901—1910	10·65	40·4	41·6	33·9	25·2	11·8	1·15
1911—1920	12·44	41·4	37·5	28·4	21·1	9·8	1·02
1921—1930	12·52	33·7	25·4	18·0	13·1	6·1	0·60
1931—1940	12·15	25·8	18·2	13·2	9·3	4·3	0·46
1940	12·94	23·6	17·3	12·6	7·9	3·0	0·27
1950	19·5	31·4	23·7	19·0	11·7	4·5	0·3
1956	19·6	31·4	26·8	18·2	10·2	3·6	0·2

[1] G. SUNDBÄRG, *Bevölkerungsstatistik Schwedens 1750—1900*, Stockholm 1907, p. 121; *Statistik Arsbok för Sverige 1958*.

13

As regards legitimate births, the fall is manifest for women in all age groups but the decrease starts earlier in the older groups. Thus, within the hundred years between 1750 and 1850 the fertility rate in the 45—49 age group dropped by one-third, while the rates in other age groups remained virtually unchanged. By 1900, a distinct reduction was also recorded in other groups above the age of 25, but the fertility rate in the 20—24 age group remained the same as before. After 1910 the decline in fertility also affected the 20—24 age group.

The illegitimate births have gradually decreased among women aged 25 and over (disregarding the rise in the period after World War II) and become gradually more frequent among females under the age of 20. The illegitimate birth rate in the 20—24 age group shows an increase in some periods and a decrease in others; in the 1950s it equals the 1871—1880 level.

Table 104 presents time trends in fertility rates classified by order of births and by duration of marriage.[1]

According to the data in Table 104, the frequency of higher order births decreases with time. This can be quite clearly observed from the fifth births. In the countries enumerated in Table 104, births up to the fourth inclusive reveal even an increasing trend; this trend is reversed for subsequent births.

An analogous phenomenon can be observed in respect to the length of the interval between marriage and birth. As a rule (France being perhaps the only exception), the proportion of children born after many years of married life has been on the decrease and the proportion of earlier births, in the first years of marriage, has grown larger.

The three phenomena—lower frequency of births at later ages, decrease in higher order births, and reduction of births after long duration of marriage—are of course interrelated. For births at later ages are commonly also births of higher order and usually occur after many years of married life.

Figures 39 and 40 illustrate the pattern of birth frequency in Australia by order of birth and by duration of marriage.

---

[1] *Recent Trends in Fertility in Industrialized Countries*, UNO, New York 1958, pp. 144—152.

TABLE 104

Years	Births per 1000 females aged 15—49 by order of birth					
	1	2	3	4	5—9	10 and subsequent
Australia						
1920—1924	26·4	20·1	18·6	9·3	17·3	1·7
1925—1929	23·9	18·2	12·5	8·4	15·9	1·5
1930—1934	20·0	15·3	9·8	6·4	11·8	1·1
1935—1939	23·2	15·4	8·9	5·2	8·8	0·8
1940—1944	27·6	19·1	10·3	5·4	7·6	0·6
1945—1949	31·9	25·1	13·9	6·8	7·8	0·5
1950—1954	30·2	26·7	16·7	8·4	7·7	0·5
Canada						
1930—1934	20·2	16·9	12·5	9·3	23·1	6·7
1935—1939	21·1	15·7	10·7	7·7	18·4	5·5
1940—1944	28·0	20·2	12·3	7·8	15·6	4·3
1945—1949	31·0	26·0	16·1	9·6	16·6	3·8
1950—1954	30·7	27·6	19·5	11·9	18·1	3·1
Denmark						
1930—1934	22·2	15·5	9·6	6·0	12·8	—
1935—1939	24·0	16·8	9·6	5·5	9·9	—
1940—1944	27·5	20·6	11·6	6·2	8·9	—
1945—1949	27·6	24·8	14·7	7·6	9·2	—
1950—1954	23·8	21·7	13·1	6·8	7·5	—
Norway						
1930—1934	17·7	12·0	7·9	5·3	10·1	
1935—1939	20·3	12·3	6·9	4·1	6·7	0·7
1940—1944	24·9	16·0	8·1	4·2	5·3	0·4
1945—1949	26·8	22·1	12·1	5·8	5·8	0·3
1950—1954	27·7	21·8	12·0	5·8	5·2	0·2
United States						
1930—1934	24·5	16·6	10·6	7·1	15·9	—
1935—1939	26·2	16·4	9·4	5·9	12·7	—
1940—1944	29·1	20·1	19·9	6·1	11·6	—
1945—1949	33·6	25·5	13·6	7·0	11·5	—
1950—1954	29·7	28·5	18·3	9·7	12·9	—

TABLE 104 (*cont.*)

Years	Births by duration of marriage as a percentage of total births				
	under 2	2—4	5—9	10—14	15 and over
Australia					
1920—1924	25·4	24·7	26·1	14·6	9·2
1925—1929	25·8	25·4	26·3	13·3	9·2
1930—1934	27·3	26·1	25·5	12·9	8·2
1935—1939	31·1	27·5	23·2	11·4	6·8
1940—1944	29·3	30·7	24·5	9·9	5·6
1945—1949	26·6	29·4	28·8	10·3	4·9
1950—1954	25·3	31·6	27·6	11·2	4·3
France					
1925—1929	24·5	30·3	31·5	7·1	6·6
1930—1934	23·6	29·3	27·7	15·0	4·4
1935—1939	21·7	28·6	28·3	14·3	7·1
1940—1944	24·0	22·8	25·9	16·9	10·4
1945—1949	35·1	24·5	19·4	12·6	8·4
1950—1954	29·12	31·0	25·1	8·7	6·0
Norway					
1925—1929	26·5	23·0	25·8	14·6	10·0
1930—1934	30·1	23·7	23·3	13·9	9·0
1935—1939	34·2	25·0	22·7	10·9	7·1
1940—1944	24·6	27·1	22·8	10·1	5·4
1945—1949	31·6	24·5	27·4	11·5	5·0
1950—1954	28·1	28·8	26·2	11·9	4·9
Sweden					
1925—1929	30·3	23·0	24·6	13·0	9·1
1930—1934	33·4	24·1	22·1	12·7	7·8
1935—1939	35·3	25·6	22·3	10·3	6·4
1940—1944	33·4	27·6	24·2	9·9	4·8
1945—1949	32·8	26·9	28·4	10·3	4·5
1950—1954	32·5	26·9	26·0	10·4	4·2

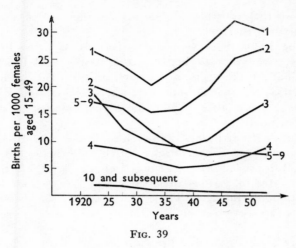

FIG. 39

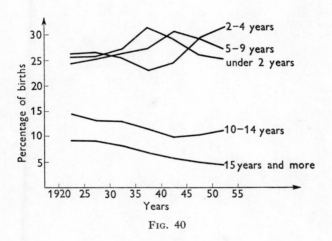

FIG. 40

The curves on the two graphs are quite irregular. Some
rise when others fall; different curves reach their lowest
points at different times; some curves continually decrease
while others alternately rise and fall. In the 1920s, third births
were nearly as numerous as second births; in the 1950s they
were much less frequent. Similarly, fifth to ninth births used
to be almost equal in number to third births and much more

numerous than fourth births; at present they are outnumbered by fourth births.

In the 1920s there were approximately as many births in the first two years as between the second and fourth and the fifth and ninth years of marriage; in the 1950s most births occurred within two to four years after the wedding. The frequency of births after 15 and more years of marriage is falling continually.

A study of birth rate trends for smaller territorial units within one country seems to prove that the existing differences also tend to prevail in the event of a changing level of fertility.

Birth rates in various departments of Norway are a good illustration of this fact. Table 105 presents the distribution of birth rates over nearly 50 years.

TABLE 105

Birth rate per 1000 population	1911—1915	1921—1925	1931—1935	1941—1945	1951—1955
			Number of departments		
8 —	—	—	1	—	—
10 —	—	—	—	—	—
12 —	—	—	3	1	1
14 —	—	1	7	—	1
16 —	—	—	7	7	6
18 —	—	2	2	5	5
20 —	3	3	—	4	4
22 —	6	9	1	3	2
24 —	4	3	—	—	1
26 —	6	1	—	—	—
28 —	1	—	—	—	—
30 —	—	1	—	—	—
32 —	—	—	—	—	—
34 —	1	—	—	—	—
Total	20	20	20	20	20
Rates: lowest	21·4	14·1	8·2	12·9	13·1
highest	34·9	30·8	22·6	23·0	25·7
Range	13·5	16·7	14·4	10·1	12·6

Changes take place more or less as if the whole configuration of rates shifted either to a higher or to a lower level, without substantially altering the proportions between the rates in various departments. The dispersion is larger in some periods and smaller in others. A department which had the lowest or the highest birth rate in one period, usually maintains its place in other periods. The table by no means reveals a consistent tendency to level out the birth rate in various parts of the country.

Gross and net reproduction rates change along with the birth rate. Over a short period the relation between these rates is linear, and the two reproduction rates are roughly proportional. The relationship results from the fact that the ratio of the net reproduction rate to the gross reproduction rate roughly equals the probability of survival from infancy to an age equivalent to the mean length of a generation; since neither the length of a generation nor mortality are subject to rapid change, the ratio of the two reproduction rates reveals no significant change. Table 106 contains the values of the three rates in Poland.[1]

TABLE 106

Type of rate	1931	1950	1951	1952	1953	1954	1955	1956	1957	1958
Birth rate	29·8	30·7	31·0	30·2	29·7	29·1	29·1	28·1	27·6	16·3
Gross reproduction rate	1·650	1·790	1·806	1·765	1·751	1·732	1·742	1·695	1·687	1·621
Net reproduction rate	1·186	1·491	1·504	1·537	1·526	1·510	1·519	1·478	1·472	1·462

A graphic representation of the contents of Table 106 is given in Fig. 41.

The curves representing the three rates are almost exactly parallel; a rise or a fall in one of them is reflected in the other two. The net reproduction rate in 1952 is the only exception showing an increase as compared with the preceding year, while the other two rates decreased over the same period. This was due to the introduction of a new life table in 1952 for the computation of net reproduction rates. Since the level of mortality presented in the new table was much lower than in the preceding period, the result was a di-

[1] *Rocznik statystyczny (Statistical Yearbook) 1959,* pp. 25 and 30.

vergence in the direction of the curves. Had the computations been made properly, i.e. had a modified life table been used for each consecutive year, the harmony between the rates would certainly have remained undisturbed.

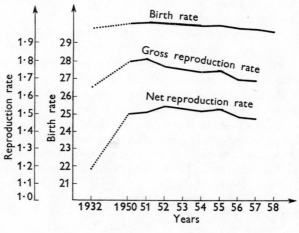

Fig. 41

A striking difference can be observed as compared with the interwar years. The span between the two reproduction rates has greatly diminished, which may be ascribed to the decline in mortality since the end of the last war; in fact, the difference between the two rates still continues to diminish at present. Changes in the birth rate are relatively small, but the gross and net reproduction rates fluctuate noticeably from year to year.

Thus, the small changes in the birth rate disguise much more substantial changes in fertility. The difference in the pattern of rates stems from the age structure of the Polish population, a structure which bears visible marks of the two world wars. The rule is that if the age distribution of a population is stable, changes in the general birth rate agree in direction and value with changes in fertility rates by age; the less stable the age distribution the weaker the correlation between the rates. The age structure of the Polish population

is definitely far from being a stable age distribution under
current conditions of mortality and fertility; that is why the
birth rate is so insensitive to changes in fertility rates by age.

Table 107 presents the rates in Japan, where the birth rate
dropped to nearly one-half its previous value in the postwar
years, and in Ceylon, where mortality also declined rapidly
after the last war. In the case of Ceylon, in view of incomplete
statistics of the population movement in that country, the
figures listed are approximate only.

TABLE 107

Type of rate	1946	1947	1948	1949	1950	1951	1952	1953	1954	1955
Japan										
Birth rate	25·3	34·3	33·7	32·8	28·2	25·4	23·5	21·5	20·1	19·4
Gross reproduction rate	—	2·259	2·105	2·092	1·765	1·582	1·444	—	—	—
Net reproduction rate	—	1·78	1·722	1·729	1·516	1·382	1·292	—	—	—
Ceylon										
Birth rate	38·4	39·4	40·6	39·9	40·4	40·5	39·5	39·4	—	—
Gross reproduction rate	3·54	—	—	—	—	3·72	3·66	—	—	—
Net reproduction rate	1·442	—	—	—	—	—	1·987	—	—	—

Beginning from 1947, the birth rate in Japan has steadily
and quite rapidly decreased.

The gross reproduction rate is also decreasing. However,
the change in the net reproduction rate does not fully agree
with that in the other two rates; after increasing slightly
until 1949, it then began to decrease. Figure 42 gives a very
clear graphic picture of the changes in the three rates.

To enable a more detailed study of the relationship between
the rates a correlation graph has been drawn (Fig. 43) showing
the values of the two reproduction rates, corresponding to
various values of the birth rate. The points for the gross reproduction rate lie very close to the straight line, but those
for the net reproduction rate reveal distinct deviations from the
straight line (Fig. 44). It should also be noted that if we drew

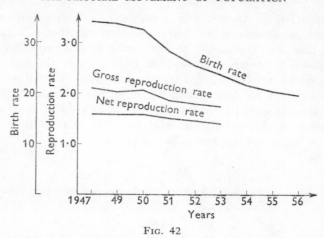

FIG. 42

the regression lines of the two reproduction rates in relation to the birth rate, the two lines would intersect near the
point which represents a rate of 20 births per 1000 population.
In other words, it is at this value of the birth rate that the
two reproduction rates would be equal, which is of course
impossible. The reason for this is that whilst it is possible
to estimate the gross reproduction rate on the basis of the
birth rate, even when the birth rate is subjected to rapid
changes, it is not possible to estimate the net reproduction
rate on the basis of the same birth rate.

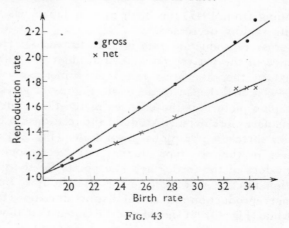

FIG. 43

The situation in Ceylon is different in that the birth rate and the gross reproduction rate remain virtually unchanged, but the net reproduction rate is subject to radical changes owing to the rapid decrease in mortality. In this connection we have found it possible to estimate the values of the gross reproduction rate not recorded for the years 1947—1950, but we have not endeavoured to compute the values of the net reproduction rate for those years.

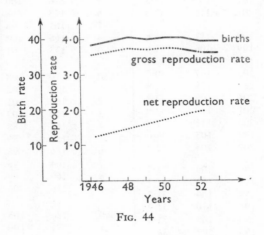

FIG. 44

The gross and net reproduction rates and the birth rate in France in the years 1806—1955 are shown in Table 108. Table 109 contains the gross and net reproduction rates in selected countries at five-year intervals between 1800 and 1955.

In Tables 108 and 109, the gross and net reproduction rates are computed per 100 females, i.e. they are 100 times higher than the rates quoted earlier in this chapter.

The pattern of reproduction rates (and of the birth rate per 1000 population, for purposes of comparison) in France is represented graphically in Fig. 45.

Fluctuations in the net reproduction rate generally follow the same trend as those in the gross reproduction rate. However, the net rate remains at approximately the same level, i.e. about 1, while the gross reproduction rate reveals a slow

TABLE 108

Year	Reproduction rate		Birth rate	Year	Reproduction rate		Birth rate
	gross	net			gross	net	
1806	197	105	31·4	1843	178	102	28·2
7	200	104	31·8	4	174	105	27·5
8	197	107	31·3	5	176	109	27·9
9	201	110	32·0	6	173	98	27·3
				7	161	96	25·4
1810	200	111	31·8	8	168	100	26·5
1	199	106	31·6	9	175	91	27·7
2	189	108	30·1				
3	192	107	30·5	1850	170	108	26·8
4	213	108	33·9	1	171	102	27·1
5	204	109	32·3	2	169	101	26·8
6	207	119	32·9	3	174	102	26·0
7	200	111	31·8	4	161	88	25·5
8	192	103	30·6	5	158	89	25·0
9	207	104	32·9	6	166	98	26·3
				7	164	95	25·9
1820	199	109	31·7	8	169	99	26·7
1	199	109	31·7	9	176	92	27·9
2	199	104	31·7				
3	196	110	31·2	1860	166	105	26·2
4	198	108	31·6	1	171	100	26·9
5	195	103	31·0	2	169	105	26·5
6	197	101	31·4	3	172	105	26·9
7	194	109	30·8	4	171	105	26·6
8	192	101	30·5	5	172	100	26·5
9	189	109	30·0	6	172	105	26·4
				7	173	107	26·4
1830	188	107	29·9	8	170	100	25·7
1	191	108	30·3	9	170	103	25·7
2	180	97	28·6				
3	185	105	29·5	1870	168	93	25·5
4	187	92	29·8	1	150	69	22·9
5	186	108	29·9	2	175	109	26·7
6	184	111	29·2	3	171	105	26·0
7	176	103	28·0	4	172	111	26·2
8	180	102	28·5	5	171	108	25·6
9	178	105	28·2	6	174	111	26·2
1840	176	103	27·9	7	170	110	25·5
1	180	104	28·5	8	168	107	25·5
2	180	103	28·5	9	168	109	25·1

TABLE 108 (*cont.*)

France

Year	Reproduction rate		Birth rate	Year	Reproduction rate		Birth rate
	gross	net			gross	net	
1880	164	104	24·6	1918	75	46	12·2
1	166	106	24·9	9	78	58	12·6
2	166	106	24·8				
3	165	106	24·8	1920	129	98	21·3
4	165	104	24·7	1	126	98	20·7
5	162	105	24·3	2	118	97	19·3
6	158	100	23·9	3	117	94	19·1
7	156	101	23·5	4	114	93	18·7
8	154	101	23·0	5	116	94	18·0
9	152	102	23·0	6	115	92	18·8
				7	113	93	18·2
1890	144	95	21·8	8	113	92	18·3
1	148	98	22·6	9	109	89	17·7
2	145	95	22·3				
3	148	98	22·8	1930	111	93	18·0
4	144	99	22·3	1	110	93	17·5
5	110	95	21·7	2	109	92	17·3
6	145	101	22·5	3	103	88	16·2
7	144	102	22·3	4	105	90	16·2
8	141	97	21·8	5	100	87	15·3
9	141	96	21·9	6	101	88	15·0
				7	102	89	14·7
1900	138	95	21·4	8	104	91	14·6
1	142	100	22·0	9	106	93	14·6
2	140	101	21·0				
3	136	98	21·1	1940	97	82	13·8
4	135	97	20·9	1	90	77	13·1
5	133	97	20·6	2	98	85	14·5
6	137	95	20·5	3	105	90	15·8
7	126	93	19·7	4	109	94	16·5
8	128	96	20·1	5	112	93	16·4
9	124	95	19·5	6	145	126	20·8
				7	146	131	21·3
1910	125	96	19·6	8	145	133	21·0
1	119	87	18·7	9	145	133	20·9
2	121	94	18·9				
3	119	92	18·8	1950	145	132	20·5
4	114	88	17·9	1	135	126	19·6
5	75	57	11·8	2	133	125	19·3
6	59	45	9·5	3	130	124	18·8
7	63	48	10·5	4	132	125	10·8
				5	131	124	18·5

TABLE 109

Years	Gross reproduction rate					Net reproduction rate				
	Eng-land	Fran-ce	Ger-many	Italy	Swe-den	Eng-land	Fran-ce	Ger-many	Italy	Swe-den
1801—1805	—	—	—	—	207	—	—	—	—	125
1806—1810	—	199	—	—	199	—	108	—	—	100
1811—1815	—	199	—	—	210	—	108	—	—	119
1816—1820	—	201	269	—	216	—	109	138	—	131
1821—1825	—	197	264	—	232	—	107	135	—	152
1826—1830	—	192	242	—	225	—	105	127	—	141
1831—1835	—	186	238	—	222	—	103	121	—	144
1836—1840	—	179	240	—	214	—	105	130	—	
1841—1845	212	177	242	—	213	130	104	133	—	
1846—1850	214	169	234	—	206	127	99	128	—	136
1851—1855	218	165	228	—		132	96	125	—	133
1856—1860	228	168	238	—	215	136	98	133	—	135
1861—1865		171	247	—	221	139	103	137	—	144
1866—1870	232	171	248	24	203	145	102	138	114	132
1871—1875	235	168	255	23	214	151	100	143	114	147
1876—1880	235	169	260	240	216	158	108	153	120	143
1881—1885	222	165	247	247	207	152	105	146	128	142
1886—1890	206	153	244	245	205	142	99	148	130	147
1891—1895	194	145	238	236	195	135	97	150	133	142
1896—1900	181	141	234	224	193	129	98	154	135	143
1901—1905	170	137	222	216	186	126	98	151	135	142
1906—1910	167	127	203	218	178	121	95	146	141	142
1911—1915	142	110	164	209	158	111	84	121		128
1916—1920	119	80	104	159	141	93	59	74	89	111
1921—1925	117	118	122	190	124	98	95	97	137	106
1926—1930	99	112	98	169	99	85	92	83	126	86
1931—1935	89	106	90	149	86	77	90	79	117	77
1936—1940	87	102	106	—	87	78	89	99	115	78
1941—1945	97	103	—	—	113	91	88	—	—	104
1946—1950	117	145	—	—	118	112	131	—	—	111
1951—1955	104	132		—	107	100	125	—	—	102

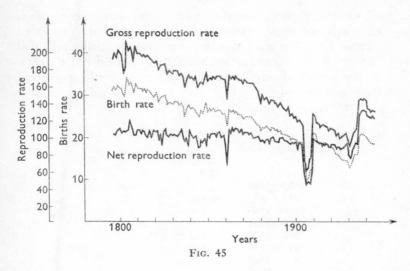

FIG. 45

but steady decline beginning from the 1820s until the years
between the two world wars, when it climbs to a level above
1·10. In consequence, the gross rate which originally was
nearly twice as high as the net rate, is now higher by ten to
twenty per cent only; this is the result of a substantial reduction in mortality.

Fluctuations of the birth rate are very similar to those
of the net reproduction rate both as regards the direction of
change and the prevailing trend throughout the period under
examination. Only in the 1860s and 1870s did the two curves
"drift apart". The explanation for this similarity can be
found in the fairly close relationship between the gross reproduction rate and the birth rate; indeed, we might venture
to estimate the gross reproduction rate on the basis of the
birth rate if the pertinent regression formula could be derived.

The values of gross and net reproduction rates in various
other countries also show a gradual reduction in the difference between the two rates. They reveal, moreover, that
a higher gross reproduction rate is not necessarily accompanied by a higher net reproduction rate; for the level of mortality varies from country to country.

Reproduction rates, like fertility rates, may be computed

both for a given period of time and for particular generations. The results of such computations for France are presented in Table 110.[1] For purposes of comparison we have included in the table the reproduction rates for a period of 30 years, (i.e. the length of one generation) after the birth of a given female generation.

TABLE 110

Years of birth	Gross reproduction rate	
	of the generation	30 years later
1826—1830	166	168
1831—1835	166	171
1836—1840	166	171
1841—1845	165	168
1846—1850	163	169
1851—1855	160	165
1856—1860	154	153
1861—1865	149	145
1866—1870	140	141
1871—1875	131	137
1876—1880	128	127
1881—1885	116	110
1886—1890	109	80
1891—1895	101	118
1896—1900	97	112
1901—1905	103	106

Apart from the perturbations caused by World War I (decrease of births in war years, rapid increase of births immediately after the war), which affected the cohorts born between 1881 and 1900, the agreement is very good. Thus, the gross reproduction rate at a given time may be regarded to be roughly equal to the gross rate for persons born one generation earlier. Such a correlation does not occur in the case of the net reproduction rate.

Computations have also been made of changes in the reproduction rate for various departments of France between the years 1860 and 1932 (Table 111[2]). The data listed in

---

[1] *Reproduction nette en Europe depuis l'origine des statistiques de l'état civil*, Paris 1941, p. 14.

[2] *Ibid.*, pp. 24—25.

the table are a good illustration of the trends in reproduction rates prevailing in smaller territorial units within one country.

Gross reproduction rates are decreasing here, and in some periods (in 1890—1892 as compared with 1860—1862) the dispersion tends to increase; other periods (1930—1932) are marked by a reduction in the dispersion. The same trend is revealed by net reproduction rates, the only difference being that their general level remains approximately unchanged, concentrating around 1 (in the table at around 100) during the entire period under consideration.

TABLE 111

Reproduc- tion rate	Gross				Net			
	1860— —1862	1890— —1892	1910— —1912	1930— —1932	1860— —1862	1890— —1892	1910— —1912	1930— —1932
	Number of departments							
60—	—	—	—	—	—	5	2	2
70—	—	—	—	—	3	9	9	7
80—	—	—	3	3	10	17	16	11
90—	—	2	5	10	27	18	20	22
100—	—	4	9	13	27	28	28	26
110—	1	5	18	21	14	8	9	13
120—	4	12	15	15	8	1	2	9
130—	9	12	16	16	—	3	3	—
140—	7	19	13	9	—	1	1	—
150—	15	11	4	1	—	—	—	—
160—	12	9	1	—	—	—	—	—
170—	14	3	4	—	—	—	—	—
180—	9	5	1	—	—	—	—	—
190—	9	5	1	—	—	—	—	—
200—	5	—	—	—	—	—	—	—
210—	4	2	—	—	—	—	—	—
220—	—	—	—	—	—	—	—	—
230—	—	1	—	—	—	—	—	—
Total	89	90	90	90	89	90	90	90

We have noted above the existence of a fair degree of consistency (i.e. a fairly close relationship) between the changes in the birth rate and in the gross reproduction rate. Such a relationship exists not only for various periods within one country but also for various countries (in the same period

14

or for various periods). The values of the two rates computed for selected countries in which vital statistics are reliable (in Demographic Yearbooks such statistics are coded C for "complete") are presented in Table 112.

TABLE 112

Country	Year	Birth rate per 1000 population	Gross reproduction rate
Algeria —European population	1948	21·8	1·400
United States	1950	23·5	1·505
Israel	1948	26·3	1·665
Japan	1950	28·2	1·765
Australia	1957	24·1	1·943
New Zealand —European population	1951	24·4	1·640
Austria	1951	14·8	0·986
Denmark	1950	18·6	1·257
England and Wales	1951	16·9	1·045
Finland	1950	24·5	1·530
France	1953	18·7	1·300
Germ. Fed. Rep.	1950	16·2	1·012
Norway	1950	19·1	1·210
Poland	1955	29·1	1·742
Portugal	1950	24·4	1·483
Spain	1940	24·5	1·418
Sweden	1950	16·4	1·105
Switzerland	1950	18·1	1·250

Figure 46 represents the relation between the two rates.

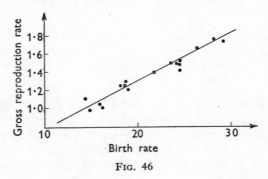

FIG. 46

The regression equation is:

$$g = 0 \cdot 053b + 0 \cdot 236$$

where:

$g =$ gross reproduction rate, and
$b =$ birth rate per 1000 population.

According to the graph, the relationship is fairly accurate, as the points lie very close to the regression line. Hence, given the birth rate, the gross reproduction rate can be estimated with considerable accuracy (Table 113).

The net reproduction rate cannot be linked by such a linear function either to the birth rate or even to the gross reproduction rate. To arrive even at an approximate estimate of the net reproduction rate we must find some other way.

As previously ascertained, the net reproduction rate is related to the number of children under 5 per 1000 women

TABLE 113

Country	Year	Children under 5 per 1000 females aged 15—49	Net reproduction rate
Algeria —European population	1948	341	1·240
United States	1950	417	1·435
Israel	1948	434	1·525
Japan	1950	527	1·516
Australia	1947	395	1·416
New Zealand —European population	1951	491	1·578
Austria	1951	293	0·911
Denmark	1950	393	1·140
England and Wales	1951	335	1·001
Finland	1950	476	1·379
France	1953	390	1·240
Germ. Fed. Rep.	1950	257	0·933
Norway	1950	387	1·107
Poland	1955	494	1·519
Portugal	1950	398	1·082
Spain	1940	322	1·010
Sweden	1950	348	1·058
Switzerland	1950	335	1·145

of childbearing age. Using the data of Table 62 for the same countries as listed in Table 112, we shall try to examine whether the relation is sufficiently close to supply a basis for our estimates.

The regression equation is:

$$n = 0 \cdot 00346c - 0 \cdot 116$$

where:

n = net reproduction rate, and

c = number of children under 5 per 1000 women of child-bearing age.

The regression line and the points representing the values of the two rates are shown on Figure 47.

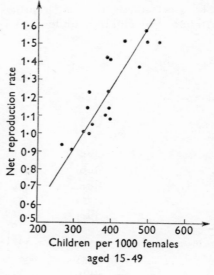

FIG. 47

The relationship is less close than in the case of the previous two rates, but the straight line does represent the general trend fairly accurately. Deviations from the line (counted vertically, i.e. on the basis of the value of the reproduction rate) and, hence, the differences between the actual value and the value derived from the regression equation, generally, do not exceed some 10% of the actual value.

By using these two equations we can estimate reproduction rates related to countries in which either the child-woman ratio at childbearing age or the birth rate is the only statistical information available. The child-woman ratio can be regarded as fairly reliable since it is calculated from census returns which usually do not contain large errors in so far as the age structure of the population is concerned (a large error may occur in the event of an insufficiently detailed study of the age distribution, e.g. when the age groups under examination are few and very large).

TABLE 114

Country	Year	Reproduction rate	
		gross	net
Algeria			
—Moslem population	1948	—	2·08
Angola	1950	—	1·76
Egypt	1947	—	1·76
Mauritius	1951	2·79	2·45
Mozambique	1940	—	2·58
Alaska	1950	—	1·84
Argentina	1947	—	1·35
Brazil	1950	—	2·14
British Honduras	1950	2·33	2·19
Chile	1940	2·063	1·19
Ecuador	1950	—	2·30
Mexico	1950	2·68	2·05
Nicaragua	1950	—	2·13
Panama	1950	—	2·29
Paraguay	1950	—	2·29
Peru	1940	—	2·15
Puerto Rico	1950	—	2·39
Venezuela	1950	—	2·34
Ceylon	1946	2·28	1·76
India	1951	—	1·79
Korea, South	1952	—	1·71
Federation of Malaya	1947	2·60	1·84
Philippines	1948	—	2·23
Turkey	1950	—	1·99
Cook Islands	1951	—	2·69
Fiji Islands	1946	2·41	2·70
New Zealand			
—Maori population	1951	—	2·79

Not everywhere is the birth rate reliable. We have confined ourselves, therefore, to estimating the gross reproduction rate only for those countries in which vital statistics are complete. Wherever an inconsistency was noted between the two estimates, e.g. the difference between the gross and net reproduction rates was too small, the gross rate, as the less accurate of the two, was excluded. In any event, the rates listed in Table 114 should be regarded with caution, as they are based on rough estimates only in the absence of reliable information.

CHAPTER 6

DEATHS

DEATHS follow births as the second factor influencing the pattern of population structure in a given area. The number of deaths is usually smaller than the number of births and larger than the number of marriages. Deaths depend on a great many demographic and non-demographic factors. The demographic factors include age, sex, marital status, profession, place of residence (urban or rural).

In so far as death records are concerned, the notion of death has undergone a certain evolution. In earlier times, (e.g. in Prussia), stillbirths were included in death records. At present, a distinction is made between stillbirths and post--natal deaths, and the former are registered separately. Although there can hardly be any doubt as to the fact of death, mortality statistics are not everywhere complete. Sometimes, this results from the fact that the statutory time allowed for death registration is too long. If a death certificate is necessary to obtain permission for burying the deceased person, as is often the case, death records are more complete. But in the event of live-born children who die in the neo-natal period there is a tendency to record their deaths as stillbirths; the tendency, whether stronger or weaker, is bound to distort deaths statistics.

The death rate is the most common but also the least accurate measure of the frequency of deaths. It is the number of deaths in a calendar year per 1000 population. Like crude nuptiality and natality rates, crude mortality rates are not strictly comparable from country to country or from one period of time to another in the same country, because they are a function of many factors which are subject to time changes (the composition of the population by sex, age, marital status and other demographic characteristics). Crude death rates should therefore be considered with caution and should not be taken as a basis for far-reaching conclusions.

The frequency of death is relatively high among infants; consequently, the larger the proportion of young children the higher the death rate, even though mortality at the later ages may remain the same in each case. If we want to know exactly the trends in mortality or the differences in mortality between two countries, the best method of obtaining an accurate reply is to use death rates by age. If it is preferable to deal with one index only, a standardized mortality rate may be computed on the basis of some uniform age structure of the population. This is absolutely necessary when studying differences in death rates for specific occupations because if we took the crude death rate as the basis for our considerations we might arrive at entirely wrong conclusions. In other cases, standardization of mortality rates although helpful is not always necessary. Moreover, there are other methods of characterizing mortality by means of one index only, completely eliminating the effect of differences in the structure of the population. Such an index is the mean expectation of life at birth.

I shall confine myself to stating, without going into the details of these problems, that the use of standardized mortality rates is restricted to comparing mortality over prolonged periods of time within one country; it is not used for comparing mortality in different countries. Life expectancy is the value used for country-to-country comparison.

Table 115[1] presents the crude death rate in various countries about the year 1957, as given in official statistics.

The incompleteness of statistics is here perhaps even more striking than in the case of birth rates. For, if a population has a stable age distribution, the death rate is the reciprocal of life expectancy at birth; and although human populations hardly ever reach actual stability, the mortality rate cannot deviate too much from the reciprocal of life expectancy at birth.

If we accept this criterion, we are immediately faced with a multitude of inconsistencies. To begin with, a death rate under 10 per 1000 population would roughly correspond to a life expectancy at birth equalling 100 years. This is a rate which can occur only in a population which has a low mortal-

---

[1] *Demographic Yearbook 1958.*

ity and an appropriate age structure, i.e. a structure characterized by very large cohorts in the reproductive age. Accordingly, we cannot question the value of the death rate for
Israel, the Netherlands, the U.S.S.R., Canada, Japan or
Poland, these countries having a mortality rate under 10,
although in each of these countries the average expectation
of life at birth does not exceed 70 years. All death rates under
5·0 seem completely improbable; but they are met with only
in under-developed countries where the registration of demographic facts is known to be very incomplete as yet. With
the exception of economically advanced countries, the death
rate between 5·0 and 9·9 recorded for the majority of countries
is also doubtful. Some of the death rates in the range between
10·0 and 14·9 in the case of under-developed countries may
also be considered questionable. It seems that, since the
birth rate in those countries is usually above 30 per 1000
population, the death rate can hardly be less than 20 per
1000. Considering the rapid growth of population, this would
correspond to a life expectancy at birth not exceeding 55
years.

In the countries where the life expectancy at birth is much
lower (e.g. 30 years), the death rate is bound to be far higher
and reach an order of magnitude of 30 to 40 per 1000 population. Among the countries listed in Table 115 there is only
one—Guinea—which notes a death rate as high as 40 per
1000 population; but this rate was not computed on the
basis of death records but by means of a sample survey
covering a small portion of the country.

If the birth rate is known for a given country and is considered to be more reliable, the estimated death rate may be
found by subtracting the annual natural increase from the
birth rate. The value of the natural increase may be computed
quite accurately on the basis of two consecutive population
censuses provided, of course, that censuses do take place in
the country in question.

Another important index, besides the general death rate,
is the infant mortality rate which is computed as a ratio
of deaths of children under one year of age to the total number
of live births. The infant mortality rate depends, perhaps
even more than the general death rate, on the completeness

TABLE 115

Deaths per 1000 population

Under 5·0	5·0—9·9	10·0—14·9	15·0—19·9	20 and more
Bechuanaland 3·5	Iraq 5·0	Czechoslovakia 10·0	Greenland 15·3	Brazil 20·6
Congo	Lebanon 5·1	Italy 10·0	Ruanda-Urundi	Guatemala 20·6
—European pop. 3·8	Hawaii 5·6	Spain 10·0	—indigenous	Ghana 20·8
Ruanda Urundi	Cuba 5·7	Switzerland 10·0	population 15·4	Burma 21·2
—European pop. 4·6	Southern Rhodesia	Venezuela 10·0	Gambia 16·0	Congo
Korea, South 4·7	—European pop. 6·0	Martinique 10·0	Norfolk Island 16·1	—indigenous
Mozambique 4·9	Alaska 6·0	Guadeloupe 10·0	Egypt 16·4	population 21·6
	Bahamas 6·2	Ceylon 10·1	Cook Islands 16·6	Sierra Leone 22·0
	Cyprus 6·3	New Zealand	China 17	Timor 22·3
	French West Africa	—European pop. 10·1	Sudan 18·5	St. Thomas 22·7
	—European pop. 6·5	Costa Rica 10·1		India 27·4
	Israel 6·5	Rumania 10·2		Guinea 40
	Angola 6·8	Honduras 10·4		
	Ifni 6·8	Samoa 10·5		
	Puerto Rico 7·0	Hungary 10·6		
	Uruguay 7·0	Yugoslavia 10·6		
	Iceland 7·0	Algeria		
	Netherlands 7·5	—Moslem pop. 10·7		

Country	Rate	Country	Rate
Fiji Islands	7·5	British Honduras	11·1
Guiana	7·6	Paraguay	11·2
U.S.S.R.	7·8	Germ. Fed. Rep.	11·3
Nicaragua	8·1	Portugal	11·4
Bermuda	8·2	England and Wales	11·5
Canada	8·2	British Guiana	11·6
Spanish Guinea	8·2	Peru	11·7
Japan	8·3	Albania	11·8
Iran	8·3	Belgium	11·9
Taiwan	8·5	Ireland	11·9
Surinam	8·6	Pakistan	11·9
Jordan	8·6	St. Helena	12·0
Norway	8·6	France	12·1
Dominican Republic	8·6	Luxemburg	12·1
Andorra	8·7	Federation of Malaya	12·4
Argentina	8·7	Cape Verde Islands	12·4
Philippines	8·8	Channel Islands	12·5
Bolivia	8·8	Madagascar	12·6
Australia	8·8	Southern Rhodesia	12·6
New Zealand	8·8	Germ. Dem. Rep.	12·6
—European pop.	9·3		

TABLE 115 (cont.)

		Deaths per 1000 population		
Under 5·0	5·0—9·9	10·0—14·9	15·0—19·9	20 and more
	Denmark 9·3	Portuguese Guinea 12·7		
	Panama 9·4	Togoland		
	North Borneo 9·4	—indigenous population 12·8		
	Thailand 9·4	Australia 12·8		
	Bulgaria 9·4	Chile 12·8		
	Finland 9·4	Mexico 12·9		
	Poland 9·5	Mauritius 13·0		
	United States 9·6	Colombia 13·1		
	Algeria	Portuguese India 13·4		
	—European pop. 9·7	Virgin Islands 13·1		
	Syria 9·9	Monaco 13·5		
		French Guinea 13·8		
		El Salvador 14·0		
		Indonesia 14·2		
		Nigeria 14·2		
		Ecuador 14·8		

of statistics in various countries; for, each of the two numbers which determine the value of the infant mortality rate may frequently contain a large error, while in the case of the general death rate we can be certain that at least the divisor, i.e. the number of population, is fairly accurate. The infant mortality rate is usually computed per 1000 or 100 births. Infant mortality rates in selected countries around the year 1957 are listed in Table 116.[1]

The comments made on the general death rate are also valid for the infant mortality rate. Some countries show unexpectedly low infant mortality rates. Thus, South Korea has the lowest infant mortality rate; in the same group of countries, with less than 50 infant deaths per 1000 births, are Turkey, Iraq, Cyprus, Taiwan and other countries where sanitary conditions are by no means satisfactory and where, consequently, a rather high infant mortality rate might have been expected. The indigenous population of Northern Rhodesia, Brazil, Burma and Aden show a very high infant mortality rate. It may be assumed that some other countries showing a lower infant mortality rate should be listed in the group of countries having 150 and more infant deaths per 1000 births; their lower infant mortality rate is certainly due to incomplete data.

It should be added that infant mortality is distinctly higher among illegitimate than among legitimate children. Moreover, the order of birth has a definite bearing on the frequency of death; mortality is usually higher among higher-order children.

There is no marked correlation between the death rate computed for the total population and the infant mortality rate. The reason is that the death rate relating to the whole population depends to a large degree on the age structure of the population, while no such dependence exists in the case of the infant mortality rate. This is clearly shown in Fig. 48; the points are widely dispersed. To the same death rate relating to the whole population correspond very different infant mortality rates, the highest infant death rate being at times several times the lowest. The reciprocal relation— the ratio of general death rate to the infant mortality rate—

---

[1] *Demographic Yearbook 1958.*

TABLE 116

Infant deaths per 1000 births

Under 50		50·0—99·9		100·0—149·9		150 and more	
Korea, South	15·4	Martinique	50·0	Colombia	100·4	Aden	151·0
Iceland	16·9	Monaco	51·3	Guatemala	100·5	Burma	157·3
Netherlands	17·2	Puerto Rico	51·4	Pakistan	100·9	Brazil	170·0
Sweden	17·4	Timor	52·2	Yugoslavia	101·7	Southern Rhodesia	
Mansel Islands	18·9	Syria	53·6	Ecuador	101·8	—indigenous popu-	
Northern Rhodesia		Spain	53·7	Costa Rica	102·7	lation	259
—European population	20·0	Panama	56·1	French West Africa	103·1		
New Zealand		Thailand	56·1				
—European population	20·0	New Zealand		North Borneo	104·0		
Norway	20·3	—Maori population	57·9	American Samoa	104·2		
Australia	21·4	Honduras	59·4	Gambia	111·9		
Southern Rhodesia		Hungary	63·1	Philippines	112·9		
—European population	22·2	Nicaragua	65·9	Ghana	113·0		
Switzerland	22·9	Argentina	66·3	Greenland	114·5		
England and Wales	23·1	Venezuela	67·3	Chile	117·2		
Denmark	23·4	Ceylon	67·5	Southern Rhodesia			
Turkey	23·9	Jordan	69·3	—indigenous popu-			
United States	26·3	Tonga	69·5	lation	120		
Finland	27·9	British Guiana	70·9	Brunei	136·4		
Iraq	28·5	Mexico	71·0	Egypt	140·4		
Cyprus	30·9	Bulgaria	72·0	Sierra Leone	144·5		

Country	Value	Country	Value	Country	Value
Canada	30·9	Paraguay	72·4	Congo	148
Ireland	33·1	Dominican Republic	73·0	Nyasaland	148·3
Czechoslovakia	33·4	Uruguay	73·0		
France	33·7	Mauritius	75·0		
Belgium	35·6	Federation of Malaya	75·5		
Taiwan	35·7				
Germ. Fed. Rep.	36·4	Poland	76·9		
		Madagascar	78·0		
Israel	38·6	Nigeria	80·1		
Luxemburg	38·6	Rumania	81·5		
Fiji Islands	38·9	El Salvador	87·0		
Japan	40·1	Portugal	88·0		
Bahamas	40·3	Portuguese India	89·2		
Alaska	41·2	Algeria			
Bermuda	41·4	—Moslem population	91·6		
French Guiana	42·1	British Honduras	92·4		
Congo		Cook Islands	92·6		
—European population	42·6	Bolivia	92·7		
Greece	44·1	Sudan	93·6		
Austria	44·2	Virgin Islands	94·0		
U.S.S.R.	45	Peru	94·8		
Algeria		Indonesia	99·6		
—European population	45·2	Spanish Guinea	99·7		
Germ. Dem. Rep.	45·2	India	99·9		
Guadeloupe	45·9				
Italy	49·8				

TABLE

Country	Year	Sex	Deaths by age per							
			Jointly	Under 1	1—4	5—9	10——14	15——19	20——24	25——29
Algeria —Moslem population	1948	j	19·7	153·8	38·3	9·9	5·8	7·6	10·2	11·5
		m	20·8	166·3	40·1	10·0	5·6	7·3	10·0	11·3
		f	18·6	140·8	36·6	9·8	6·0	8·0	10·4	11·7
Argentina	1947	j	9·9	77·9	6·4	1·4	1·2	2·3	3·1	3·2
		m	11·0	84·1	6·5	1·5	1·2	2·3	3·1	3·2
		f	8·8	71·6	6·3	1·3	1·2	2·4	3·0	3·3
Australia	1952	j	9·4	24·6	1·6	0·6	0·6	1·1	1·4	1·4
		m	10·5	27·7	1·7	0·7	0·6	1·5	2·0	1·8
		f	8·4	21·3	1·5	0·6	0·5	0·6	0·7	1·0
Austria	1952	j	12·0	54·1	2·0	0·7	0·6	1·0	1·5	1·5
		m	13·1	61·2	2·2	0·8	0·7	1·4	2·0	1·9
		f	11·0	46·7	1·8	0·5	0·4	0·7	1·2	1·2
Belgium	1952	j	11·9	47·1	1·7	0·6	0·5	0·7	1·1	1·3
		m	12·9	52·4	1·8	0·7	0·5	0·9	1·3	1·5
		f	11·0	41·5	1·6	0·5	0·4	0·5	0·8	1·1
Denmark	1952	j	9·0	29·3	1·5	0·6	0·4	0·7	1·0	1·1
		m	9·4	33·1	1·7	0·7	0·5	0·9	1·4	1·4
		f	8·7	25·3	1·3	0·4	0·3	0·6	0·7	0·8
Egypt	1947	j	21·5	208·4	49·7	5·3	4·3	4·3	5·6	6·9
		m	23·5	219·2	52·3	5·9	5·0	5·2	7·1	8·6
		f	19·6	197·3	47·2	4·7	3·5	3·5	4·1	5·5
Canada	1952	j	8·7	10·1		0·8	0·7	1·0	1·4	1·4
		m	10·0	11·3		1·0	0·8	1·4	1·9	1·8
		f	7·5	8·8		0·7	0·5	0·6	0·9	1·0
El Salvador . .	1950	j	14·8	106·4	24·9	6·8	2·3	4·1	6·0	6·5
		m	15·5	112·0	25·3	6·5	2·4	4·4	7·2	7·1
		f	14·1	100·5	24·5	7·0	2·3	3·8	4·9	6·0
England and Wales	1952	j	11·3	28·3	1·2	0·5	0·4	0·7	1·0	1·1
		m	12·2	31·7	1·3	0·6	0·5	0·9	1·3	1·3
		f	10·5	24·7	1·0	0·6	0·3	0·5	0·8	1·0
Federation of Malaya	1947	j	19·5	175·4	24·8	8·3	4·2	4·7	7·3	9·6
		m	20·3	191·3	24·8	8·3	4·2	4·4	6·3	8·5
		f	18·6	159·3	24·8	8·3	4·1	5·1	8·2	10·6
Finland	1952	j	9·5	32·9	1·9	0·7	0·6	1·1	1·7	2·3
		m	10·2	35·6	2·2	0·8	0·7	1·3	2·1	2·9
		f	9·0	30·0	1·6	0·6	0·5	0·9	1·2	1·6
Fiji Islands . . .	1953	j	9·2	55·2	5·3	1·9	1·7	1·7	3·1	3·7
		m	10·2	63·1	6·5	1·9	2·5	1·6	2·0	2·7
		f	8·2	46·9	6·0	1·8	1·7	1·9	4·3	4·6
France	1952	j	12·2	42·0	2·3	0·6	0·5	0·9	1·3	1·6
		m	12·9	47·0	2·5	0·7	0·5	1·1	1·6	1·8
		f	11·6	36·8	2·2	0·5	0·4	0·7	1·0	1·3
Iceland	1950	j	7·9	22·8	1·3	0·9	0·7	0·9	1·4	2·2
		m	8·2	21·5	1·5	1·4	1·0	1·3	2·5	3·3
		f	7·5	24·1	1·2	0·4	0·4	0·5	0·3	1·1
Italy	1951	j	10·3	67·4	4·4	0·9	0·8	1·1	1·5	1·8
		m	11·0	72·0	4·5	1·0	0·9	1·3	1·7	2·0
		f	9·7	62·6	4·4	0·9	0·6	1·0	1·4	1·6

117

1000 population

30——34	35——39	40——44	45——49	50——54	55——59	60——64	65——69	70——74	75——79	80——84	85 and over
11·4		13·5		21·1		38·5			71·7	139·5	
11·9		15·7		24·8		43·3			80·4	160·3	
11·0		11·4		17·2		33·7			63·3	122·3	
3·4	4·5	6·1	9·3	13·6	19·5	29·0	41·2	63·0	92·8	148·7	224·2
3·6	4·8	7·0	11·2	16·4	24·2	34·7	49·1	72·9	108·3	159·5	236·1
3·3	4·1	5·0	7·0	10·1	13·9	22·3	32·9	53·1	79·5	140·2	217·3
1·6	2·3	3·3	5·6	8·9	13·9	22·1	34·0	51·5	84·9	136·2	258·5
1·9	2·6	3·8	6·6	11·0	18·0	28·6	43·7	64·3	101·8	152·4	274·9
1·3	1·9	2·8	4·5	6·8	10·1	15·8	25·3	40·8	62·3	124·4	247·7
1·8	2·4	3·5	5·7	8·9	12·9	20·5	33·2	54·4	92·1	148·3	247·8
2·1	2·7	3·9	6·8	11·5	17·6	26·6	41·8	64·3	100·8	159·5	270·0
1·6	2·1	3·2	4·7	6·6	9·4	15·9	27·0	47·4	86·0	140·5	234·4
1·6	2·2	3·3	5·5	8·7	13·3	20·5	31·4	52·4	85·0	138·4	222·8
1·7	2·6	4·0	6·9	11·3	17·7	25·9	38·5	60·5	95·4	152·7	241·3
1·5	1·7	2·6	4·1	6·2	9·5	15·9	25·5	45·7	76·8	128·1	211·8
1·4	1·8	2·5	4·3	6·7	10·3	16·8	27·0	47·4	81·7	129·7	243·4
1·5	1·9	2·7	4·7	7·7	12·0	19·0	30·3	51·1	84·4	132·4	247·5
1·2	1·7	2·4	3·9	5·7	8·7	14·8	24·0	44·0	79·3	127·3	240·4
9·5	10·2	12·1	12·0	16·3	16·5	23·6	40·9	56·7	117·0	159·4	689·9
10·8	12·4	14·2	15·2	20·3	22·1	30·3	50·2	70·7	134·2	183·6	644·8
8·2	8·1	9·9	8·7	12·7	11·0	18·0	31·5	45·7	100·2	141·7	723·0
1·7	2·3	3·4	5·4	8·6	13·0	20·1	30·0	46·4	74·8	120·4	212·7
2·1	2·6	3·9	6·3	10·6	16·3	24·5	35·6	52·2	83·2	132·5	223·7
1·4	1·9	2·8	4·4	6·4	9·6	15·4	23·9	40·4	66·4	109·5	204·2
7·8	7·8	10·4	11·0	14·4	16·7	27·1	34·8	55·0	76·6	91·1	149·7
7·9	8·4	10·7	12·5	16·2	18·1	25·3	36·6	56·8	80·6	97·5	144·9
7·7	7·2	10·1	9·6	12·7	15·4	28·8	32·9	53·3	72·7	86·5	152·8
1·4	1·9	2·9	4·8	8·1	12·9	20·4	32·7	51·8	85·5	137·7	242·0
1·6	2·2	3·3	5·7	10·4	17·4	27·5	43·4	63·2	105·1	158·5	273·5
1·2	1·6	2·5	3·9	6·0	9·3	14·9	24·7	41·8	72·7	125·0	227·6
11·2	12·3	15·3	18·1	26·7	—	—	—	63·2	—	—	—
10·8	11·9	16·1	19·7	28·9	—	—	—	64·9	—	—	—
11·7	12·8	14·1	15·4	23·3	—	—	—	61·0	—	—	—
2·4	3·1	4·3	6·4	10·0	15·8	24·7	39·1	61·6	99·9	157·9	264·0
3·2	4·3	5·8	8·9	13·7	22·3	33·5	51·2	73·6	113·5	176·2	271·9
1·8	2·2	2·9	4·3	6·8	10·8	18·3	31·3	54·4	92·4	148·7	260·6
4·1	5·8	5·4	8·2	12·8	15·4	43·3	32·8	68·1		84·3	
3·6	5·5	6·6	9·2	14·8	17·5	46·8	33·9	59·9		74·5	
4·6	6·1	4·2	7·1	10·4	12·8	38·3	30·8	85·5		111·0	
1·9	2·7	3·9	6·0	9·2	13·0	19·0	29·6	47·9	79·2	128·4	227·2
2·1	3·2	4·8	7·7	12·0	17·7	25·6	38·6	60·1	97·0	154·6	276·2
1·6	2·2	3·1	4·4	6·6	9·4	14·3	23·4	39·8	67·8	114·0	207·1
2·2	3·2	4·2	5·6	6·4	9·0	17·0	22·8	42·4	64·5	110·3	178·7
3·0	3·3	5·0	6·5	6·7	10·5	22·7	28·3	50·9	69·0	116·6	197·2
1·4	3·1	3·5	4·6	6·1	7·5	11·8	18·2	35·7	61·0	106·2	168·8
2·1	2·5	3·6	5·6	8·2	12·3	18·9	31·1	63·1	93·7	185·9	
2·3	2·8	4·4	7·0	10·5	15·5	22·7	35·0	58·4	99·5	198·0	
1·9	2·2	3·0	4·3	6·2	9·7	15·8	27·8	48·6	88·9	176·7	

15

TABLE

Country	Year	Sex	Deaths by age per							
			Jointly	Under 1	1—4	5—9	10—14	15—19	20—24	25—29
Israel	1953	j	6·3	36·7	2·4	0·6	0·5	1·1	1·5	1·4
		m	6·6	38·1	2·5	0·4	0·7	1·6	2·1	1·6
		f	6·0	35·3	2·3	0·8	0·4	0·7	0·9	1·1
Japan	1951	j	9·9	57·2	8·3	1·8	1·0	1·9	3·5	4·1
		m	10·4	60·9	8·4	1·9	1·0	2·0	3·7	4·3
		f	9·4	53·3	8·3	1·7	1·0	1·9	3·3	3·9
Mauritius	1952	j	14·9	112·0	13·7	2·3	1·9	3·6	5·3	5·7
		m	15·3	122·8	13·0	1·9	1·0	3·0	4·7	4·6
		f	14·4	100·9	14·4	2·7	2·6	4·2	6·0	6·9
Netherlands	1953	j	7·7	22·4	1·6	0·8	0·6	0·7	0·8	0·9
		m	8·0	25·6	1·8	0·9	0·7	0·9	1·1	1·1
		f	7·3	19·0	1·5	0·6	0·4	0·5	0·6	0·7
New Zealand	1953									
—European population		j	8·8	20·4	1·3	0·4	0·5	1·0	1·1	1·1
		m	9·8	23·5	1·4	0·5	0·5	1·4	1·6	1·5
		f	7·9	17·2	1·2	0·4	0·4	0·5	0·7	0·7
—Maori population	1953	j	10·8	78·3	5·4	2·1	2·3	2·0	4·8	3·5
		m	12·0	90·7	5·7	1·8	2·0	2·5	6·3	3·6
		f	9·6	64·8	5·7	2·3	2·6	1·5	3·4	3·3
Norway	1952	j	8·5	24·6	1·5	0·6	0·5	0·7	1·1	1·2
		m	8·7	26·7	1·5	0·8	0·6	0·9	1·5	1·5
		f	8·4	22·2	1·4	0·4	0·4	0·4	0·6	1·0
Poland	1951	j	8·9	74·3	2·5	0·8	0·6	0·9	1·6	1·6
		m	9·7	82·3	2·6	0·9	0·8	1·3	2·0	2·4
		f	8·3	65·6	2·4	0·7	0·5	0·8	1·2	1·4
Portugal	1951	j	12·4	98·7	12·9	1·9	1·2	2·0	3·2	3·3
		m	13·1	105·7	13·2	1·9	1·3	2·0	3·7	3·9
		f	11·8	91·2	12·5	1·8	1·1	1·9	2·7	2·8
Sweden	1951	j	9·9	21·6	1·2	0·6	0·5	0·8	1·1	1·1
		m	10·0	24·2	1·4	0·8	0·5	1·0	1·4	1·4
		f	9·4	18·8	1·1	0·4	0·4	0·6	0·8	0·9
Switzerland	1952	j	9·9	30·2	1·7	0·6	0·5	0·9	1·3	1·3
		m	10·4	34·0	1·9	0·7	0·6	1·2	1·8	1·8
		f	9·4	26·1	1·5	0·5	0·4	0·6	0·8	0·9
United States	1951	j	9·7	7·3		0·6	0·6	1·1	1·5	1·6
		m	11·1	8·2		0·7	0·7	1·4	2·0	2·0
		f	8·2	6·4		0·5	0·4	0·7	1·0	1·2
Yugoslavia	1952	j	11·8	101·9	10·2	1·8	1·2	2·0	3·2	3·4
		m	12·3	108·5	10·0	1·8	1·2	2·0	3·2	3·4
		f	11·3	95·0	10·4	1·8	1·2	2·1	3·2	3·3

117 (*cont.*)

1000 population

30——34	35——39	40——44	45——49	50——54	55——59	60——64	65——69	70——74	75——79	80——84	85 and over
1·2	1·6	2·6	3·9	7·7	11·8	19·1	30·2	53·5	—	115·3	—
1·3	1·5	2·4	4·3	8·9	13·7	21·2	34·6	55·5	—	117·5	—
1·1	1·8	2·8	3·4	6·3	9·6	17·1	26·4	51·8	—	113·4	—
4·2	4·7	5·7	7·9	10·9	16·5	26·5	41·5	64·2	94·2	168·6	
4·3	4·9	6·3	8·8	12·5	19·3	30·5	50·0	76·4	108·5	182·3	
4·1	4·5	5·2	7·0	9·2	13·7	20·8	34·5	55·3	84·7	161·4	
6·9	8·2	11·4	15·2	21·9	30·7	40·1	54·3	96·7	128·3	120·3	119·6
5·3	9·0	14·0	18·5	27·7	37·2	48·2	77·1	141·1	140·2	100·7	93·3
8·6	7·3	8·4	11·2	15·3	24·2	33·4	40·0	72·6	123·2	127·1	128·8
1·2	1·7	2·4	3·8	6·1	9·7	16·4	25·6	44·7	77·7	126·9	224·8
1·3	1·7	2·7	4·2	6·9	11·3	17·5	27·9	47·9	80·9	131·9	233·5
1·2	1·6	2·2	3·4	5·4	8·2	13·4	23·5	41·8	74·8	122·5	218·0
1·3	1·7	2·9	4·9	7·4	12·1	18·6	29·4	47·3	74·4	122·2	197·1
1·6	1·9	3·3	5·3	8·8	14·9	23·7	36·4	55·9	86·4	134·2	207·2
1·0	1·4	2·5	4·4	6·0	9·6	14·1	23·1	39·4	63·9	112·2	189·8
4·0	5·8	10·0	15·6	16·8	31·5	36·7	60·4	85·9	116·7	113·0	367·7
4·3	7·1	8·2	19·1	18·1	29·8	36·7	69·9	94·3	145·8	109·1	420·0
3·7	4·6	11·9	11·5	15·2	33·7	36·7	49·2	76·3	77·8	116·7	342·9
1·3	1·7	2·5	3·7	5·6	8·8	13·8	22·3	39·5	65·1	112·9	207·6
1·6	2·2	2·9	4·4	6·9	10·2	15·9	25·7	42·8	67·9	119·4	209·2
1·0	1·2	2·1	2·9	4·4	7·5	11·9	19·4	36·7	62·9	108·1	206·4
2·1	2·7	3·7	5·4	8·6	13·7	22·1	34·7	65·7	90·7	140·4	176·2
2·5	3·2	4·6	6·7	11·9	17·6	28·5	43·6	68·1	100·0	158·9	195·6
1·7	2·3	3·0	4·3	6·4	10·3	21·2	28·8	48·2	85·4	130·7	167·7
3·6	4·3	5·5	6·9	9·7	13·0	21·6	32·1	61·3	93·8	169·9	246·9
4·3	5·1	7·1	9·1	13·0	18·0	27·2	40·9	72·4	110·6	188·8	258·7
3·0	3·4	4·0	5·0	7·0	10·1	17·4	26·1	53·6	83·6	159·8	242·1
1·4	1·7	2·5	4·3	6·4	10·3	16·5	26·9	48·0	79·9	137·2	250·6
1·6	1·9	2·9	4·7	7·1	11·8	19·0	29·8	49·1	82·0	142·4	259·0
1·2	1·6	2·2	3·8	5·8	9·8	14·3	24·3	43·2	78·0	132·9	244·5
1·5	2·0	2·9	4·7	7·6	12·2	18·7	30·7	51·7	83·4	140·3	235·9
1·7	2·4	3·5	5·5	9·3	14·9	22·6	37·2	59·9	94·7	152·5	250·3
1·3	1·7	2·3	3·9	6·1	9·8	15·5	25·4	45·5	75·7	132·4	224·3
2·0	2·8	4·3	6·6	10·5	15·5	22·7	33·9	49·9	79·5	119·1	194·4
2·4	3·3	5·3	8·2	13·2	20·0	28·5	42·0	59·4	90·7	130·6	207·4
1·6	2·3	3·4	5·0	7·8	11·1	17·0	26·2	41·3	69·9	109·8	186·4
3·7	4·7	5·0	6·8	10·1	14·2	23·5	34·4	56·7	87·8	155·5	259·7
3·7	3·9	5·6	8·0	12·1	17·2	27·4	38·6	61·8	94·6	161·7	268·7
3·7	3·6	4·4	5·6	8·4	11·8	20·5	31·4	53·0	82·7	150·6	253·3

is much more distinct, because the variations are relatively smaller. In no event, however, can one rate be "corrected" on the basis of the other.

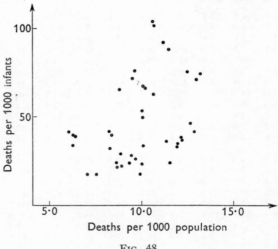

Fig. 48

Figure 48 covers those countries only whose statistic are considered to be complete by the Statistical Office of the United Nations. If the information relating to the remaining countries were included in the graph, the pattern would be even more distorted.

Except for the very backward countries where female mortality at confinement is presumably very high, both the general death rate and the infant mortality rate are commonly lower among females than among males.

Moreover mortality is to a large extent a function of age. Table 117[1] presents the distribution of deaths by age in selected countries in recent years.

The trend in death rates by age is generally quite consistent. Very high in infancy, the mortality rate drops rapidly thereafter to reach a minimum in the 10—14 age group,

---

[1] *Demographic Yearbook 1958.*

and starts increasing again, subsequently at first slowly, then, increasingly faster, and at the latest ages the death rate exceeds that in the first year of life. Some deviations from this pattern can be observed in small countries or small subpopulations. An irregular pattern of mortality is noted, for example, among the Maori population in New Zealand, where deaths in the 20—24 age group are more frequent than in the 25—29 age group. Similar deviations occur in Egypt, Mauritius and El Salvador.

Obviously, the probability of death in life tables must follow a comparable pattern. However, since one of the stages in the computation of life tables is to level out the data, no deviations by age are revealed in them.

As a rule, death rates for various ages are also higher among men than among women. Exceptions to this rule are observed among Moslem women between 10 and 29 years of age in Algeria, among women under 35 in Mauritius, between 15 and 39 years of age in the Federation of Malaya, between 15 and 39 in the Fiji Islands, and in the Maori population in New Zealand among females between 5 and 15 years of age; the remaining exceptions are rare and sporadic. Since a higher female mortality is invariably observed at the earlier ages, it can be surmised that it may be the outcome of excessive childbirth mortality and that even at present confinement is still a grave threat to a woman's life in under-developed countries. Higher female mortality in the other age groups is only sporadic, and is the result of special conditions prevailing in the given country, or due to chance.

Figure 49 represents graphically the death rate as a function of age and sex in Algeria and Denmark.

The graph clearly reveals the minimum mortality in the 10—14 age group and the uneven rate of growth of mortality at the later ages, particularly its slower rise between 25 and 35 years of age; there is even a certain decline in mortality between these ages among Algerian women. The curves also show that female mortality at the later ages is far lower than male mortality.

The rates listed in Table 117 illustrate the distribution of mortality by 5-year groups; the two exceptions are the first age group—children under 1 including one birth cohort

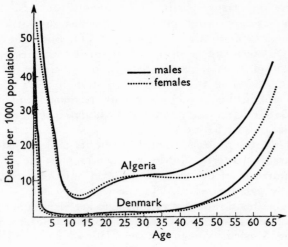

FIG. 49

only, and the 1—4 age group which covers four cohorts. Changes in mortality over short intervals of time, within the first year of life, are of interest. Such infant mortality rates are given in Table 118.[1]

The rates are not completely comparable because not every country applies the same differentiation of the period of infancy as that used in the table. The following classification is often preferred: 0 days, 1—4 days, 5 days to 1 month, etc.; sometimes 28 days (4 weeks) are used instead of 1 month. In the case of Poland the differentiation is fairly detailed, accounting for consecutive months of age among other details, but these had to be concentrated to fit the classification used in Table 118; also, an interval of 10 days is applied in Polish statistics instead of 7 days.

The values contained in the various columns of Table 118 are hard to collate because each of them refers to a different interval of time—1 day, 6 days, 23 days, 5 months, and 6 months. In order to make them comparable, they must be made to refer to a common time period. A period of one day seems the most convenient. We have made the necessary

---

[1] *Statistical Yearbook 1958.*

TABLE 118

Country	Year	Sex	Infant deaths below 1 year of age per 1000 births					
			jointly	under 1 day	1—7 days	7 days 1 month	1—5 months	6—11 months
1	2	3	4	5	6	7	8	9
Egypt	1953	j	148·5	1·0	9·2	12·6	60·5	65·2
		m	146·6	1·1	10·1	13·5	59·2	62·7
		f	150·5	0·9	8·2	11·6	61·9	67·9
Canada	1956	j	31·9	9·8	6·9	3·4	8·6	3·2
		m	35·0	10·9	8·0	3·6	9·2	3·3
		f	28·7	8·7	5·8	3·2	8·0	3·1
Chile	1953	j	102.4	11·3	13·8	16·6	48·6	22·2
		m	119·7	12·6	14·9	17·3	51·7	23·3
		f	104·9	9·7	12·6	16·0	45·5	21·1
Costa Rica . .	1956	j	71·6	5·2	9·2	8·8	30·7	17·6
		m	79·1	6·8	11·0	9·6	50·6	
		f	64·8	3·6	7·3	8·0	45·8	
Dominican Republic . . .	1955	j	73·8	3·0	11·1	13·4	28·5	17·8
		m	79·5	3·6	12·6	14·4	30·3	18·7
		f	67·7	2·4	9·5	12·4	26·6	16·9
El Salvador . .	1953	j	82·7	1·4	14·2	13·2	28·2	25·8
		m	90·8	1·7	15·9	14·8	30·7	27·6
		f	74·3	1·1	12·3	11·4	25·5	23·9
Mexico	1955	j	83·3	2·0	14·7	12·3	30·3	24·1
		m	88·5	2·3	16·7	13·4	31·5	24·5
		f	77·9	1·6	12·5	11·1	29·1	25·6
United States .	1955	j	26·4	10·0	7·0	2·1	5·2	2·1
		m	29·6	11·2	8·1	2·4	5·7	2·2
		f	23·0	8·8	5·8	1·9	4·7	2·0
Ceylon	1950	j	81·6	31·3	15·5	12·7	16·5	12·5
		m	88·5	35·6	17·1	13·4	16·8	12·8
		f	74·3	26·8	13·9	11·9	16·3	17·6
Israel	1956	j	35·9	4·7	8·8	5·1	11·6	4·3
		m	36·9	5·4	9·9	5·1	11·0	4·1
		f	34·8	4·0	7·6	5·2	12·2	4·6
Japan	1955	j	39·8	3·4	9·7	9·3	12·4	5·1
		m	42·3	3·8	10·6	8·6	12·9	5·3
		f	37·1	2·9	8·8	8·8	11·8	4·8
Federation of Malaya . . .	1954	j	83·4	4·9	11·2	14·1	26·0	16·8
		m	92·4	5·6	12·6	16·0	40·6	17·7
		f	73·4	4·1	9·8	12·2	31·3	16·0

TABLE 118 (cont.)

1	2	3	4	5	6	7	8	9
Thailand . . .	1955	j	56·1	1·6	6·6	8·9	25·6	13·4
		m	60·9	1·7	7·2	9·7	28·6	12·7
		f	50·7	1·4	5·8	7·9	22·6	12·2
Austria	1956	j	43·3	13·4	8·9	4·2	12·3	4·5
		m	48·9	15·3	10·0	4·8	14·1	4·7
		f	37·4	11·3	7·7	3·6	10·5	4·2
Belgium . . .	1955	j	40·7	10·5	6·4	5·8	13·8	4·1
		m	46·4	12·1	7·7	6·3	15·8	4·4
		f	34·8	8·9	5·1	5·2	11·7	3·8
Bulgaria . . .	1956	j	72·0	3·9	12·3	15·7	27·0	13·1
		m	77·7	4·8	14·3	16·8	28·4	13·1
		f	65·9	2·9	10·0	14·5	25·6	12·8
Czechoslovakia	1955	j	34·1	5·8	7·0	4·6	12·5	4·1
		m	38·4	6·7	8·5	5·1	13·6	4·4
		f	29·4	4·9	5·3	4·1	11·3	3·8
Denmark . . .	1956	j	24·9	6·5	8·8	2·4	4·8	2·4
		m	29·1	7·5	10·6	2·6	5·8	2·7
		f	20·5	5·4	6·9	2·2	3·8	2·2
England and Wales . . .	1953	j	26·8	7·4	7·4	2·8	6·4	2·7
		m	29·8	8·1	8·6	3·1	7·0	2·9
		f	23·6	6·7	6·0	2·6	5·8	2·4
Finland . . .	1955	j	29·7	6·2	9·2	3·1	7·1	4·0
		m	33·5	7·0	10·9	3·6	7·9	4·1
		f	25·7	5·3	7·5	2·6	6·4	3·9
France	1955	j	34·3	3·3	8·8	4·3	11·1	6·8
		m	38·4	3·8	10·0	4·8	12·6	7·2
		f	30·0	2·8	7·5	3·8	9·5	5·4
Germ. Fed. Rep.	1955	j	41·5	15·6	8·2	4·1	10·0	3·7
		m	45·9	17·2	9·6	4·4	10·8	4·1
		f	36·9	14·0	6·9	3·7	9·0	3·3
Hungary . . .	1956	j	58·8	11·9	10·4	9·3	20·1	7·1
		m	64·3	13·3	11·6	10·0	22·0	7·5
		f	52·9	10·4	9·2	8·3	18·0	6·7
Iceland	1952	j	20·6	2·7	6·4	2·0	7·1	2·5
		m	21·8	3·3	5·6	1·9	8·4	2·8
		f	19·2	2·1	7·3	2·1	5·7	2·1
Ireland	1952	j	35·6	7·5	8·2	7·1	9·8	3·1
		m	40·0	8·5	9·6	7·7	11·0	3·2
		f	31·0	6·4	6·7	6·4	8·5	3·0

TABLE 118 (*cont.*)

1	2	3	4	5	6	7	8	9
Italy	1956	j	20·6	2·7	6·4	2·0	7·1	2·5
		m	21·8	3·3	5·6	1·9	8·4	2·8
		f	19·2	2·1	7·3	2·1	5·7	2·1
Netherlands . .	1956	j	19·0	5·6	5·5	1·9	4·0	2·0
		m	21·6	6·2	6·6	2·1	4·5	2·2
		f	16·2	4·9	4·3	1·7	3·6	1·7
Norway . . .	1956	j	20·6	4·0	6·8	1·8	5·3	2·7
		m	22·8	4·7	7·6	1·8	6·0	2·6
		f	18·3	3·3	5·8	1·7	4·5	2·9
Poland	1956	j	71·2	11·3	9·3	9·6	31·0	10·0
		m						
		f						
Portugal . . .	1956	j	87·8	6·1	9·5	13·9	36·9	21·7
		m	94·3	6·7	10·6	15·3	39·0	22·7
		f	81·0	5·5	8·4	12·4	34·0	20·6
Sweden . . .	1955	j	17·4	5·0	6·4	1·5	2·8	1·7
		m	19·4	5·7	7·3	1·7	3·1	1·6
		f	15·4	4·2	5·6	1·3	2·6	1·8
Switzerland . .	1956	j	26·5	10·5	5·8	2·6	4·8	2·8
		m	29·0	11·8	6·4	2·6	5·3	2·9
		f	23·9	9·2	5·3	2·5	4·2	2·8
Yugoslavia . .	1955	j	112·8	6·5	14·0	21·0	46·2	24·9
		m	117·2	7·2	15·6	22·1	47·7	24·6
		f	108·1	5·8	12·5	19·8	44·6	25·2
Australia . . .	1956	j	21·7	8·0	5·6	2·0	3·9	3·2
		m	23·6	8·5	5·6	2·1	4·2	2·2
		f	19·7	7·4	4·7	1·9	3·7	2·1
Cook Islands .	1956	j	148·3	45·9		16·8	41·3	44·3
		m	163·6	58·3		21·5	39·9	42·9
		f	134·1	33·5		12·2	42·7	45·7
Fiji Islands . .	1954	j	48·9	4·9	8·8	5·8	16·4	13·1
		m	51·8	5·7	9·8	6·4	17·1	12·8
		f	45·9	4·2	7·7	5·1	15·6	13·4
New Zealand —white population . .	1954	j	20·0	12·5		1·8	3·9	1·8
		m	22·3	14·5		2·1	3·8	1·8
		f	17·6	10·4		1·5	3·9	1·7
—Maori population . .	1954	j	58·6	—	20·0	—	21·4	1·2
		m	67·5	—	24·2	—	23·9	19·4
		f	49·2	—	15·5	—	18·8	14·8

computations for two extreme cases—Sweden where infant mortality (and general mortality, too) is very low, and Yugoslavia which has a high infant mortality rate. For the purpose of comparison, we have computed the corresponding values for Poland (infant mortality statistics in Poland for periods shorter than one year cover male and female infants jointly). The case of Egypt, although its infant mortality is higher than in Yugoslavia, has not been taken into consideration in our computations because Egypt's vital statistics seemed too unreliable. The results obtained using the method for computing compound interest are given in Table 119.

TABLE 119

Duration of life of infant	Infant deaths per 1000 per day		
	Sweden	Yugoslavia	Poland
0 days	5·0	6·5	11·3
1—7 days	1·06	2·33	1·16
8 days to 1 month	0·071	1·00	0·48
1—5 months	0·018	0·304	0·204
6—11 months	0·0093	0·136	0·055

A comparison of the rates in Sweden and Yugoslavia shows that differences in mortality for the first day of life are relatively small; the death rate among Yugoslav infants is 30% higher than that in Sweden. The gap between the two increases in the subsequent groups; mortality between 1 and 5 months of age in Yugoslavia is already 17 times higher than in Sweden, following which the disparity slightly decreases. This is due to the fact that the struggle for the life of a newly-born child in the first days of its life has so far yielded no tangible results; hence, differences between individual countries in this respect are comparatively small. For the later periods in the infant's life the differences are quite apparent between the countries which make wide use of the latest medical knowledge and those which are not yet in a position to avail themselves of it. Another way of defining this is that the fight against endogenous deaths (i.e. those depending on the vitality of the infant) is most difficult and not very effective, while important achievements have been made by medicine in fighting exogenous deaths (i.e. those caused by extraneous, environmental factors).[1] Thus, in Sweden the mortality among infants between 6 and 11 months of age is 538 times less than that in the first day of life and only 48 times less for Yugoslavia.

In comparison with these two countries, infant mortality in the first day of life in Poland appears to be unusually high; it is more than twice as high as in Sweden and nearly twice as high as in Yugoslavia. On the other hand, the death rate in the second six months of life in Poland is only one two-hundredth of its value in the first day of life.

Presumably the younger the age the less accurate the death records. The least reliable are statistics of infant mortality in the first day of life, if only because of the effect of variations in registration procedure and the tendency not to count live-born infants who die before registration. The most complete are statistics of infant mortality in the second six months of life. The relation between the frequency of deaths in the second six months of life and that of one to six months of age is shown in Fig. 50.

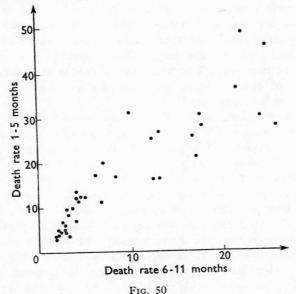

FIG. 50

[1] Compare S. Szulc, Umieralność niemowląt (Infant Mortality), *Przegląd Statystyczny* (*Statistical Review*), 1956 and 1957.

The relationship is distinct, though not very marked, in the case of countries where infant mortality is relatively low (the points in the left-hand portion of the graph). In the right-hand portion of the graph the points are widely dispersed; they represent countries in which infant mortality is higher. However, if we take into account the fact that countries having a higher infant mortality are more backward and, consequently, have available less reliable statistics, the problem appears in an entirely different light. The wide dispersion of the points may be the reflection of incomplete statistics rather than of the actual state of affairs. The graph shows that if we extrapolated the correlation characteristic of the countries where mortality is low by drawing, for instance a straight line, most of the points located in the right-hand portion of the graph would be below the line. This may be interpreted as meaning that while statistics of infant mortality in the 6—12 months of life are relatively accurate for all countries, statistics of infant mortality in the first six months of life are very incomplete for many countries. The point representing infant mortality in Poland would lie somewhere on the extended extrapolation line, which would point to the reliability of infant mortality statistics in Poland.

We shall now examine briefly the relation between marital status and mortality. The frequency of deaths at various ages depends to a high degree on marital status. This is borne out by the contents of Table 120.

Mortality among married men and women is the lowest in every country for every age group. This phenomenon may be due to various causes. It may, for example, be the outcome of natural selection, since persons of a weak constitution and poor health are not inclined to marry, nor are those who cannot afford to support a family.

Bachelors, spinsters, widows and widowers reveal a higher mortality; the death rate among bachelors and spinsters is lower at the earlier ages, and among widows and widowers at the later ages. Remarkably, mortality among widows and widowers declines up to a certain age, in contrast to the trend in general mortality which increases continually with increasing age. No such deviation is observed among bachelors and spinsters.

TABLE 120

Status	Deaths per 1000 population by age groups					
	15—19	20—24	25—34	35—44	45—54	55—64
El Salvador 1950						
Males, total	3·5	6·3	7·0	8·9	13·9	28·4
single	3·7	8·3	13·9	26·2	43·6	79·5
married	—	1·5	2·6	3·7	6·7	15·9
widowed and divorced	—	—	14·5	12·4	12·9	29·3
Females, total	2·8	3·9	5·4	7·3	11·3	23·1
single	3·2	5·9	11·8	18·3	22·9	40·1
married	1·3	2·0	2·6	3·4	6·3	15·7
widowed and divorced	—	—	5·6	5·1	9·4	13·3
Japan 1955						
Males, total	1·5	2·7	2·9	4·0	9·0	21·6
single	1·5	2·8	5·3	18·0	36·5	97·2
married	—	1·2	1·8	3·4	7·9	18·9
widowed and divorced	—	10·5	8·5	15·4	19·8	33·1
Females, total	1·1	1·9	2·4	3·4	6·4	14·1
single	1·1	2·4	5·3	12·1	23·9	57·2
married	0·9	1·3	1·7	2·9	5·5	13·0
widowed and divorced	—	4·4	3·9	3·9	7·5	16·4
Portugal 1950						
Males, total	2·4	3·9	4·3	6·0	10·3	21·0
single	2·4	4·2	6·3	11·2	19·1	32·7
married	—	2·8	3·2	4·8	8·9	18·6
widowed and divorced	—	—	9·5	12·6	16·2	21·1
Females, total	2·1	2·9	3·2	3·8	5·9	13·1
single	2·0	3·1	4·1	5·6	7·7	16·3
married	2·6	2·7	2·6	3·2	5·1	11·7
widowed and divorced	—	—	6·0	5·9	7·6	14·4

Table 121 presents the corresponding death rates for France, classified by 5-year age groups up to 90 years and over (the rates computed on the basis of small portions of the population, i.e. less reliable, are given in brackets).

The general trend in these statistics is similar to that in the countries listed in Table 120, i.e. apart from widowers and widows, mortality among all males and females, regardless of marital status, increases with increasing age. Among widows and widowers mortality is relatively high at the earlier ages; a decrease in mortality is then observed, followed by a final increase. Mortality among widowed and divorced males in France is very low, even lower than among married males; it is only from 80 years onwards that the relation is reversed.

TABLE 121

Age groups	Deaths per 1000 population in France in 1952							
	Males				Females			
	total	single	mar-ried	widowers and divorcees	total	single	mar-ried-	widowers and divorcees
15—19	1·1	1·1	1·0	—	0·7	0·7	0·7	(13)
20—24	1·6	1·8	1·0	—	1·0	1·1	0·8	(3·4)
25—29	1·9	2·9	1·3	(4·4)	1·3	2·0	1·1	1·8
30—34	2·4	4·6	1·8					
35—39	3·3	6·5	2·7	2·5	2·2	3·3	2·0	2·9
40—44	4·8	8·5	4·1	2·1	3·1	5·0	2·8	3·9
45—49	7·7	13·5	6·6	5·8	4·4	5·6	4·1	5·6
50—54	12·9	18·9	11·8	10·1	6·6	8·0	6·2	7·8
55—59	17·7	25·9	16·1	18·5	9·4	10·2	8·6	10·9
60—64	25·6	34·6	25·4	23·6	14·3	14·9	13·2	15·6
65—69	38·3	46·1	35·2	27·9	23·3	24·3	21·3	24·8
70—74	59·9	78·5	54·7	42·4	39·7	42·4	35·8	41·1
75—79	95·1	117	85·8	68·3	68·0	71·1	57·0	70·4
80—84	152	163	135	172	115	119	92·1	117
85—89	242	258	206	388	198	189	135	193
90 and over	347	330	317	933	283	269	188	287

Mortality among widows and divorcees is higher than among married women and approximately the same as among spinsters, with the exception of the earlier age group in which mortality among widows and divorcees is slightly lower than among spinsters.

A graphic representation of female mortality in relation to age and marital status is given in Fig. 51.

The mortality rate—be it the general death rate per 1000 population, the infant mortality, or the death rate by age—reveals great differences even within one country. This is shown by the example of Norway. Table 122 presents the general death rates and infant mortality rates distributed by various departments of Norway in the years 1951—1955.

Here, too, the relation between the two death rates is not pronounced: those departments where the general death rate is low do not necessarily have a low infant mortality rate as well, and *vice versa*.

Life tables furnish a picture of the distribution of mortality by age. They show the process of diminution of the

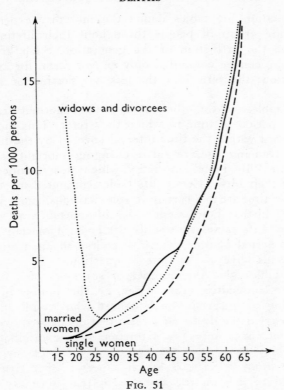

FIG. 51

TABLE 122

Deaths per 1000 population	Number of departments	Infant deaths per 1000 births	Number of departments
7·5— 7·9	4	15·0—19·9	3
8·0— 8·4	5	20·0—24·9	14
8·5— 8·9	5	25·0—29·9	1
9·0— 9·4	5	30·0—34·9	1
9·5— 9·9	—	35·0—39·9	—
10·0—10·4	1	40·0—44·9	1
Total	20	Total	20

original birth cohorts subjected to the current rates of mortality. Life tables may be constructed for a given time interval, i.e. a year or several years, or for a cohort born within a specific period of time.

Generation life tables depict the mortality experience of a definite group of people throughout their lifetime, from birth to the extinction of the generation. Such life tables, as a rule, can be computed only *ex post facto*, for an extinct generation; they are none the less a reflection of a certain reality.

Life tables, on the other hand, contain mortality rates only for the period of time to which they refer. This means that those born within the time interval covered by the table will, with advancing age, reveal a changing mortality, different from the "life table" mortality which was obtained at the time of their birth. Hence, life tables computed for a definite period of time are to a certain degree fictitious, since no generation of births shows such order of mortality as set forth in them. Life tables show only the level of mortality during a given period of time, which of course affects a great many generations alive at the time in question.

Life tables give the number of survivors of a cohort of births to consecutive years of age, i.e. the number of persons belonging to a certain birth cohort who would survive to a given age if the death rates remained unchanged over a long period of time, until the extinction of the original cohort. Life tables also reveal the average life expectancy, i.e. the average number of years which a person of a given age is expected to live on the assumption that mortality remains unchanged. The third quantity in life tables is the probability of death within a given year at various ages. We present below two abridged versions of life tables computed for selected countries, giving the first two life table quantities only (Tables 123 and 124).[1]

The number of survivors decreases continually with increasing age, more or less rapidly depending on the current death rate for a given age in the given country. The most rapid decrease is noted in infancy and for the aged, and the slowest in the 10—15 age group. Given the number of survivors per 100,000, 10,000 or 1000 births, it is very easy to find the probability of survival from birth to any age.

In Poland, for example, the number of women surviving to 30 years of age is 89,937; since the life table is given per

<hr>

[1] *Demographic Yearbook 1954.*

100,000 births, the probability that a woman will survive to the age of 30 years equals 89,937 : 100,000 = 0·89937. Hence, the probability of survival is obtained simply by shifting the decimal point.

If, instead of the probability of survival from birth to a given age, we wish to determine the probability of survival from one age to a later one, we must find the ratio of the corresponding numbers of survivors. Thus the probability that a woman aged 15 in Poland will survive to the age of 60 is the number of female survivors at 60 years of age (78,321) divided by the number of female survivors at 15 years of age (91,573), or 78,321 : 91,573 = 0·855.

During infancy and in the first years of life, life expectancy increases (the higher the general death rate the longer the initial period of increasing life expectancy); afterwards it declines, first slowly and then at an approximately even pace. It is only for the later ages that the decrease becomes again increasingly slower.

Trends in the age distribution of survival and life expectancy in India—a typical high-mortality country, and in Canada—a typical low-mortality country, are presented in Figs. 52 and 53. The male population only has been taken into account in the graphs. For the purpose of comparability, the

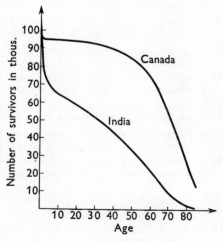

FIG. 52

Country	Years	Sex	Number of survi								
			0	1	2	3	4	5	10	15	
Congo . . .	1950—1952	m	100,000	86,525	—	—	—	76,197	72,111	69,627	6(
		f	100,000	88,549	—	—	—	78,111	74,108	71,735	6(
Canada . . .	1950—1952	m	100,000	95,675	95,349	95,077	95,126	94,914	94,480	94,083	9.
		f	100,000	96,577	96,289	96,141	96,031	95,943	95,625	95,363	9(
El Salvador .	1949—1951	m	100,000	90,238	—	—	—	81,308	78,815	77,824	7(
		f	100,000	91,337	—	—	—	82,650	80,004	79,058	7(
United States	1949—1951	m	100,000	96,661	96,425	96,279	96,169	96,077	95,726	95,368	9(
		f	100,000	97,406	97,197	97,076	96,982	96,908	96,652	96,431	9(
Argentina . .	1947	m	100,000	90,713	89,420	88,891	88,602	88,407	87,753	87,226	8(
		f	100,000	92,072	90,797	90,268	89,983	89,804	89,224	88,709	87
Ceylon . . .	1920—1922	m	100,000	80,509	76,523	72,770	69,474	67,167	62,273	59,387	5(
		f	100,000	81,672	77,155	72,755	68,767	66,169	60,755	57,617	54
Ceylon . . .	1952	m	100,000	91,114	89,016	—	—	85,256	83,333	82,781	82
		f	100,000	92,696	90,056	—	—	85,483	83,300	82,703	81
India	1941—1950	m	142,759	115,635	108,576	104,616	102,006	100,000	92,539	87,138	82
		f	146,896	121,189	111,448	105,983	102,518	100,000	91,599	86,688	83
Israel	1953	m	1000	963	959	957	955	954	950	947	
		f	1000	966	962	960	958	957	955	953	
Japan	1953	m	100,000	94,890	94,064	93,543	92,948	92,604	91,817	91,451	90
		f	100,000	95,510	94,679	94,054	93,574	93,237	92,547	92,205	91
England and Wales . .	1952	m	10,000	9,691	9,669	9,656	9,646	9,639	9,611	9,587	9
		f	10,000	9,759	9,741	9,731	9,724	9,718	9,698	9,681	9
Finland . . .	1950—1951	m	100,000	95,639	95,285	95,065	94,913	94,805	94,272	93,880	93
		f	100,000	96,643	96,280	96,109	96,002	95,901	95,561	95,243	94
France . . .	1950—1951	m	10,000	9,479	9,427	9,407	9,395	9,386	9,352	9,319	9
		f	10,000	9,598	9,551	9,535	9,524	9,515	9,488	9,464	9
Norway . . .	1946—1950	m	100,000	96,582	96,263	96,047	95,883	95,747	95,259	94,903	94
		f	100,000	97,434	97,179	96,995	96,870	96,793	96,499	96,271	95
Poland . . .	1955—1956	m	100,000	91,512	90,939	90,703	90,533	91,397	89,922	89,531	88
		f	100,000	93,268	92,730	92,507	92,348	92,221	91,826	91,573	91
Portugal . .	1949—1952	m	100,000	89,536	86,664	85,445	84,887	84,524	83,662	83,112	82
		ʟ	100,000	90,749	87,853	86,685	86,141	85,801	85,981	84,483	83
Sweden . . .	1946—1950	m	100,000	97,337	97,111	96,961	96,832	96,728	96,325	96,028	9(
		f	100,000	97,947	97,772	97,650	97,549	97,473	97,236	96,998	9(
New Zealand —white population	1950—1952	m	100,000	97,501	97,302	97,155	97,061	96,979	96,660	96,332	9(
		f	100,000	98,005	97,801	97,695	97,615	97,553	97,342	97,193	9(
—Maori population	1950—1952	m	100,000	92,024	90,415	89,917	89,559	89,288	88,339	87,589	8(
		f	100,000	92,960	91,473	91,117	90,811	90,565	89,825	88,863	87

e	30	35	40	45	50	55	60	65	70	75	80	85
88	59,911	55,849	51,284	46,385	40,909	34,648	27,612	20,382	13,716	7,597	3,001	704
96	61,724	58,121	53,910	49,254	43,880	38,310	31,475	24,452	17,865	11,300	5,670	2,093
86	91,752	90,824	89,649	87,877	85,084	80,762	74,444	65,815	55,020	41,835	26,993	13,510
27	93,993	93,311	92,354	90,939	88,911	86,027	81,789	75,525	66,576	53,950	37,712	20,768
18	70,930	68,124	65,190	61,703	57,866	53,403	48,480	42,173	35,313	26,207	17,978	11,004
36	73,503	70,669	68,047	64,734	61,426	57,562	53,562	46,018	38,653	29,584	21,000	13,452
91	92,861	91,760	90,207	87,819	84,158	78,781	71,246	61,566	49,950	36,756	23,237	11,750
83	94,993	94,206	93,101	91,469	89,075	85,694	80,890	74,119	64,873	52,111	36,486	20,668
29	83,581	82,081	80,152	77,275	73,150	67,157	59,643	49,910	38,854	26,618	14,873	5,677
07	84,972	83,602	81,888	79,767	77,153	73,326	68,369	61,177	51,697	39,204	25,791	11,699
07	50,678	47,230	43,404	39,176	34,458	29,394	24,347	19,174	13,419	7,549	3,108	840
96	46,604	42,320	38,325	34,615	31,141	27,436	22,810	17,339	11,533	5,973	2,086	439
43	80,129	78,797	77,186	75,292	72,624	69,121	64,280	57,617	48,684	37,328	24,433	5,129
00	77,828	75,635	73,511	71,403	69,110	66,223	62,261	56,461	48,022	36,616	12,927	—
58	73,394	67,968	61,977	55,512	48,265	40,139	31,405	22,456	14,193	7,379	3,213	993
17	74,475	67,752	60,448	53,139	45,901	38,699	31,307	23,442	15,899	9,444	4,693	1,834
29	922	916	909	898	879	841	785	706	593	449	282	131
46	941	936	927	914	899	871	830	762	667	514	319	173
94	87,964	86,486	84,834	82,662	79,546	74,940	68,218	58,934	46,446	31,797	—	—
24	89,257	87,865	86,319	84,446	81,921	78,431	73,529	66,625	56,525	42,869	—	—
80	9,419	9,345	9,243	9,094	8,837	8,390	7,691	6,703	5,390	3,857	2,252	974
19	9,572	9,515	9,437	9,319	9,140	8,868	8,466	7,861	6,944	5,630	3,899	2,142
53	90,414	88,711	86,799	83,945	79,992	73,850	65,599	54,872	42,087	28,634	15,710	5,420
05	93,110	92,043	90,852	89,347	87,327	83,365	79,819	72,824	62,083	46,775	28,681	13,030
00	9,079	8,955	8,794	8,554	8,198	84,284	7,990	6,094	4,946	3,234	2,039	827
55	9,290	9,197	9,081	8,931	8,712	7,679	7,979	7,371	6,473	5,169	3,486	1,787
26	92,377	91,356	90,196	88,673	86,491	8,407	79,071	72,189	63,856	51,362	35,354	19,190
53	95,285	94,642	93,950	91,916	90,264	87,940	84,590	79,362	71,216	58,861	42,222	23,784
43	86,982	85,841	84,411	82,608	79,900	75,625	69,092	59,961	48,276	34,514	20,930	10,293
58	90,010	89,205	88,163	86,882	85,091	82,399	78,321	71,825	62,266	49,271	34,196	19,956
58	79,175	80,077	75,466	72,907	69,633	65,378	59,802	52,379	42,471	29,950	17,220	7,229
57	81,335	80,077	78,712	77,118	75,153	72,550	68,920	63,411	55,222	42,986	28,495	13,755
49	93,692	92,773	91,697	90,280	88,079	84,672	79,627	72,189	61,628	47,690	30,803	14,729
40	95,399	94,655	93,684	92,420	90,530	87,732	83,637	77,384	67,910	53,829	36,008	18,000
98	94,181	93,348	92,250	90,803	88,381	84,435	78,196	69,427	57,405	42,955	27,089	13,139
47	96,083	95,497	94,685	93,485	91,501	88,525	84,121	77,680	68,580	55,569	38,548	21,009
78	81,533	78,966	75,860	72,424	67,912	61,116	52,518	41,693	30,524	20,086	11,061	4,492
54	83,515	81,454	78,508	74,462	68,677	61,737	53,013	43,049	30,351	24,304	15,628	7,832

16*

TABl

Country	Years	Sex	Life expectan								
			0	1	2	3	4	5	10	15	20
Congo	1950—1952	m	37·64	42·45	—	—	—	44·04	41·40	37·78	34·
		f	40·00	44·14	—	—	—	45·87	43·23	39·58	36·
Canada	1950—1952	m	66·33	68·33	67·56	66·68	65·79	64·86	60·15	55·39	50·
		f	70·83	72·33	71·55	70·66	69·74	68·80	64·02	59·19	54·
El Salvador . .	1949—1951	m	49·94	54·31	—	—	—	56·14	52·85	48·49	44·
		f	52·40	56·35	—	—	—	58·14	54·99	50·62	46·
United States .	1949—1951	m	65·47	66·73	65·89	64·99	64·06	63·12	58·35	53·56	48·
		f	70·96	71·84	71·00	70·09	69·15	68·21	63·38	58·52	53·
Argentina . . .	1947	m	56·9	61·7	61·6	61·0	60·2	59·3	54·7	50·0	45·
		f	61·4	65·7	65·7	65·0	64·2	63·3	58·7	54·0	49·
Ceylon	1920—1922	m	32·72	39·53	40·56	41·62	42·58	43·02	41·25	38·13	34·
		f	30·67	36·44	37·54	38·78	40·00	40·62	39·00	35·99	32·
Ceylon	1952	m	57·6	62·2	62·6	—	—	62·3	58·7	54·1	49·
		f	55·5	58·9	59·6	—	—	59·7	56·2	51·6	47·
India	1941—1950	m	32·45	39·00	40·50	41·02	41·05	40·86	38·97	36·24	33·
		f	31·66	37·30	39·52	40·54	40·89	40·91	39·45	36·56	32·
Israel	1953	m	67·98	69·57	68·88	68·04	67·16	66·23	61·49	56·70	52·
		f	70·50	72·00	71·29	70·44	69·56	68·65	63·78	58·89	54·
Japan	1953	m	61·9	64·3	63·8	63·2	62·6	61·8	57·3	52·6	48·
		f	65·7	67·7	67·3	66·8	66·1	65·3	60·8	56·0	51·
England and Wales . . .	1952	m	67·06	68·20	67·35	66·44	65·51	64·56	59·74	54·88	50·
		f	72·35	73·14	72·27	71·34	70·40	69·44	64·58	69·69	54·
Finland . . .	1946—1950	m	58·59	61·09	60·47	59·68	58·85	57·97	53·44	48·77	44·
		f	65·87	67·97	67·37	66·58	65·72	64·82	60·18	55·48	51·
France	1950—1951	m	63·0	66·1	65·4	64·6	63·6	62·7	57·9	53·1	48·
		f	69·3	71·2	70·6	69·7	68·8	67·8	63·0	58·2	53·
Norway . . .	1946—1950	m	69·25	70·70	69·93	69·09	68·20	67·30	62·63	57·86	53·
		f	72·65	73·56	72·75	71·89	70·98	70·05	65·24	60·39	55·
Poland	1955—1956	m	61·8	66·5	66·0	65·1	64·3	63·3	58·7	53·9	49·
		f	67·9	71·7	71·1	70·2	69·4	68·5	63·7	58·9	54·
Portugal . . .	1949—1952	m	55·52	60·98	61·99	61·87	61·27	60·53	56·13	51·48	47·
		f	60·50	65·64	66·79	66·69	66·10	65·36	60·97	56·32	51·
Sweden . . .	1946—1950	m	69·04	69·92	69·09	68·19	67·28	66·35	61·62	56·80	52·
		f	71·58	72·08	71·20	70·29	69·36	68·42	63·58	58·73	53·
New Zealand —white population .	1950—1952	m	68·29	69·03	68·17	67·27	66·33	65·30	60·60	55·79	51·
		f	72·43	72·90	72·05	71·12	70·18	69·23	64·37	59·47	54·
—Maori population .	1950—1952	m	54·05	57·69	57·71	57·02	56·25	55·42	50·99	46·40	42·
		f	55·88	59·08	59·03	58·26	57·45	56·61	52·05	47·59	43·

y age and sex

25	30	35	40	45	50	55	60	65	70	75	80	85
31·22	27·69	24·52	21·48	18·48	15·61	12·97	10·63	8·52	6·46	4·70	3·34	2·25
33·20	29·78	26·47	23·33	20·30	17·47	24·64	12·27	10·08	7·88	6·02	4·62	3·64
46·20	41·60	37·00	32·45	28·05	23·88	20·02	16·49	13·31	10·41	7·89	5·84	4·27
49·67	44·94	40·24	35·63	31·14	26·80	22·61	18·64	14·97	11·62	8·73	6·38	4·57
40·94	37·39	33·83	30·24	26·80	23·41	20·15	16·94	14·09	11·32	9·28	7·55	5·80
42·60	38·82	35·27	31·53	28·02	24·39	20·86	17·40	14·67	11·97	9·87	7·80	5·95
44·36	39·78	35·23	30·79	26·55	22·59	18·96	15·68	12·74	10·11	7·83	5·94	4·41
48·99	44·28	39·63	35·06	30·64	26·40	22·33	18·50	14·95	11·71	8·94	6·67	4·90
41·3	36·9	32·5	28·2	24·2	20·4	17·0	13·8	11·1	8·5	6·4	4·6	3·7
45·3	41·1	36·7	32·4	28·2	24·1	20·2	16·5	13·1	10·1	7·6	5·3	3·9
31·56	28·35	25·23	22·23	19·36	16·66	14·09	11·50	8·92	6·65	4·90	3·63	2·63
30·09	27·58	25·11	22·48	19·62	16·53	13·42	10·61	8·16	6·00	4·31	3·15	2·28
45·0	40·6	36·3	32·0	27·7	23·6	19·7	16·0	12·5	9·3	6·4	2·3	2·0
43·2	39·3	35·4	31·3	27·2	23·0	18·9	14·9	11·2	7·7	4·2	2·4	—
29·78	26·58	23·50	20·53	17·63	14·89	12·39	10·13	8·18	6·51	5·13	3·99	3·06
29·30	26·18	23·52	21·06	18·61	16·16	13·69	11·33	9·29	7·53	6·03	4·77	3·69
47·65	43·02	38·28	33·55	28·92	24·50	20·50	16·78	13·38	10·45	8·01	6·26	5·62
49·30	44·56	39·79	35·13	30·59	26·07	21·83	17·79	14·15	10·81	8·28	6·82	5·47
43·6	39·3	34·9	30·6	26·3	22·2	18·4	15·0	11·9	9·4	7·6	—	—
47·0	42·6	38·2	33·9	29·6	25·4	21·4	17·7	14·2	11·3	9·1	—	—
45·44	40·72	36·02	31·39	26·86	22·67	18·64	15·11	11·97	9·27	6·97	5·15	3·62
50·03	45·27	40·62	35·84	31·26	26·82	22·57	18·52	14·76	11·38	8·45	6·09	4·35
40·35	36·30	32·16	28·02	24·01	20·28	16·85	13·75	11·03	8·65	6·63	4·98	3·66
46·69	42·36	37·98	33·59	29·20	24·88	20·74	16·79	13·17	10·04	7·47	5·42	3·93
43·8	39·3	34·8	30·4	26·2	22·2	18·5	15·1	11·9	9·1	6·7	4·8	3·4
48·7	44·1	39·5	35·0	30·5	26·2	22·1	18·1	14·4	11·1	8·2	5·9	4·2
48·74	44·22	39·68	35·16	30·72	26·43	22·32	18·39	14·74	11·43	8·58	6·30	4·55
50·96	46·29	41·61	36·96	32·41	27·95	23·62	19·45	15·55	12·03	8·99	6·51	4·64
44·7	40·2	35·7	31·3	26·9	22·8	18·9	15·4	12·4	9·7	7·6	6·0	4·7
49·5	44·8	40·2	35·6	31·1	26·7	22·5	18·5	15·0	11·8	9·3	7·3	5·7
42·81	38·62	34·42	30·26	26·23	22·35	18·63	15·12	11·90	9·06	6·78	4·97	3·64
47·50	43·18	38·82	34·45	30·11	25·83	21·66	17·66	13·96	10·64	7·92	5·65	4·12
47·60	43·02	38·42	33·84	29·33	24·99	20·89	17·05	13·53	10·40	7·68	5·50	3·89
49·26	44·57	39·90	35·29	30·73	26·32	22·08	18·03	14·27	10·89	8·04	5·76	4·11
46·56	41·89	37·24	32·65	28·13	23·83	19·82	16·19	12·90	10·05	7·57	5·55	3·62
49·83	45·06	40·32	35·64	31·06	26·68	22·49	18·53	14·84	11·46	8·53	6·16	4·24
38·28	34·25	30·28	26·41	22·54	18·86	15·67	12·81	10·47	8·39	6·48	4·79	3·41
39·21	35·11	30·93	27·00	23·32	20·07	17·03	14·41	12·16	9·98	7·77	5·71	3·98

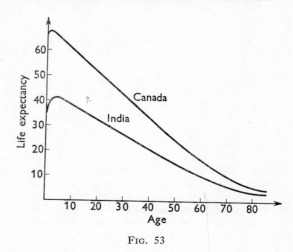

FIG. 53

rates relating to India have been computed per 100,000
births.

The highly regular course of the curves in the two graphs
leads us to believe that the various life table quantities may
be closely related. Let us try to verify whether this is true.

We shall begin by examining the relation between the
probabilities of surviving to different ages. Taking as an
example the probabilities of males surviving to 15 and 30
years of age, we have drawn a graph showing this relationship
for the countries listed in Table 121. The graph is shown
in Fig. 54.

The relation is very close and distinctly linear. Deviations
from the regression line shown on the graph are insignificant.
Thus, knowing the probability of survival to 15 years of
age it is possible to derive with great accuracy the probability
of survival to 30 years of age, and *vice versa*.

Similar close functional relations are also observed between
the probabilities of survival to other ages than those used in
the graph. Accordingly, it is safe to say that survival to various
ages is very closely related, especially when the interval between
the ages considered is not too long. To prove that the relation
becomes less marked with an increasing interval between the
ages we have drawn a graph analogous to that in Figure 54,

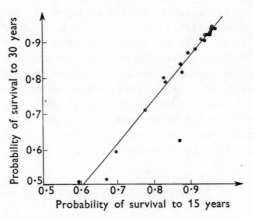

FIG. 54

except that it shows the relation between the probability of survival to 15 and to 60 years of age (Fig. 55).

Here the dispersion is much greater than in Fig. 54. It is noteworthy that the model tables prepared by the Statistical Office of the United Nations are based on the regression

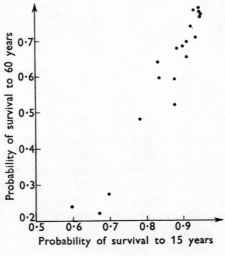

FIG. 55

between life table values at 5-year intervals, i.e. they take into account the fact that for short intervals of time the relationship is so close as to be nearly functional.

Figure 56 shows analogous relations between life expectancies at various ages (the notation for life expectancy at age x is e_x) namely for 0 and 15 years of age, on the one hand, and for 0 and 60 years on the other. The graph is so constructed that the points in the upper part refer to the relation between e_0 and e_{15} and those in the lower portion to the relation between e_0 and e_{60}. The regression lines are also drawn.

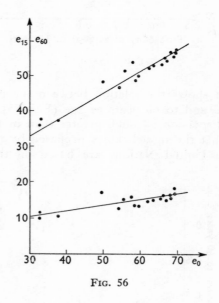

FIG. 56

According to Fig. 56 the relationship is not very close, but it is much less pronounced between e_0 and e_{60} than between e_0 and e_{15}. The probable interpretation is that there is virtually no relation between life expectancy in old age and that at birth. At any rate, a longer life expectancy at birth does not necessarily imply a longer life expectancy at either earlier or later years of life.

Figure 57 represents the relation between two different quantities from the life table—the life expectancy at birth

(e_0) and the probability of survival from birth to 30 years of age (P_{30}). We have selected the age of 30 years because it is a period approximately equivalent to the length of a female generation. The correlation is close and linear.

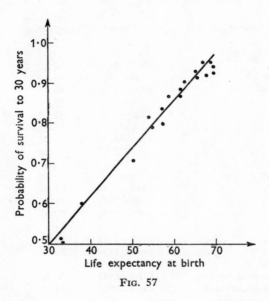

FIG. 57

The regression equation between the life expectancy at birth and the probability of survival to an age equal to the length of a generation is:

$$e_0 = 87 \cdot 1 \, P_{30} - 14 \cdot 4.$$

Knowing the probability of survival from birth to 30 years of age it is possible to estimate from the above equation, the life expectancy at birth.

We shall now examine the relation between two indices which do not depend on the age structure of the population. They are the life expectancy at birth and the infant mortality rate. If we confine our study to the countries analysed earlier in this chapter (excluding the Congo, because its infant mortality rate is not recorded in the Demographic Yearbook) and if we assume that the life expectancy at birth equals the mean value of e_0 for males and females, we obtain the results presented in Table 125.

TABLE 125

Country	Years	Life expectancy at birth	Deaths per 1000 births
Canada	1950—1952	68·60	39·2
El Salvador U	1949—1951	51·17	84·3
United States	1949—1951	68·21	29·6
Argentina	1947	59·15	77·1
Ceylon.	1920—1922	31·70	192·3
do.	1952	56·55	139·9
India U	1941—1950	32·05	139·7
Israel	1953	69·24	35·9
Japan	1953	63·8	49·4
England and Wales	1952	69·70	27·5
Finland	1940—1950	62·23	51·7
France	1950—1951	66·45	51·4
Norway	1946—1950	70·95	31·0
Poland	1955—1956	64·9	76·5
Portugal	1949—1952	58·01	98·0
Sweden	1946—1950	70·31	23·9
New Zealand			
—white population	1950—1952	70·36	22·4
—Maori population U. . .	1950—1952	54·96	74·1

It is quite apparent that the relation between the two indices is not very close; while the expectation of life at birth in Canada and the United States, for instance, is nearly the same, the infant mortality rates in the two countries differ considerably. The same is true in the case of Norway and Sweden; contrary to what might have been reasonably expected, Norway too has a longer life expectancy at birth and a higher infant mortality rate. The letter U in Table 125 denotes countries in which vital records are stated to be "unreliable" in the quality code used by the Statistical Office of the United Nations.

The relation between the life expectancy at birth and the infant mortality rate is represented in Fig. 58. The points denoting national vital statistics regarded as unreliable are marked with crosses.

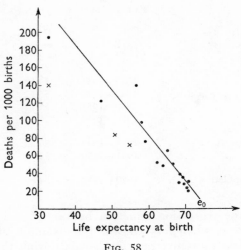

FIG. 58

Although the dispersion of the points is rather wide, the general trend is quite distinct and obviously linear. If we exclude the points denoting countries marked U, the corresponding regression equation is:

$$f = -5{\cdot}18e_0 + 391{\cdot}6$$

where:

f = infant mortality rate, and
e_0 = life expectancy at birth.

In Fig. 58 the points representing countries in which statistics are stated to be incomplete lie below the regression line; this corroborates the quality classification used by the Statistical Office of the United Nations.

If no other information is available, the regression equation may serve to make at least a rough estimate of the level of infant mortality, provided that the life expectancy at birth is known. It makes it possible to correct the official data on infant mortality in countries marked U (El Salvador, India and the Maori population in New Zealand) as well as to arrive at estimates of the infant mortality rate in several other countries where only the life expectancy at birth is known. The results of these computations are listed in Table 126.

TABLE 126

Country	Years	Life expectancy at birth	Estimated infant mortality rate
Brazil	1949—1951	52·88	117
Costa Rica	1949—1951	55·72	103
El Salvador	1949—1951	51·17	128
Congo	1950—1952	38·82	183
South Africa —Asian population	1945—1947	50·22	131
India	1941—1950	32·05	226
New Zealand —Maori population	1950—1952	54·96	108

Finally, the regression equation between f and e_0 may be used to find e_0 when f is known. For example, it is known that the infant mortality rate in Canada during the 17th and 18th centuries was 248 per 1000 births. The information is

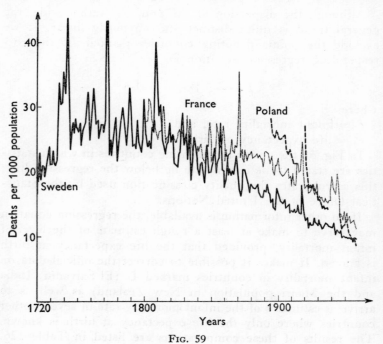

Fig. 59

TABLE 127

Year	Sweden	Year	Sweden	Year	Sweden
1721	18·4	1745	23·3	1775	24·8
2	22·9	6	26·4	6	22·5
3	18·8	7	27·5	7	24·9
4	22·0	8	26·0	8	26·6
5	20·9	9	28·1	9	28·5
6	19·2	1750	26·9	1780	21·7
7	20·3	1	26·2	1	25·0
8	21·7	2	27·3	2	27·3
9	23·8	3	24·0	3	28·1
1730	21·1	4	26·3	4	29·7
1	21·1	5	27·4	5	28·3
2	23·1	6	27·7	6	25·3
3	21·1	7	29·9	7	23·9
4	20·9	8	32·4	8	26·7
5	21·7	9	26·3	9	33·1
6	27·0	1760	24·8	1790	30·4
7	23·7	1	25·8	1	25·5
8	30·5	2	31·2	2	23·9
9	30·6	3	32·9	3	24·3
1740	35·5	4	27·2	4	23·6
1	32·2	5	27·7	5	27·9
2	39·0	6	25·1	6	24·6
3	43·7	7	25·6	7	23·8
4	25·3	8	27·2	8	23·1
		9	27·1	9	25·2
		1770	26·1		
		1	27·8		
		2	37·4		
		3	52·4		
		4	22·4		

Year	Sweden	Denmark	France	Germany (Prussia)
1800	31·4	28·5	—	—
1	26·1	27·7	27·7	—
2	23·7	23·2	27·7	—
3	23·8	23·5	31·2	—
4	24·9	23·7	31·0	—
5	23·5	23·2	28·8	—
6	27·5	22·3	26·8	—
7	26·2	22·9	27·6	—
8	34·8	25·2	26·5	—
9	40·0	25·1	25·9	—

TABLE 127 *(cont.)*

Year	Sweden	Denmark	France	Germany (Prussia)
1810	31·6	28·7	24·9	—
1	28·8	24·4	26·1	—
2	30·3	27·0	26·2	—
3	27·4	22·8	26·4	—
4	25·1	24·7	29·8	—
5	23·6	21·6	26·0	—
6	28·7	20·7	24·5	27·7
7	24·2	19·0	25·3	29·0
8	24·4	18·9	25·3	29·1
9	27·4	19·5	26·1	30·4
1820	24·5	20·9	25·4	26·3
1	25·6	24·0	24·3	25·0
2	22·6	24·3	25·3	27·4
3	21·0	17·7	24·0	27·3
4	20·8	18·6	24·5	26·9
5	20·5	19·2	25·9	21·2

Year	Sweden	Denmark	France	Germany (Prussia)	England
1826	22·6	21·1	26·5	29·0	—
7	23·0	20·0	24·9	29·4	—
8	26·7	23·6	26·2	29·7	—
9	29·0	26·8	25·0	30·5	—
1830	24·1	25·3	25·0	30·4	—
1	26·0	30·1	24·6	35·6	—
2	23·4	26·3	28·5	32·4	—
3	21·7	23·3	24·7	31·5	—
4	25·7	23·5	27·8	31·8	—
5	18·5	22·9	24·5	28·2	—
6	20·0	22·3	22·3	27·4	—
7	24·6	21·7	25·3	31·4	—
8	24·1	20·0	24·2	27·8	22·2
9	23·6	20·5	22·7	29·9	21·9
1840	20·3	21·0	23·7	28·6	22·6
1	19·4	19·8	23·2	27·8	21·6
2	21·1	20·2	24·0	28·8	21·7
3	21·4	19·3	23·1	29·0	21·2
4	20·3	19·3	22·0	26·1	21·5
5	18·8	19·3	21·1	27·5	20·9
6	21·8	21·5	23·2	29·6	23·0
7	23·7	21·7	23·9	41·8	24·7
8	19·7	21·1	23·6	33·5	23·0

TABLE 127 (cont.)

Year	Sweden	Denmark	France	Germany (Prussia)	England
1849	19·8	22·4	27·4	30·9	25·1
1850	19·8	19·1	21·4	27·9	20·8
1	20·7	18·4	22·3	26·8	22·0
2	22·7	19·6	22·6	33·1	22·3
3	23·7	25·0	22·0	30·8	22·9
4	19·8	18·4	27·4	29·2	23·5
5	21·4	20·0	26·0	32·0	22·6
6	21·8	18·7	23·1	27·8	20·5
7	27·6	21·8	23·7	30·1	21·8
8	21·7	23·2	24·1	29·6	23·1
9	20·1	20·3	26·8	27·8	22·4
1860	17·6	20·2	21·6	25·6	21·2
1	18·5	18·4	23·2	27·2	21·6
2	21·4	18·3	21·7	26·4	21·4
3	19·3	18·1	22·5	28·0	23·0
4	20·2	23·2	22·7	28·2	23·7
5	19·4	23·0	24·7	29·7	23·2
6	20·0	20·7	23·2	35·9	23·4
7	19·6	19·8	22·7	24·1	21·7
8	21·0	19·2	24·1	25·0	21·8
9	22·3	19·0	23·5	24·3	22·3
1870	19·8	19·0	28·4	25·5	22·9
1	17·2	19·4	35·1	29·6	22·6
2	16·3	18·4	22·0	29·0	21·3
3	17·2	18·6	23·3	28·3	21·0
4	20·3	20·0	21·4	26·7	22·2
5	20·3	21·0	23·0	27·6	22·7

Year	Sweden	Denmark	France	Germany	England	Poland
1876	19·6	19·7	22·6	26·3	20·9	—
7	18·7	18·7	21·6	26·4	20·3	—
8	18·1	18·4	22·5	26·2	21·6	—
9	16·9	19·7	22·5	25·6	20·7	—
1880	18·1	20·4	22·9	26·0	20·5	—
1	17·7	18·3	22·0	25·5	18·9	—
2	17·3	19·2	22·2	25·7	19·6	—
3	17·3	18·4	22·2	25·9	19·6	—
4	17·5	18·3	22·6	26·0	19·7	—
5	17·7	17·8	22·0	25·7	19·2	—
6	16·6	18·1	22·6	26·2	19·5	—
7	16·1	18·2	22·0	24·2	19·1	—
8	16·0	19·5	21·9	23·7	18·1	—

TABLE 127 (cont.)

Year	Sweden	Denmark	France	Germany	England	Poland
1889	16·0	18·5	20·7	24·7	18·2	—
1890	17·1	19·0	22·8	24·4	19·5	—
1	16·8	20·0	22·9	23·4	20·2	—
2	17·9	19·5	22·8	24·1	19·0	—
3	16·8	19·0	22·5	24·6	19·2	—
4	16·4	17·6	21·2	22·3	16·6	—
5	15·2	16·9	22·2	22·1	18·7	27·5
6	15·6	15·7	20·0	21·8	17·1	25·7
7	15·3	16·2	19·5	21·3	17·4	25·5
8	15·1	15·5	20·9	20·5	17·5	25·1
9	17·6	17·3	21·1	21·5	18·2	26·0
1900	16·8	16·8	21·9	22·1	17·9	25·5
1	16·0	15·7	20·1	20·7	16·1	24·9
2	15·4	14·6	19·5	19·4	15·7	24·9
3	15·1	14·6	19·3	20·0	15·3	25·0
4	15·3	14·1	19·4	19·6	15·4	25·2
5	15·6	15·0	19·6	19·8	15·3	25·6
6	14·4	13·5	19·9	18·2	15·5	23·4
7	14·6	14·1	20·2	18·0	15·1	22·7
8	14·9	14·6	18·9	18·1	14·8	22·5
9	13·7	13·3	19·1	17·2	14·6	23·0
1910	14·0	12·9	17·8	16·2	13·5	22·3
1	13·8	13·4	19·6	17·3	14·6	21·7
2	14·2	13·0	17·9	15·6	13·3	(21·1)
3	13·6	12·5	17·7	15·0	13·8	(21·1)
4	13·8	12·5	20·7	19·0	14·0	—
5	14·7	12·8	21·0	21·4	15·7	—
6	13·6	13·4	19·8	19·2	14·3	—
7	13·4	13·2	20·2	20·6	14·2	—
8	18·0	13·0	24·0	24·8	17·3	—
9	14·5	13·0	19·3	15·6	14·0	26·9
1920	13·3	12·0	17·2	15·1	12·4	27·0
1	12·4	11·0	17·7	13·9	12·1	20·9
2	12·8	11·9	17·5	14·4	12·8	19·9
3	11·4	11·3	16·7	13·9	11·6	17·3
4	12·0	11·2	16·9	12·2	17·9	
5	11·7	10·8	17·4	11·9	12·2	16·7
6	11·8	11·0	17·4	11·7	11·6	17·8
7	12·7	11·6	16·5	12·0	12·3	17·3
8	12·0	11·0	16·4	11·6	11·7	16·4
9	12·2	11·2	17·9	12·6	13·4	16·7
1930	11·7	10·8	15·6	11·0	11·4	15·5
1	12·5	11·4	16·2	11·2	12·3	15·5
2	11·6	11·0	15·8	10·8	12·0	15·1
3	11·2	10·6	15·8	11·2	12·3	14·2

TABLE 127 (*cont.*)

Year	Sweden	Denmark	France	Germany	England	Poland
1934	11·2	10·4	15·1	10·9	11·8	14·5
5	11·7	11·1	15·7	11·8	11·7	14·1
6	12·0	11·0	15·3	11·8	12·1	14·3
7	12·0	10·8	15·0	11·7	12·4	14·1
8	11·5	10·3	15·4	11·6	11·6	13·9
9	11·5	10·1	15·5	12·3	12·1	—
1940	11·4	10·4	18·9	12·7	14·4	—
1	11·3	10·3	17·3	12·0	13·5	—
2	9·9	9·6	16·9	12·0	12·3	—
3	10·2	9·6	16·3	12·1	13·0	—
4	11·0	10·2	19·4	—	12·7	—
5	10·8	10·5	16·1	—	12·6	—
6	10·5	10·2	13·4	—	12·0	13·4
7	10·8	9·7	13·1	—	12·3	11·3
8	9·8	8·6	12·4	—	11·0	11·2
9	10·0	8·9	13·7	—	11·8	11·6
1950	9·0	9·2	12·6	—	11·7	11·6
1	9·9	8·8	13·4	—	12·4	12·4
2	9·6	9·0	12·3	—	11·3	11·1
3	9·7	9·0	13·0	—	11·4	10·2
4	9·6	9·1	12·0	—	11·3	10·3
5	9·4	8·7	12·1	—	11·7	9·6
6	9·6	8·9	12·4	—	11·7	9·0
7	9·9	9·3	12·0	—	11·5	9·5
8	9·6	9·2	11·1	—	11·3	9·4

fairly exact, as it is based on parochial registers which already
then kept a complete and reliable record of vital statistics.
By using $f = 248$ in the regression equation we obtain the
life expectancy at birth $e_0 = 27·8$ years. The result seems
to be quite probable.

Death rates per 1000 population in selected countries for
a prolonged period are presented in Table 127.

Like natality and nuptiality, mortality reveals sharp annual
fluctuations in the distant past. The fluctuations diminish visibly only after the second half of the 19th century. Sudden
upswings followed by rapid declines in the death rate are
obviously a reflection of war years. The effect of business cycles
cannot, however, be traced, the rates instead of a rhythmic
pattern revealing only small and irregular fluctuations.

Trends in the death rates in three countries are shown

in Fig. 59. Although Poland has higher mortality for every age group, her death rate is now lower than that in Sweden and France.

In the distant past, very high mortality rates were prevalent everywhere. This is illustrated by Canada's death rates in the 17th and 18th centuries (Table 128).

TABLE 128

Years	Death rates in Canada per 1000 population
1681—1690	20·0
1691—1700	17·4
1701—1710	23·6
1711—1720	24·8
1721—1730	23·8
1731—1740	26·3
1741—1750	34·0
1751—1760	39·6
1761—1770	33·8

The table depicts what appears to be a strange phenomenon—an increasing trend in the rates. On closer examination the explanation is very simple. In the earlier years the influx of immigrants to Canada was very large and young people constituted the bulk of the population. This was bound to result in a relatively low level of mortality. After the flow of immigrants had stopped and the ageing of the population began, the death rate reached a normal level to be expected under the conditions of mortality at the time. The death rate was, of course, enormously high in comparison with the present death rate in Canada or elsewhere. The infant death rate computed in relation to the number of births (i.e. independent of the age structure of the population) in Canada at that time was also very high—248 per 1000 births.

We mentioned previously that female mortality is commonly lower than male mortality. This directly affects the death rate which is also lower among females than among males. It is interesting to observe the changes in the ratio of male to female deaths over longer periods of time. The rates for England and Wales over a period of more than a hundred years are listed in Table 129.

The quotients in the last column of the table are not ratios of crude death rates, but of standardized rates adjusted to a common base.

TABLE 129

| Years | England and Wales | | | |
| | Deaths per 1000 population | | | Ratio m : f |
	total	males	females	
1841—1845	21·4	22·1	20·6	1·096
1846—1850	23·3	24·1	22·6	1·088
1851—1855	22·7	23·5	21·8	1·099
1856—1860	21·8	22·6	21·0	1·095
1861—1865	22·6	23·7	21·5	1·116
1866—1870	22·4	23·7	21·2	1·132
1871—1875	22·0	23·3	20·7	1·150
1876—1880	20·8	22·1	19·5	1·160
1881—1885	19·4	20·5	18·3	1·152
1886—1890	18·9	20·0	17·8	1·164
1891—1895	18·7	19·8	17·7	1·161
1896—1900	17·7	18·8	16·6	1·178
1901—1905	16·0	17·1	15·0	1·191
1906—1910	14·7	15·6	13·8	1·198
1911—1915	14·3	15·4	13·3	1·226
1916—1920	14·4	16·5	12·8	1·282
1921—1925	12·1	12·9	11·4	1·240
1926—1930	12·1	12·9	11·4	1·260
1931—1935	12·0	12·7	11·4	1·276
1936—1940	12·5	13·5	11·6	1·337
1941—1945	12·8	15·1	11·1	1·414
1948	11·0	11·9	10·1	1·409

Both male and female death rates fell during the period under examination, but since the decrease among women was more rapid than among men, the quotient of the two rates grew less and less favourable for males.

Characteristically, a similar trend exists in infant mortality rates. The rates for England and Wales for the same period are given in Table 130.

Differences between infant death rates by sex are not as large as in the case of general mortality rates, but the time trend—namely, the continual increase in the ratio of male

TABLE 130

Years	England and Wales			Ratio m : f
	Infant deaths in the first year of life per 1000 births			
	total	males	females	
1841—1845	148	162	132	1·22
1846—1850	157	172	142	1·22
1851—1855	156	172	141	1·22
1856—1860	152	166	137	1·21
1861—1865	151	166	136	1·22
1866—1870	157	170	142	1·20
1871—1875	153	167	138	1·21
1876—1880	145	159	130	1·22
1881—1885	139	152	125	1·22
1886—1890	145	159	131	1·22
1891—1895	151	165	135	1·22
1896—1900	156	170	141	1·21
1901—1905	138	151	124	1·22
1906—1910	117	129	105	1·23
1911—1915	110	121	97	1·25
1916—1920	90	101	79	1·28
1921—1925	76	86	66	1·30
1926—1930	68	77	59	1·30
1931—1935	62	70	54	1·29
1936—1940	55	62	48	1·29
1941—1945	50	56	44	1·28
1948	34	38	30	1·27

to female infant death rates, to the disadvantage of males—
is quite pronounced.

Death rates by age groups have also been subject to considerable change over longer periods of time. Death rates (jointly
for males and females) relating to England and Wales are
listed in Table 131.

A study of time trends in death rates by age groups reveals
that the periods of decrease and the periods of increase in the
death rate are nearly the same for all age groups, i.e. all death
rates by age groups either simultaneously increase or simultaneously decrease. The more obvious deviations from this rule
occur in the latest age groups, in which changes in mortality
are generally relatively smaller. This is shown in Fig. 60
(on a logarithmic scale).

TABLE 131

England and Wales

Deaths per 1000 population by age groups

Years	0—4	5—9	10—14	15—19	20—24	25—34	35—44	45—54	55—64	65—74	75—84	85 and more
1841—1845	63·7	8·7	5·0	7·2	8·8	9·7	12·1	16·1	28·7	62·0	137·1	295·3
1846—1850	68·7	8·4	5·6	7·7	9·8	10·9	13·6	18·1	31·4	65·9	145·8	306·6
1851—1855	68·9	8·6	5·2	7·4	9·0	10·1	12·7	17·2	29·6	62·9	148·2	299·5
1856—1860	66·9	8·3	4·7	6·7	8·3	9·4	12·0	16·1	28·4	60·9	136·6	283·4
1861—1865	69·1	8·4	4·7	6·6	8·4	9·8	12·6	17·1	30·2	62·4	139·1	298·8
1866—1870	68·1	7·6	4·3	6·2	8·0	9·9	12·9	17·6	30·6	63·3	141·7	294·8
1871—1875	64·9	6·9	4·0	5·8	7·7	9·6	13·1	18·0	31·6	65·3	141·6	305·2
1876—1880	61·9	6·1	3·5	4·9	6·5	8·4	12·3	17·5	31·6	64·7	142·9	311·5
1881—1885	56·6	5·7	3·2	4·6	6·0	8·0	11·8	17·2	31·0	63·5	136·1	277·7
1886—1890	56·9	4·9	2·8	4·1	5·3	7·2	11·0	17·1	3·18	66·3	139·0	290·3
1891—1895	57·8	4·6	2·6	4·0	5·0	5·7	11·0	17·3	32·5	67·3	140·8	274·1
1896—1900	57·5	4·1	2·4	3·5	4·5	6·0	10·0	16·2	30·5	64·1	133·6	267·5
1901—1905	50·2	3·8	2·2	3·1	4·0	5·5	8·9	15·0	28·7	59·5	127·3	258·5
1906—1910	41·7	3·4	2·0	2·9	3·6	4·8	7·8	13·7	27·6	58·1	127·0	262·8
1911—1915	37·5	3·4	2·1	2·9	3·6	4·6	7·3	13·1	26·2	57·3	126·2	257·9
1916—1920	31·4	3·8	1·7	3·8	5·2	6·5	7·5	12·1	24·0	54·5	124·8	250·7
1921—1925	24·7	2·5	2·5	2·6	3·3	3·8	5·7	10·1	21·5	51·6	123·7	255·0
1926—1930	20·9	2·4	1·6	2·5	3·1	3·5	5·4	9·9	20·7	52·2	123·4	281·4
1931—1935	18·1	2·18	1·41	2·33	2·96	3·20	4·82	9·4	20·1	49·0	119·3	255·7
1936—1940	15·6	1·84	1·20	2·01	2·72	2·87	4·35	9·1	20·4	48·5	119·7	263·4
1941—1945	14·0	1·50	1·08	1·96	3·06	3·04	3·95	8·0	18·1	43·0	104·5	213·0
1948	8·7	0·75	0·60	1·20	1·55	1·82	2·79	6·7	16·4	39·4	94·1	191·9
1955	5·9	0·4	0·4	0·6	0·9	1·1	2·2	6·2	14·3	43·5	104·7	233·7

Since the decline in mortality in the 55—64 age group was comparatively smaller than in the 0—4 age group, the death rate in the former group is now higher than in the latter, while the reverse was true at the beginning of the period under examination, and even until World War I. Similarly,

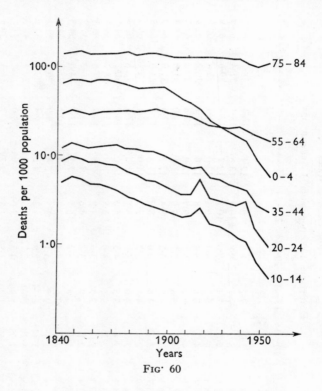

Fig· 60

TABLE

| Generation born in the years | England and | | | | |
| | Deaths per 1000 population | | | | |
	0—4	5—9	10—14	15—19	20—24
1841—1845	63·7	8·4	5·2	6·7	8·4
1846—1850	68·7	8·6	4·7	6·6	8·0
1851—1855	68·9	8·3	4·7	6·2	7·7
1856—1860	66·9	8·4	4·3	5·8	6·5

mortality in the 15—19 age group is now somewhat higher
than in the 5—9 age group, contrary to what was observed
in the years 1911—1915. Finally, mortality in the earliest
age group (0—4 years) dropped in recent years below the
level of mortality in the 45—54 age group, and prior to this
below the mortality in the 55—64 and 65—74 age groups.

Figure 60 clearly indicates that the younger the age and
the smaller the interval between the age groups under consideration, the closer the relationship between the respective
death rates of the age groups. Changes in the later age groups
are relatively small, and their trends are sometimes inconsistent with the trends in the death rates of other age groups.

Given several tables of the same type as Table 128, it is
possible to construct a table of death rates specific to various
generations which, in turn, will be the basis for computing
a cohort life table. It is advisable to classify the rates by five-
-year (or ten-year) age groups and to tabulate the death rates
for 5-year intervals of time. The death rates relating to the
same cohort may then be found by moving diagonally from
the upper left-hand corner to the lower right-hand corner of
the table. The death rates for four generations, each including
five birth cohorts, are presented in Table 132 for England
and Wales.

Where a classification by five-year age groups was available
the rates were taken directly from the life table; death rates
for ten-year age groups were determined by computing the
arithmetic means of two superimposed rates. Since mortality decreases with time, the death rate of a given cohort
is lower than the rate which was prevalent at the birth of the

132

Wales

by age groups

25—34	35—44	45—54	55—64	65—74	75—84	85 and over
9·7	12·0	17·2	29·6	57·7	124·2	268·5
9·0	11·4	16·7	28·1	55·9	123·5	259·5
8·2	11·0	15·6	26·9	53·0	121·3	238·2
7·6	10·5	14·3	25·1	51·9	119·5	202·4

said generation, but higher than the rate obtained after the extinction of the generation.

Correspondingly, the life expectancy at birth relating to a given cohort will vary between the life expectancy at birth in the years when the said cohort was born and the life expectancy at birth in the years after the extinction of the cohort, but it will be closer to the former.

In France, for example, the life expectancy for a cohort born in 1880 averaged 43·0 years among males and 47·8 years among females. However, the French life table for the years 1898—1903 (barely 20 years after the birth of the cohort) shows a lower mortality, the life expectancy at birth being 45·31 years among males and 48·69 years among females. Similarly, in Norway the life expectancy at birth for the 1860 cohort averaged 48·4 years for males and 51·4 years for females. This agrees very closely with the mortality rate which prevailed in Norway in 1871—1880 and 1881—1890. During those two decades the life expectancy at birth was 48·3 and 48·7 years for males and 51·3 and 51·2 years for females.[1] It follows that a cohort life table corresponds to a current life table relating to a period some 15 years after the birth of the given cohort.

We ascertained earlier in this chapter that fairly significant differences in the death rate occur even within one country. We shall quote two examples to illustrate how these differences change with time.

The first of them refers to the death rate in various departments of Norway between 1911 and 1955 (Table 133).

Besides the general declining trend which is a reflection of diminishing mortality, the table reveals a trend towards a decreasing dispersion of the rates. Thus, instead of a shift of the whole configuration of rates between the various departments, the time trend can be observed in an increasing levelling out of the rates in all departments. This trend was sharply disturbed only in the years 1941—1945, as a result of hostilities. Some areas in Norway suffered particularly

---

[1] For data on life expectancy at birth classified by generations in various countries see *Evolution de la mortalité en Europe depuis l'origine de l'état civil*, Paris 1941, p. 62.

TABLE 133

Deaths per 1000 population	Norway								
	Number of departments								
	1911– –1915	1916– –1920	1921– –1925	1926– –1930	1931– –1935	1936– –1940	1941– –1945	1946– –1950	1951– –1955
7·5— 7·9	—	—	—	—	—	—	—	1	4
8·0— 8·4	—	—	—	—	—	—	—	—	5
8·5— 8·9	—	—	—	—	1	1	1	6	5
9·0— 9·4	—	—	—	1	—	—	—	8	5
9·5— 9·9	—	—	1	—	3	1	3	1	—
10·0—10·4	—	—	—	1	6	7	6	3	1
10·5—10·9	—	1	2	7	6	6	2	—	—
11·0—11·4	1	—	7	5	—	3	5	1	—
11·5—11·9	—	—	4	2	3	1	1	—	—
12·0—12·4	4	—	1	1	1	1	1	—	—
12·5—12·9	3	1	4	2	—	—	—	—	—
13·0—13·4	6	3	—	1	—	—	—	—	—
13·5—13·9	2	3	—	—	—	—	—	—	—
14·0—14·4	2	6	—	—	—	—	1	—	—
14·5—14·9	1	1	—	—	—	—	—	—	—
15·0—15·4	—	2	1	—	—	—	—	—	—
15·5—15·9	—	3	—	—	—	—	—	—	—
16 and more	1	1	—	—	—	—	—	—	—
Total	20	20	20	20	20	20	20	20	20

heavy casualties; this caused a much higher mortality in those areas, while in the remaining part of the country the death rate remained virtually unchanged or even decreased.

This example suggests a reservation that, since departments are fairly large territorial units, they certainly do not afford uniform conditions of mortality. Our second example will, therefore, refer to smaller territorial units in England and Wales (Table 134). The period covered by the table is much longer—just over 100 years.

In this case the situation is entirely different. Even accounting for the fact that the number of administrative units in 1949 is more than twice as large as in the two preceding periods named in the table, the single visible trend is a general decrease in the death rate for all territorial units; no trend towards a reduction in the dispersion of rates can be observed.

Table 135 contains rates illustrating changes in infant mortality in Norway, classified by departments.

TABLE 134

Deaths per 1000 population	England and Wales		
	Number of administrative units		
	1841—1860	1891—1900	1949
5·0— 5·9	—	—	3
6·0— 6·9	—	—	4
7·0— 7·9	—	—	15
8·0— 8·9	—	—	50
9·0— 9·9	—	—	118
10·0—10·9	—	—	227
11·0—11·9	—	—	329
12·0—12·9	—	9	300
13·0—13·9	—	22	237
14·0—14·9	—	73	138
15·0—15·9	3	135	88
16·0—16·9	14	148	47
17·0—17·9	48	79	22
18·0—18·9	85	60	14
19·0—19·9	92	52	8
20·0—20·9	108	24	1
21·0—21·9	87	13	2
22·0—22·9	44	6	3
23·0—23·9	27	4	—
24·0—24·9	29	4	—
25·0—25·9	22	1	—
26·0—26·9	14	1	—
27·0—27·9	12	—	—
28·0—28·9	6	—	—
29·0—29·9	3	—	—
30·0 and more	6	4	—
Total	600	635	1606

Here, too, we note a constant decrease in infant mortality along with an increasing concentration of rates; interrupted only during World War II (1941—1945). As previously ascertained in the case of England and Wales, this trend towards concentration of rates is however not universal, it may not occur in any other country but Norway. The differentiation of the death rate within one country leads to a differentiation of other rates which characterize the level of mortality, first of all to the differentiation of life expectancy values. Such data for smaller territorial units are seldom available.

TABLE 135

Infant deaths per 1000 births	Norway								
	Number of departments								
	1911–-1915	1916–-1920	1921–-1925	1926–-1930	1931–-1935	1936–-1940	1941–-1945	1946–-1950	1951–-1955
15—19	—	—	—	—	—	—	—	—	3
20—24	—	—	—	—	—	—	—	—	14
25—29	—	—	—	—	—	—	2	7	1
30—34	—	—	—	—	1	7	6	7	1
35—39	—	—	—	2	5	6	7	2	—
40—44	1	—	6	4	7	3	2	—	1
45—49	1	2	4	8	2	2	1	1	—
50—54	3	6	5	1	3	1	1	—	—
55—59	4	1	3	2	—	—	—	1	—
60—64	4	7	1	1	1	—	—	—	—
65—69	2	—	—	1	—	—	—	—	—
70—74	2	1	—	—	—	—	—	—	—
75—79	1	—	—	—	—	1	—	—	—
80—84	—	1	—	—	—	—	1	—	—
85—89	—	—	—	—	—	—	—	—	—
90—94	—	—	—	1	1	—	—	—	—
95—99	—	—	—	—	—	—	—	—	—
100 and more	2	1	1	—	—	—	—	—	—
Total	20	20	20	20	20	20	20	20	20

The most comprehensive tables are those for the United States. However, the detailed distribution of rates by states refers to the white population only; statistics on the remaining population are distributed in six groups of states.[1]

Rates relating to all states have been tabulated for the period between 1939—1941, and rates relating to all states but one (Texas), for the years 1929—1931. The results are presented in Table 136.

Two trends are revealed in the table—a visible increase in life expectancy and a certain concentration of rates. It should be noted that life expectancy among males in various states in 1939—1941 follows a pattern almost identical to the

---

[1] These data are quoted by L. I. DUBLIN, A. J. LOTKA and M. SPIEGEL-MAN in Length of Life, Ed. Ronald Press, New York, 1949, pp. 324—343; from this work are also taken the statistics illustrating trends in life expectancy at birth over longer periods of time.

TABLE 136

Life expectancy at birth	Number of states			
	Males (white)		Females (white)	
	1929—1931	1939—1941	1929—1931	1939—1941
48·00—48·99	1	—	—	—
49·00—49·99	1	—	—	—
50·00—50·99	—	—	—	—
51·00—51·99	—	—	—	—
52·00—52·99	—	—	1	—
53·00—53·99	—	—	—	—
54·00—54·99	—	—	—	—
55·00—55·99	2	—	1	—
56·00—56·99	1	1	—	—
57·00—57·99	4	1	—	—
58·00—58·99	13	1	—	—
59·00—59·99	11	—	1	—
60·00—60·99	4	1	—	1
61·00—61·99	5	9	11	—
62·00—62·99	2	12	12	—
63·00—63·99	3	14	10	1
64·00—64·99	1	3	3	—
65·00—65·99	—	5	7	2
66·00—66·99	—	2	2	11
67·00—67·99	—	—	—	17
68·00—68·99	—	—	—	10
69·00—69·99	—	—	—	6
70·00—70·99	—	—	—	1
Total	48	49	48	49

expectation of life among females in 1929—1931, i.e. a decade earlier.

We give additionally in Table 137 [1] statistics relating to various departments of France in the period between 1860 and 1932. The rates listed are not values of life expectancy at birth but of the closely related probability of death before 30 years of age. By subtracting the value of this probability from 1 we obtain the probability of survival from birth to an age equivalent to the length of a generation.

The table initially reveals a certain increase in the dispersion of rates rather than a trend towards their concentration.

---

[1] *Evolution de la mortalité en Europe depuis l'origine de l'état civil*, Paris 1941, pp. 24—25.

TABLE 137

Probability of death before 30 years of age	France			
	Number of departments			
	1860—1862	1890—1892	1910—1912	1930—1932
0·100—0·124	—	—	—	3
0·125—0·149	—	—	—	26
0·150—0·174	—	—	5	47
0·175—0·199	—	—	11	13
0·200—0·224	—	—	16	1
0·225—0·249	—	2	22	—
0·250—0·274	—	6	19	—
0·275—0·299	1	8	13	—
0·300—0·324	4	20	3	—
0·325—0·349	16	16	1	—
0·350—0·374	22	14	—	—
0·375—0·399	15	7	—	—
0·400—0·424	10	11	—	—
0·425—0·449	7	2	—	—
0·450—0·474	5	2	—	—
0·475—0·499	3	1	—	—
0·500—0·524	4	1	—	—
0·525—0·549	2	—	—	—
Total	89	90	90	90

A gradual reduction in the dispersion becomes visible only in the years 1910—1912 and subsequent years. This is evidence that an improved mortality rate does not necessarily result in a levelling out of the death rate throughout the country.

A rough estimate of life expectancy at birth, based on the values in Table 137 relating to the probability of death before 30 years of age, in accordance with the formula on page 251, will give us the lower and upper limits of the range of variations in life expectancy at birth throughout the whole of France at different periods of time. This is shown in Table 138.

For comparison, we have included in the table the values of life expectancy at birth taken from the life tables for females, referring to approximately the same years. The values taken from life tables are in every case closer to the upper than to the lower limit. At first, the disparity between mini-

272   THE NATURAL MOVEMENT OF POPULATION

TABLE 138

Years	Life expectancy at birth		
	minimum	maximum	life table value females
1860—1862	26·1	47·6	40·55
1890—1892	29·1	52·8	48·72
1910—1912	43·9	58·5	54·41
1930—1932	55·8	63·1	59·02

mum and maximum life expectancy at birth slightly increases, following which it considerably decreases.

To complete our considerations on the subject of death rates, we now give a table illustrating the trends in infant mortality rates classified by days and weeks of age for England and Wales during the past decade (Table 139).[1]

TABLE 139

Year	Infant deaths per 1000 births			
	under 1 day	1—6 days	1—4 weeks	4 weeks— 1 year
1949	7·9	8·1	3·6	14·2
1950	7·5	8·2	3·5	1·20
1951	7·8	8·2	3·5	11·7
1952	7·8	7·8	3·2	10·0
1953	7·6	7·5	2·9	9·6
1954	7·9	7·5	2·8	8·2
1955	7·9	7·1	2·7	8·1
1956	7·6	6·9	2·7	7·2
1957	7·9	6·6	2·5	7·0
1958	7·7	6·4	2·4	6·8

As may be seen from the table, in the first day of the infant's life, medicine is still helpless in the fight against death; but some success is already achieved in the first week of the child's life, and at the age of one month and over medicine scores an impressive success, infant mortality having dropped at that age by one half within ten years.[2]

[1] *Annual Abstract of Statistics 1959.*
[2] Cf. S. Szulc, Umieralność niemowląt (Infant Mortality), *Przegląd Statystyczny (Statistical Review)*, 1956 and 1957.

TABLE 142

Life table for Poland in 1896—1897 (1900—1901)

Age	number of survivors			average life expectancy at birth		
	total	males	females	total	males	females
0	10,000	10,000	10,000	34·2	33·1	35·4
5	6046	5794	6310	50·3	50·8	49·9
10	5781	5540	6033	47·5	47·9	47·2
15	5650	5420	5889	43·6	43·8	43·2
20	5501	5284	5727	39·5	40·0	39·4
25	5309	5105	5528	36·0	36·3	35·7
35	4909	4742	5087	28·5	28·7	28·4
45	4405	4276	4544	21·3	21·3	21·2
55	3680	3543	3833	14·6	14·7	14·4
65	2547	2472	2621	9·1	9·3	8·9
75	1178	1188	1163	—	—	—

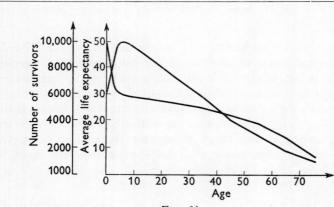

FIG. 61

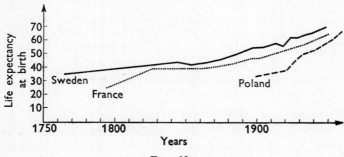

FIG. 62

278   THE NATURAL MOVEMENT OF POPULATION

TABLE 143

Years	Total	Males	Females
1896—1897 (1900—1901)*	34·2	33·1	35·4
1921	39·3	—	—
1927	45·9	—	—
1931—1932	49·8	48·2	51·4
1933—1934	51·2	49·5	52·8
1938	52·1	—	—
1948	59·1	55·6	61·5
1952—1954	61·5	58·6	64·2
1955—1956	64·9	61·8	67·8
1958	66·3	—	—

* Note that the estimated life expectancy at birth, based on the infant mortality rate (which in 1896—1897 and 1900—1901 was 223), computed in accordance with the formula on page 253, equals $e_0 = 32·5$ years, i.e. a value quite close to the one listed in the life table.

Figure 62 shows the trends in life expectancy at birth in three countries over longer periods of time (the average rates, relating jointly to men and women, as approximately representing the mortality of the total population).

We shall now proceed to make a comparison between life expectancy at birth relating to different cohorts and the corresponding values taken from life tables. The computed values of life expectancy classified by cohorts are listed in Table 144.

TABLE 144

Country	Sex	Life expectancy at birth for persons born in						
		1750	1780	1800	1820	1840	1860	1880
England	m	—	—	—	—	39·5	42·8	—
	f	—	—	—	—	42·7	46·5	—
France	m	—	—	—	39·4	38·2	41·4	43·0
	f	—	—	—	41·0	41·3	42·7	47·8
Sweden	m	33·5	34·1	37·2	41·4	44·3	46·6	—
	f	36·7	41·8	40·8	45·3	47·9	49·5	—

A comparison of the rates relating to Sweden in Table 144 with those in Table 140 reveals no consistent relation between the life expectancy of a certain generation and the life expectancy at different periods of time. Thus, the life expectancy for the cohort born in 1820 is almost exactly the same as that in the period between 1846 and 1860, that is 25 to 30 years later. The life expectancy for a cohort born in 1840 corresponds roughly to the mortality about the year 1870, that is also some 30 years later. However, in the case of a cohort born in 1860 the life expectancy corresponds to the level of mortality obtaining only 20 years after the birth of the said cohort. A similar inconsistency is observed in France. Moreover, the impact of war upon the life expectancy of a cohort is so strong that it obscures the pattern of existing interrelations.

Let us see now whether there is any relationship between the death rate and the life expectancy at birth.[1] We shall base our analysis on the statistics relating to Sweden. The mean death rates for the periods covered by life tables and the values of life expectancy at birth have been computed, and the results are collated in Table 145.

Figure 63 shows the corresponding correlation graph for the death rate and the life expectancy at birth in Sweden. The graph includes points illustrating an analogous correlation for Poland; to distinguish them from the former, these points are marked with crosses. The relation is distinct and quite close, but not linear.

For a stationary population structure the relation between the death rate and the life expectancy at birth is approximately inverse; the relation between these two values is therefore hyperbolic. In the case under examination, although the structure of the population is certainly not stationary, a hyperbolic relation is, of course, theoretically justified, but not necessarily in its simplest, inversely proportional form. A more general form of the hyperbola may be derived from the equation

$$e_0 = a + \frac{b}{z + c}$$

---

[1] The first to examine the relation between the death rate (after necessary adjustment) and life expectancy at birth was probably J. BROWNLEE (*The Use of Death Rates as a Measure of Hygienic Conditions*, London 1922). In the Polish literature the subject is dealt with by S. SZULC in his "O standaryzacji współczynników" (On Standardizing Rates), *Kwartalnik Statystyczny* (*Statistical Quarterly*) 1930 and *Zagadnienia Demograficzne Polski* (*Demographic Problems of Poland*), op. cit., p. 103.

where:

e_0 = life expectancy at birth,

z = death rate relating to total population, and

a, b, c are constants.

In the case of Poland the equation takes the form

$$e_0 = 5 \cdot 31 + \frac{955 \cdot 62}{z + 6 \cdot 42}.$$

TABLE 145

Years	Death rate per 1000 population	Life expectancy at birth
1755—1776	28·6	34·45
1816—1840	24·5	41·53
1841—1845	20·2	44·27
1846—1850	20·0	43·48
1851—1855	21·7	42·59
1856—1860	21·6	42·81
1861—1870	19·2	44·60
1871—1880	18·3	47·05
1881—1890	16·9	50·01
1891—1900	16·4	52·28
1901—1910	14·9	55·75
1911—1915	14·0	57·86
1916—1920	14·6	56·21
1921—1925	12·1	61·83
1926—1930	12·1	62·26
1931—1935	11·6	64·27
1936—1940	11·7	65·61
1941—1945	10·6	—
1946—1950	10·0	70·31

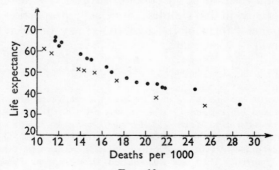

FIG. 63

It should be emphasized that this hyperbolic relation becomes evident over prolonged periods of time, as the observations referring to Sweden cover a period of some 200 years, and to Poland, some 60 years. Despite the perturbations caused by the two world wars the form of the hyperbola is quite pronounced even in the case of Poland.

The above formula is not universal, i.e. the values of the constants in the formula must be derived for each individual country. The values of parameters a, b, and c for Poland will be of no use in the case of Sweden, since the whole hyperbola which represents the relation between the two rates in Sweden lies above the corresponding hyperbola for Poland.

Evidence of fairly good consistency between the equation and the statistical material is furnished by the rate which, computed from the formula, deviates from the recorded value by no more than 1·0 (Poland). In most cases the deviation is much below 1·0. However, a grave error might result by using the equation derived for one country to estimate life expectancy in another country.

Time trends in life expectancy at various ages, not only at birth, may be examined on the example of statistics relating to Norway over a period of more than a hundred years, between 1831 and 1955 (Table 146).

The general trend is quite clear: changes in the life expectancy at birth are followed as a rule by similar changes in the life expectancy for other ages, 1, 5, 10 and more years. However, such is the character of the time trend that the life expectancy at 5 or 10 years of age, formerly longer than that at birth, is now shorter. Gradual improvement in mortality rates leads to the elimination of the life expectancy paradox i.e. that life expectancy begins to decline, not in early infancy but several years after birth.

Trends in life expectancy in Norway at various ages over intervals of some 30 years for the entire period under study are illustrated in Figure 64.

The pattern of time trends in life expectancy is not completely consistent. A comparison of life expectancy for males at various ages in 1856—1865 and in 1871—1880 reveals an increase in life expectancy among males at 0, 1, 5, 30, 40, 50, 60, and 70 years of age, no change among males at 10

TABLE 146

Years	Norway life expectancy by age									
	0	1	5	10	20	30	40	50	60	70

					Males					
1831—1840	41·8	—	50·9	47·4	39·5	32·9	26·7	19·6	13·8	8·8
1841—1850	44·5	—	52·0	49·4	41·5	34·6	27·6	20·7	14·4	9·0
1856—1865	47·4	52·3	53·7	50·8	43·2	36·3	29·1	22·0	15·2	9·4
1871—1880	48·3	53·4	54·1	50·8	43·1	36·8	29·7	22·5	15·6	9·9
1881—1890	48·7	53·4	54·2	51·2	43·9	37·7	30·4	23·1	16·1	10·1
1891—1900	50·4	55·3	54·7	51·0	43·6	37·7	30·6	23·3	16·6	10·3
1901—1910	54·8	58·7	56·9	52·9	45·2	38·8	31·5	23·9	16·8	10·6
1911—1920	55·6	60·0	56·7	52·6	44·8	38·8	31·6	24·1	17·0	10·4
1921—1930	61·0	63·5	60·7	56·3	47·7	40·4	32·4	24·4	17·0	10·6
1931—1940	64·1	66·2	63·1	58·6	49·6	41·5	33·1	24·9	17·2	10·7
1941—1950	69·2	70·7	67·3	62·6	53·2	44·2	35·2	26·4	18·4	11·4
1951—1955	71·1	71·9	68·4	63·6	54·1	44·8	35·5	26·6	18·5	11·6

					Females					
1831—1840	45·6	—	53·9	50·4	42·2	35·1	28·2	21·4	14·8	9·3
1841—1850	47·9	—	55·0	51·8	43·9	36·2	29·4	22·2	15·2	9·5
1856—1865	50·0	54·2	55·6	52·8	45·3	37·8	30·7	23·4	16·2	10·1
1871—1880	51·3	55·7	56·3	53·1	45·4	38·2	31·1	23·8	16·7	10·5
1881—1890	51·2	55·2	56·1	53·3	45·9	38·8	31·8	24·4	17·2	10·9
1891—1900	54·1	58·3	57·7	54·1	46·5	39·4	32·3	24·9	17·5	11·0
1901—1910	57·7	60·8	59·0	55·1	47·2	40·2	32·9	25·3	17·8	11·2
1911—1920	58·7	61·2	59·1	55·0	47·2	40·3	33·0	25·3	17·8	11·1
1921—1930	63·8	65·8	62·9	58·4	49·8	42·1	34·0	25·9	18·2	11·4
1931—1940	67·5	69·1	65·9	61·2	52·1	43·5	34·9	26·3	18·4	11·4
1941—1950	72·6	73·6	70·0	65·2	55·6	46·3	37·0	27·9	19·4	12·0
1951—1955	74·7	75·2	71·6	66·7	57·0	47·3	37·8	28·0	19·9	12·3

years of age, and a decline among males at 20 years of age. The most significant change in life expectancy is observed in childhood and adolescence, and the least significant in old age.

Trends in life expectancy may be analysed from another angle by examining how this value changes at various ages in reation to life expectancy at birth. The graphs in Fig. 65 show these trends most clearly.

Apart from some slight deviations, the relations are almost exactly linear; the change becomes gradually less important at the later ages. In terms of increased life expectancy, infants

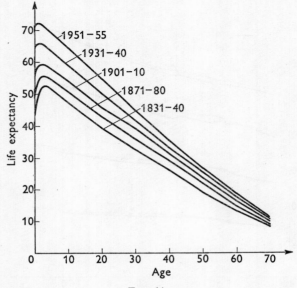

FIG. 64

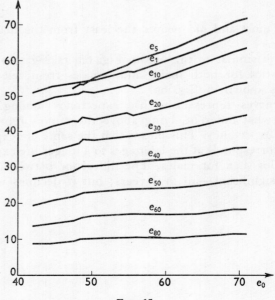

FIG. 65

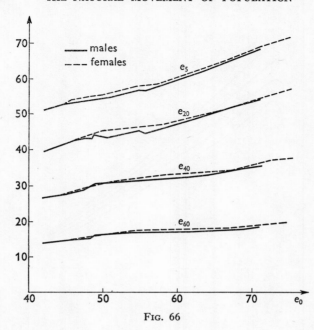

FIG. 66

gain the most and old people the least from the decrease in mortality.

A graph similar to the one in Fig. 65, taking into account the statistics for both males and females from selected age groups is shown in Fig. 66.

The curves representing life expectancy among females are somewhat different, lying above the curves representing male life expectancy. This means that the same life expectancy at birth corresponds at the later ages to a longer life expectancy for females than for males. The difference between the two is quite significant—up to 2 years; but it declines with age.

CONCLUDING REMARKS

I HAVE endeavoured in this book to give a brief outline of some demographic problems relating to the general pattern of the natural movement of populations. These are what we might call macrodemographic problems.

I have used statistics as a basis and have presented in this book only such considerations and conclusions as could be derived from the data on hand. I have tried to avoid dealing with controversial subjects on which there is a lack of complete information and which, therefore, call for further detailed research. These controversial topics include some fundamental demographic problems, such as the impact of social and economic factors upon the intensity of demographic processes. Notwithstanding the many sagacious studies and the extensive literature on the subject, there is no agreement among demographers concerning the nature and scope of the trends in demographic phenomena dependent upon various socio-economic conditions. However, these are already problems partly within the scope of microdemography.

When selecting the subject matter for this book I was guided not only by the more or less universal character of a problem but also by the fact whether or not it could be examined without making too elaborate use of the mathematical and statistical apparatus. I have made an effort to restrict myself to the simplest methods of analysis, i.e. to averages and regressions. However, even these methods make it possible to arrive at many illuminating and fundamental conclusions.

I am well aware of the fact that this book does not give an exhaustive review of all demographic problems which might be analysed by these simple methods. In demography, as in other sciences, much remains to be discovered and elucidated by future generations of researchers.

INDEX

287

288